ON THE SIDE OF ICE

On the Side of ICE

Policing Immigrants in a Sanctuary State

Peter Mancina

NEW YORK UNIVERSITY PRESS
New York

NEW YORK UNIVERSITY PRESS
New York
www.nyupress.org

© 2025 by New York University
All rights reserved

Please contact the Library of Congress for Cataloging-in-Publication data.

ISBN: 9781479837571 (hardback)
ISBN: 9781479837618 (paperback)
ISBN: 9781479837632 (library ebook)
ISBN: 9781479837625 (consumer ebook)

This book is printed on acid-free paper, and its binding materials are chosen for strength and durability. We strive to use environmentally responsible suppliers and materials to the greatest extent possible in publishing our books.

The manufacturer's authorized representative in the EU for product safety is Mare Nostrum Group B.V., Mauritskade 21D, 1091 GC Amsterdam, The Netherlands.
Email: gpsr@mare-nostrum.co.uk.

Manufactured in the United States of America

10 9 8 7 6 5 4 3 2 1

Also available as an ebook

For Mike, Maureen, Bea, and Evla

CONTENTS

List of Acronyms ix
Prologue: The Immigration Enforcement Traffic Stop xi
Introduction: Sanctuary Policing, Force Multiplication, and Force Division 1
1. Immigration Control's Force Multipliers 21
2. Force Multiplication in a Sanctuary State 54
3. Capturing Migrants with Police Body-Worn Cameras 66
4. Parking and Standing in the Street for ICE 87
5. The Morality of Sanctuary Style Force Multiplication 106
6. Sanctuary Policing and Force Division 127
7. The Authority of Sanctuary Policy 153
Conclusion 181
Acknowledgments 191
Methodology: Surveillant Anthropology 193
Notes 217
References 231
Index 241
About the Author 257

LIST OF ACRONYMS

BEST   Border Enforcement Security Task Force
BWC   Body-worn camera
BPD   Benjamin Township Police Department
CBP   US Customs and Border Protection
CCTV   Closed-circuit television
CIA   US Central Intelligence Agency
DHS   US Department of Homeland Security
DOL   US Department of Labor
ERO   Enforcement Removal Operations, ICE
FBI   US Federal Bureau of Investigation
HSI   Homeland Security Investigations, ICE
ICE   US Immigration and Customs Enforcement
INS   US Immigration and Naturalization Service
IRS   US Internal Revenue Service
LEA   Law enforcement agency
LESC   Law Enforcement Support Center, ICE
NCIC   National Crime Information Center
SUV   Sport Utility Vehicle
TCIU   Transnational Criminal Investigative Units, ICE-HSI
USCIS   US Citizenship and Immigration Services

PROLOGUE

The Immigration Enforcement Traffic Stop

It is March 4, 2020, more than one year after New Jersey Attorney General Gurbir Grewal issued his much-praised "Immigrant Trust Directive," a state sanctuary style policy with the force of law that limits the instances when local, county, regional, and state law enforcement officers can assist US Immigration and Customs Enforcement (ICE) in locating, arresting, and detaining immigrants to enforce federal immigration laws. It is 9:00 am, and Birchwood Police Department Officer Tim Rizzer turns on his chest-mounted body-worn camera, or BWC, and makes a traffic stop of a small white unmarked delivery truck, known as a box truck, in front of a row of grey residential track homes.[1] On this sunny morning, Officer Rizzer walks from the driver's side of his patrol car behind the stopped truck and up on the sidewalk as he approaches the truck's passenger side door. There, he sees two Latin American men in their thirties sitting in the cab of the truck. The passenger manually rolls down his window to talk to Rizzer. The officer says in a friendly manner, "What's up guys, how are ya'?" They respond, "Good morning." The officer continues, "I'm Officer Rizzer; you got yer driver's license and registration on ya,' boss?"

As the driver reaches down toward the cupholders mounted near the radio to a document holder in between their seats, Rizzer, speaking in English, continues, "Is this your vehicle or is this a company truck?" The two look at him and cooperatively respond, "Company, company truck," with Spanish accents, indicating that they speak English as a second language. Officer Rizzer then states, "The registration expired in 2017." The passenger looks to the driver and says something inaudible. The driver quickly raises his eyebrows and makes a facial expression to indicate mild surprise and that he understands. The driver continues to look through the documents from the document holder to find the registration papers and passes a document to the passenger, who in turn hands it to Rizzer. Rizzer tells them, "This is the insurance card. Do you have the registration card?" The driver finds another paper and passes it to Rizzer, who repeats that the second paper also pertains to the insurance. He then uses his hand to make a sign of the size of the type of card he is asking them to produce. After a few seconds, they look again at the papers, and the passenger says, "We only have this," referring to the insurance papers they had already given him.

Maintaining a straight and friendly manner, Rizzer asks, "OK, who owns the truck?" "Uh, his boss," the passenger replies, referring to the driver's boss. "Where is he at?" Rizzer asks. "He's not here. He's in another country on vacation. He'll be back tomorrow or today, he back," says the passenger. "Where's the company out of?" Rizzer then asks and receives a response inaudible to his BWC. "OK, can you call somebody there to get it registered?" In Spanish, the passenger asks the driver, "¿Puede llamar alguien para que tener la licencia?" (Can you call someone to get the license?) Rizzer explains, "They can call, um, whoever's at the office can call PennDot, and they can get it registered online." The car had been registered in Pennsylvania, and PennDot is the online vehicle registration system managed by the Pennsylvania Department of Transportation.

The officer then asks the driver, "Do you have a license on you?" The driver hands over an identification card from Brazil. The officer looks at it and says, "Is your first name José?" The driver responds, "My first name is Reyes." Reyes is a common surname in Latin America, and using the term "first name" may have been confusing for the driver, who had thought "first name" required him to respond with his surname first and his given name second, as is the practice in some countries. The officer then asks, "Your *first* name is Reyes?" The driver nods, and the passenger nods, saying, "Reyes." Rizzer then repeats the question, "Your first name is Reyes?" Then the passenger says, "The *last* name is Reyes, the first name is . . ." And he looks to the driver to finish his sentence. The driver says, "Senan," and the passenger chimes in, "First name is Senan, last name is Reyes," and he points to the identification card from Brazil that Rizzer is holding. Rizzer then shows the passenger the card, pointing to the biggest name on it, "José," and says, "Where do you see that on there, 'cause I don't see that? You just said your name was Fernando?" having misheard the name that the driver and passenger had told him. The passenger then points to a portion of the card where the name Senan Reyes is written in the upper corner and then the officer says, "OK, do you have any license out of any state? In New Jersey or Pennsylvania, anything?" The passenger speaks to Senan in Spanish to clarify Rizzer's question. Senan responds to the passenger saying, "Todavía no. Tengo amigos . . ." (Not yet. I have friends . . .) But while he is still speaking, the passenger tells Rizzer, "Not yet, but it is coming. They are mailing it."

Rizzer asks the passenger, "OK, and do you have a license or no?" The passenger responds, "No, I do not." Rizzer says, "OK, 'cause you got to wear a seat belt at all times, OK? Back when you guys passed me, you didn't have a seat belt on." The passenger nods and says, "OK." The officer says, "That's why I'm asking, do you have an ID on you?" The passenger, who misunderstands the question and thinks the question is directed toward Senan, turns to Senan and asks him again in Spanish, "¿No tiene un ID ni una persona que puede venir?" (You don't have an ID, or even someone who can come?) The passenger then tells Rizzer, "He can call the wife." The officer then says to the passenger while pointing at the passenger, "No, do *you* have an ID I'm asking." The passenger says, "Uh, no, I don't have an ID." Rizzer says, "OK, you don't have a PA [Pennsylvania] ID or nuttin'? Nothin' with yer name on it?" The passenger shakes his head and smiles uncomfortably. Rizzer then asks the passenger, "You ever been issued tickets in New Jersey?" The passenger then asks the driver in Spanish, and the driver tells him "No," leading the passenger to tell the officer in English, "No, he hasn't." Rizzer then again points at the passenger and says, "No, I mean *you*, I'm askin'." "*Me?*" says the passenger. "Yeah," says Rizzer. "Oh, no, before I had a little problem to immigration and I go outside for working my papers. Yes." Rizzer then says to the passenger, "So you don't have anything with your name on it, I'm asking?" The passenger responds, "No," and shakes his head.

The passenger then says, "So you said the registration is expired?" to clarify why they had been pulled over in the first place. "It's been expired since 2017. What's your first name?" says Rizzer. The passenger says while pointing to his chest, "*My* first name? Juan." "Middle name?" "Pablo." "Last name?" "Mendoza." Then, anticipating that Rizzer may misunderstand the name, as before, Juan offers to write it down so the spelling is correct. After Senan hands Juan a pen, Juan writes his name on the back of the insurance papers he had previously given to the officer.

"What's your date of birth?" asks Rizzer. Juan then provides it to him verbally. "You say you had a problem with immigration?" Rizzer asks. "Yes," Juan responds. "What happened there?" says Rizzer. Juan offers, "I had a little fight with somebody, and it go to a couple months . . . and they give me a bill for go outside." "OK, and where was that at?" Rizzer asks. Before answering this question, Juan continues his story, saying, "And now I have this," and he points down to his ankle where he is wearing an ankle monitoring bracelet. It is unclear if it was put on him by a local law enforcement agency or by ICE. ICE routinely uses ankle bracelets as an alternative to immigration detention, allowing ICE to know that the person they have placed in removal proceedings is within a limited territory in which ICE allows individuals to circulate before their court dates and potential removal. If the person with the monitoring bracelet were to leave this area, the ankle monitor, if issued by ICE, would alert ICE and track the person's location.

Rizzer then says, "You got an ankle bracelet?" "Yes," replies Juan. "OK, then you should have an ID card or sumpin', right?" Rizzer says. "Yes, I no have nothing," replies Juan with an uncomfortable chuckle before he averts his eyes downward. "OK, what state are you on probation?" Rizzer asks. "Uh, probation is for couple months, ah . . ." Juan responds. "Outta what state?" asks Rizzer. "Jersey," Juan says, and then, realizing Rizzer didn't understand, he begins to write that down on a piece of paper too. He then points at the word and says, "This morning, I go to my court." "Yeah, but where's court at?" Rizzer says. Shaking his head, Juan replies, "I don't know." He then takes out his phone to use a translation app to look up how to say something. "You were speaking pretty good English. I'm just trying to find out where you are on probation out of," says Rizzer, "You got an ankle bracelet, so it's gotta be somewhere in the United States, right?" Juan nods. It would seem as if Rizzer believed that the ankle bracelet was given to him by a local, county, or state law enforcement agency rather than by ICE. Rizzer continues, "So what state?" "Newark," Juan says. "Newark, New Jersey," Rizzer repeats back to Juan.

Rizzer then takes Senan's Brazilian ID back to his patrol vehicle, an SUV with the number "205" painted on the front driver's side. The bodycam video shows us that a second officer, a white male in his sixties, has arrived at the scene but has been standing silently near and behind Rizzer as he was questioning Juan and Senan. That second officer's vehicle, an SUV identical to Rizzer's, was parked immediately behind Rizzer's vehicle, indicating that he had arrived separately as backup. Rizzer enters his patrol vehicle and sits in the driver's seat in front of a mounted laptop wirelessly connected to the internet. He uses the Brazilian ID and the piece of paper where Juan wrote his name to type their names into a criminal background check search console on the laptop. The ID card has been blurred from the video produced by the BWC using video editing software by the police agency's public records custodian to avoid disclosing Senan's private information. Soon after, a visual blurring editing effect is added to the visual area of the footage to hide the mounted laptop. Rizzer examines both sides of the Brazilian ID card, and a beeping noise can be heard in the car. Rizzer holds the ID card in his left hand while using his right to type information from it. From the laptop, an auto-alert with a computerized voice states "NCIC alert," indicating that the individual that he just searched for in the National Crime Information Center NCIC database has a "hit," an entry under one of its many file systems.

The NCIC is a database that allows police officers nationwide to look up warrants and other criminal background information countrywide and is managed by the US Department of Justice.[2] ICE routinely uploads administrative ICE warrants into the NCIC database file named "Immigration Violator" if, for instance, an individual who is subject to removal proceedings or court check-ins misses a hearing. In such cases, immigration judges will order the individual to be removed in absentia, meaning "in their absence." ICE will then issue an administrative ICE warrant for their arrest and will place a digital alert in the NCIC for all law enforcement agencies (LEA) at all jurisdictional levels to respond to the warrant and alert ICE of their contact with the individual.

ICE warrants are not criminal warrants and have no force of law requiring that the agency respond to them or notify ICE.[3] An agency response is completely voluntary, as they are not required to participate in immigration enforcement, which is a federal mandate. To minimize local law enforcement cooperation in immigration enforcement, New Jersey, like many other US states, generally prohibited local, county, and state law enforcement from participating in civil immigration enforcement operations and providing nonpublic, personally identifying information of individuals they encounter to ICE if it is merely to enforce civil immigration laws. Responding to these administrative warrants, including those that are identified through NCIC background checks, plays no part in the local prosecution of traffic infractions such as expired registration or other state crimes, so detaining Senan—even keeping him in his car waiting—on the basis of an ICE warrant would violate the state Attorney General's Immigrant Trust Directive.

Officer Rizzer then silently reads the NCIC alert to himself and says to the other officer, after about twenty seconds of silence, "Alright, it looks like he's got an immigration violation, failure to appear for removal." The other officer says quickly, "What's that?" inviting Rizzer to repeat what he said because he didn't hear him. "The driver has a . . . ICE warrant, it looks like," says Rizzer. Then, reading the warrant from his patrol laptop, he says, "Outside administration warrant of removal from the United States." His body camera then makes a buzzing beep noise. Continuing to read the NCIC hit and ICE warrant, Rizzer says, "Contact for immediate hit confirmation. Failure to appear for removal from the United States . . . alien unlawfully present due to order of removal from the USA. Contact Bureau of Immigration and Customs Enforcement. That's for the driver. I'm going to assume the passenger has the same thing," says Rizzer—a rather big assumption. Within ten seconds, Officer Rizzer uses his patrol car radio to contact central dispatch for his agency. A male voice responds, and Rizzer says, "Can you check first name Sierra Echo November Alpha November, last name is Romeo Echo Yankee Echo Sierra, 7, 22 of 87. Ah, nothin' in hand. He might be a hit out of ICE. I'm gonna call them." He then puts down the radio, and the dispatch radios back, "Middle initial?" Officer Rizzer then responds, "Negative, I'm gettin' an ICE hit for immediate removal from the United States, stand by." The dispatcher then responds, "10-4." Rizzer sighs and then says, "Ahhhh, it's always sumpin'."

Officer Rizzer then returns to typing on his patrol car laptop while holding the Brazilian ID card. Again, an audio alert sounds "NCIC alert" from his laptop. A combination of silence, a beeping patrol car, the buzzing of his body cam, and keystrokes on the laptop fill the space. Then, within three minutes of finding the ICE warrant and ten minutes after first engaging the passenger and driver of the pulled-over vehicle, Officer Rizzer takes out his cell phone and, with one hand, begins to dial the main number for ICE included in the ICE administrative warrant alert—8-7-7-9-9-9-5-3-7-2. Rizzer, whether he knows it or not, is violating the state Attorney General's Immigrant Trust Directive.

As can be heard in the BWC audio recording, Officer Rizzer receives an automated choice menu for navigating to an ICE representative. He then switches the audio to his phone's speaker, which allows the BWC to capture ". . . at 8-0-2-8-7-2-6-0-2-0. To forward your NCIC call now, press 1. To replay this message, press 2 now." Officer Rizzer presses one, and a male voice answers the phone almost immediately. "Hi, L-E-S-C." LESC, which stands for Law Enforcement Support Center, is an ICE division that runs a call center. That center is the point of contact to ICE for all local agencies in the United States and a point of exchange of information that can be shared from these local agencies through the LESC to ICE field officers. Rizzer then says, "Hi, I'm an officer in Birchwood, New Jersey. I have a subject stopped, and it says I need to contact you for immediate hit confirmation." The LESC rep responds with, "Huhh. Ohhhh kay, ahm. Which part of New Jersey did you say you were from?" Rizzer responds, "We're in South Jersey, in Birchwood." After a brief silence, Rizzer continues, "I'm currently roadside with the individual and NCIC came up to contact you guys." The LESC rep says, "Yep, ah what is the, what is your best callback contact number?" Rizzer says, "Ah, it's area code 649 . . . 792 . . . 4329." The LESC rep says, "And what is your name, sir?" "It's Officer Rizzer, R-I-Z-Z-E-R," Rizzer responds. Rizzer puts down the Brazilian ID card and paper with the passenger's name written on it and takes the phone into his hand, speaking into the microphone and holding the phone like a slice of pizza. LESC says, "R-I and what did you say was the rest of it?" "Z-Z-E-R, badge 2-90," responds Rizzer. LESC says, "2-90, and do you know your ORI?" The "ORI" is a police agency acronym for Originating Agency Identifier that will quickly confirm the agency that Rizzer works for. Rizzer responds, "Yeah, it's NJ0050700." "K," says the LESC rep. After about twenty seconds of silence, the LESC rep clears his throat and says, "Now, what is the Nick number you are seeing?" referring to the case number on the NCIC hit on Rizzer's laptop. Rizzer is heard making noises as he tries to find it, "Ahhhhhh, chsh chsh, chsh, chsh." "Alright, ORI case number . . . ah! Nick number is N-1-5-

0-5-9-9-4-8-2. It says alien unlawfully present due to order of removal." LESC rep responds, "Yeah, that normally means, ahh, they're in absentia, never showed up to court, so they [the individual in removal proceedings] didn't get the opportunity to say their side, so the judge just went ahead and ordered them removed." Rizzer then asks the LESC rep, "OK, so then is this an active warrant?" The LESC rep then says, "Yeah, they are administrative so the only ones who can act on it is an immigration officer. So, I just got to look into it here to confirm who it is, and if it turns out to be the person, then I'll reach out to the local office and ask one of my [ICE] field agents how they want to proceed." Rizzer then responds, "OK."

The LESC rep then continues to ask Rizzer, "Any local charges, or is it just?" Rizzer jumps in to respond, "It's just gonna be motor vehicle at this point." "OK, what was the reason for the stop?" the LESC rep asks. "Unregistered vehicle," says Rizzer. "OK, do they have a valid driver's license?" asks the LESC rep. "I do not believe so; I have some kind of paper form of a Brazilian . . . a Brazilian sumptin' [something]" Rizzer says with mild ridicule. The LESC representative chuckles, "What, like a consulate card or something like that?" Rizzer says, "Yeah, somethin' like that, half of it is in English, half of it's not." A consulate card is a form of identification that nationals of a particular foreign country, including undocumented immigrants, can obtain from one of their nation's consulate offices in the United States. The LESC rep can then be heard over the phone talking to himself as he notes down certain information, "Ah, in absentia . . . alright."

Rizzer then says to the LESC rep, "Are you sure if the passenger's got anything? Cause it's not comin' back [the NCIC database isn't providing any information on him], and he's got an ankle bracelet, so he should be comin' back." The other Birchwood officer then chimes in from out of the body camera's view, perhaps outside the passenger window of the patrol vehicle on the sidewalk, "It doesn't necessarily have to come back." Rizzer then says to the LESC rep, "I just want to confirm that . . . whether what he gave me is the truth." Rizzer then picks up his patrol car radio and checks in with his agency dispatch, saying, "I sent you a second of notes. I got nothin' on him," referring to Juan's background check, including in the NCIC. Dispatch then responds back on the radio, "10-4, Be advised I'm on hold now with . . . the ICE."

Rizzer then realizes that both he and his agency's dispatcher had called ICE about Senan and Juan. Rizzer responds to his dispatch, "I have an [ICE] agent on my end. You can disregard." "10-4," responds the dispatcher. The LESC rep, overhearing this conversation between Rizzer and his dispatch, chimes in, "Uh, you talkin' to someone else?" Rizzer responds, "Uh yeah, I was just talkin' to dispatch, sorry." LESC then says, "Oh, I overheard that they were on hold with ICE, so I was curious who they were calling," and then chuckles. "Yeahhhh, I just told him he could hang up 'cause I got you on the phone."

Following another brief silence, the LESC rep says, "K, alright, what is a good email I can send some photos to?" Rizzer responds, "2-90 at B-P-D dot org." Another message comes loudly over the patrol car radio, "Can you open up the south door, please?" from another officer back at the Birchwood Police Station. As such, it is very likely that the communication between Rizzer and dispatch about the ICE immigration warrant and each of their calls to ICE could also be heard on this radio line by the other patrol officers on duty at this time. The LESC rep then says, "OK, I just sent those to you now [the photos]. And he is the one operating the vehicle?" "Yes," says Rizzer. The LESC rep then asks, "What's the vehicle's information?" "Ahhh, it is a 2000 and 6 Chevy Box Truck, Pennsylvania registration, HPR, Hotel, Papa, Romeo, 4-0-2-6," says Rizzer. LESC then asks, "Did he say where he lives or anything like that?" "Ah, I didn't get that far," responds Rizzer. "Oww kay [Oh kay]," says the LESC rep.

The other Birchwood officer then opens the passenger door and softly asks Rizzer to hit the mute button on his phone for the call with LESC. After Rizzer mutes the call, the other officer says, "They're not going to want him 'cause he didn't do nothin'. They put out these detainers and these warrants that . . . you can't prosecute 'em, take 'em away unless they're doin' a criminal act." This may indicate that the Birchwood officer mistook the provisions of the New Jersey Immigrant Trust Directive, which disallows local police from cooperating with ICE on the basis of an administrative warrant or a detainer, for ICE's own directives that aren't limited to only deporting people who committed criminal acts. ICE also targets people like Senan who have no criminal history and who may only be ordered removed in absentia after failing to appear in immigration court. ICE often relies on local police to voluntarily act as ICE's "force multipliers" or local partners, auxiliaries, surrogates, or emissaries to identify, arrest, detain, and turn over to ICE *any deportable immigrant* that they make contact with on the street or house in local jails, regardless of criminal background.

The second officer then asks Rizzer, "What's this guy sayin'?" "That he's gonna contact ICE and see what they want us to do with 'em," Rizzer says. From this statement, it appears that Rizzer either didn't fully understand that LESC *was* ICE and that he was talking to ICE already or that he just believed that the process was going to move forward with immigration field agents.

After about a minute, Officer Rizzer unmutes his phone and sets it down next to his laptop, saying, "I'mma start pennin'," referring to writing the violation tickets for Senan. The second officer then provided Rizzer with other information about Senan and Juan. It appears that while Rizzer was talking with the LESC rep, the second officer had walked up to the truck to further question the two men about their full names. Rizzer, looking at a piece of paper that the second officer handed to him, says, "Now it's Mendez?" The second officer says, "That's his full name," referring to Juan having two last names as is common for Latin Americans: A child's surname is often comprised of the father's patronym and the mother's patronym. Rizzer then takes the paper with Juan's full name and birth date as well as a small flip spiral notebook and places them in front of him on the steering wheel of his vehicle. After making a few keystrokes on his patrol vehicle laptop, the second officer mentions, "And his bracelet is from a bail bondsman, so it's nothin' official." "Really?!" Rizzer responds with surprise. "That's what he said," explains the second officer. "Never heard of that," Rizzer replies.

Officer Rizzer continues typing on his laptop with his right hand. Then, setting down the piece of paper, flipping closed his mini spiral notebook and putting it in a pocket of his uniform below the BWC, he takes out a black clipboard with a flip-up hard black top, which covers police forms. He opens the strap that kept the clipboard from opening on its own and pulls out a long, narrow pad with a blue card on top from which he can fill out a ticket, which is a traffic court summons for Senan. He reinserts the pad partially back into his clipboard, allowing the top two pages of the ticket pad to rest flatly on the hard surface of the clipboard's cover. The top page is a white ticket that he will keep, while behind it is a yellow carbon copy that he will issue to Senan.

He then asks the other officer sitting with him, "John's gonna be able to tow that?" referring to the box truck. No auditory response from the other officer can be heard. Officer Rizzer then takes the Brazilian ID card into his hands and looks at it. He says to his partner, "What do you think about this?" as he flips it over to inspect the back of the card and then stares at the front, holding it on both sides with both of his hands. The other officer says, "It's expired," potentially avoiding any comments on the card's authenticity, the foreignness of it, or whether it is a driver's license of any kind. It didn't matter what it *was*, given that the expiration reduced it to an inactive legal tool of any kind whatsoever. After a few seconds, the other officer follows up with, "Anyway, " after which Officer Rizzer says, "Right, but," and the other officer quickly tells him, "Just write 'em 'unlicensed.'"

Officer Rizzer then says, "Usually they're hardcopy, aren't they?" referring to the fact that the nature of the ID was printed merely on cardstock without any lamination. He flicks it with his thumb to gauge the card's thickness and durability. He then sets the Brazilian ID on the keyboard of his laptop and returns to writing tickets with a metallic pen in his slightly thick, white right hand. The other officer says, "Yeah, well, some countries they . . ." and trails off. Rizzer begins writing the driver's name on the ticket. "Passenger's got a local address though," says the other officer. "Does he?" replies Rizzer, as he takes the Brazilian ID back into his hands and places it on top of the ticket, reexamining the front side as if to gather more information to include. He then writes the driver's birthday on the ticket.

After writing a few more things on the ticket, Rizzer stops to pick up his phone, looks at it, and places it on the keys of his laptop, with the LESC representative still on the line. A sigh from the rep is heard on the phone speaker, while Rizzer resumes writing the ticket behind blurred visual blocks added to the BWC video by the agency records custodian. The LESC rep then says, "Did that email show up on your end? . . . orrrr ?" Rizzer then responds, "I'm not going to be able to access that right now." The rep, who was a bit surprised at Rizzer's response, says, "Oh. . . . hmm. . . . OK . . . ahhhhh." Rizzer continues writing the ticket and begins to type on his laptop keyboard, after which the laptop dings. The LESC rep, who by now is slightly confused and annoyed but polite, says, "So you won't be able to pull up the photos?" Rizzer, seeming to think about it more, says, "Uhhhhhhh, hang on one sec," to which the LESC rep says in a stunted and quiet way, "Ahaight."

After Rizzer types a few keystrokes on his laptop, the LESC rep states, "So if you could just look at 'em and make a determination based on your training experience whether or not it looks like the subject of our warrant, and if you say 'yes,' we'll go forward, if you think it doesn't then that's the end of it." After typing while the LESC rep was talking, Rizzer then says, "Uhhhhh, I got it, hold on." He hits the space bar on his laptop and quickly replies, "Yeah, that's him," having seen the photos the rep sent him. The LESC rep then says, "That's him? OK. [sighs] Alrightee," and then "Ahhhhh, chsh, chsh, chsh, chsh chsh," as he thinks of what to do next. Rizzer turns the laptop so that the other officer in his vehicle can see what is on the screen, which is blocked out by the visual blurring blocks placed by the video's editor. It is presumably the images of the driver that the LESC rep sent to Rizzer's email address. The rep then asks Rizzer, "Which county do you fall in?" to which he responds, "Point Easton." "K . . . Mount Laurel," says the LESC, rep as he is thinking through which of his ICE field offices to contact based on Rizzer's location. "Ahhh tuh, tuh, tuh, tuh, tuhhhhh. Alright, why don't you stay on hold while I reach out to my field agents out there," says the rep. "OK," Rizzer replies. At this point, the driver and passenger have been waiting for fifteen minutes for Rizzer to return to them.

Rizzer's agency dispatch then calls on the radio "205," referring to his patrol vehicle number. Rizzer picks up and says, "205" quickly and affirmatively. Loud piano music is coming from the phone while Rizzer remains on hold for the LESC rep to give him a response about what the ICE field officers say that he should do. Dispatch then says, "Juan is negative ATS / ACS [Automated Traffic System/Automated Complaint System], ah can't find anything on him. NCIC does have a contact in ACSO. Ah, he's negative." This would indicate that there is no criminal history or judicial warrant for the passenger's arrest in the state's ATS/ACS, a system that lists criminal warrants issued by criminal court judges throughout New Jersey and that's run by the state's courts. Nor does there seem to be any ICE administrative warrant in the NCIC for him.

At that point, the LESC rep returns to the phone call and begins speaking at the same time as Rizzer's dispatch, prompting Rizzer to ask, "I'm sorry, what was that, sir?" "Ah, yeah, I was just asking where you are located at; where's the stop at," the LESC rep says. "We're at 5th and New Jersey," responds Rizzer. Rizzer's dispatch, then over the radio, says again, "He's negative ATS/ACS." The LESC rep goes on to ask Rizzer, "Alright . . . in Jersey?" to which Rizzer replies, "Yeah, Birchwood." The LESC rep puts Rizzer back on hold, and Rizzer returns to writing the traffic violation ticket for Senan, while piano music resumes over the phone speaker. When he finishes writing the first ticket, he lifts up the top sheet, removes the carbon copy sheet from the bottom at its perforated edge toward the top of the pad and sets the copy to the side of his laptop. He flips the other pages of that ticket up and over the top of the pad and sets a new set of ticket pages on the flat face of the clipboard's cover to write a second ticket. He begins to write up a second ticket for the driver. After a minute, he pauses from his writing, picks up his radio, and says, "205." When the dispatcher responds, Rizzer says, "Can you notify John for that registration?" referring to the tow truck driver. "Advise him it's gonna be a box truck," Rizzer continues. "10-4," responds the dispatcher. Rizzer puts the radio back on his middle console and returns to his ticket writing. Once he finishes writing up the tickets, Rizzer takes his phone, which is still playing on-hold piano music, in his left hand with the two tickets and begins typing on his laptop with his right hand. He then clears a third set of ticket sheets on his clipboard, preparing to fill out a third ticket for Senan.

At that moment, the dispatch calls to Rizzer, saying, "205," but since the LESC rep took Rizzer off hold at the same time and began speaking, Rizzer responds to LESC first. Ignoring his dispatch, Rizzer says, "Ga'head sir." After some silence, he probes again, "Hello?" to which the LESC rep responds, "OK, so I just talked to one of my officers out of Mount Laurel, and since you're not, since you don't have any local charges, since you're just a stop, you are probably going to cite and release." The LESC rep is referring to the fact that rather than taking the driver and passenger into police custody and to the station into detention, Rizzer would likely just give Senan the traffic tickets and let the two leave on their own. Rizzer answers, "Right. " "Ahm," the rep continues, "that he's [the ICE field officer] not going to be able to get out there, he's not going to want to hold you up. All he's asking for is if we could get any good information so that we could get it to our field ops team and they can follow up with it, um where he's [the driver] livin', cell phone, where he's workin'," to which Officer Rizzer responds, "OK." The LESC rep continues, "If you can get that information then that way, they can chase him down later." Rizzer responds, "OK, sounds good."

LESC then prompts Rizzer, "Ah, I can wait if you want to get out and grab that and I can just write it down," referring to the information that he requested Rizzer collect from Senan and Juan. "Aaahm, yeah, gimme one minute; I'm about to issue [the tickets], and then can I put you on hold?" Rizzer tells the rep. The rep responds, "Yeah, no problem." "Alright, gimme one minute," says Rizzer. After setting his phone down unmuted next to his laptop console, Rizzer finishes writing up the third ticket for Senan and removes the yellow carbon copy from the bottom of the ticket pages, collects the other tickets he had previously written, along with Senan's Brazilian ID card, and opens the car door. Twenty-three minutes after taking Senan's ID and other papers back to his patrol car, Rizzer walks back to the truck's driver's side door as cars driving on the road pass him quickly on his left-hand side.

As Senan manually rolls down his window, the other officer accompanying Rizzer can be seen just outside of Juan's window on the other side of the truck. Rizzer tells Senan in a friendly tone, "Alright man, look. I issued some summons, OK? This vehicle is going to get towed cause it's unregistered. Alright, three years ago it got unregistered." Juan then says, "Someone is coming?" "It's gonna get towed," repeats Rizzer, as he gestures with his hand, waving it downward while holding the tickets to punctuate each word he says. Senan then nods his head, affirming that he understands. Rizzer continues, ". . . to John's Autobody. So, all I ask is that you just leave one key for the truck, OK?" Senan then nods again and strokes his chin as if he were considering the situation. "Once the car gets registered, you can ah, you can go get it out of impound, OK?" says Rizzer, and Senan nods. "He'll give you a card when he gets here, OK?" Rizzer then hands Senan the papers and ID that he had taken before and says, "Here's all your credentials back." Rizzer is holding the yellow paper tickets, and he says, "You are being issued quite a few summons, OK? Um, 'unlicensed driver,' 'unregistered vehicle,' and 'failure to exhibit the registration to the vehicle.'" As he is listing the summonses,

Senan nods, understanding. Rizzer continues, "Alright, you are going to have a court date on the 17th at 1:00 pm. It is mandatory, OK? You understand that?" Senan nods again and says, "Yep." Rizzer hands him the three long, narrow yellow tickets.

Without skipping a beat, Rizzer then continues in the same friendly tone, "Listen, I got a couple of questions for ya, 'k? For the report. What's the name of the fiberglass company [the company that they work for]?" Juan leans forward from the passenger seat to speak past Senan to Rizzer, "Fibernew." Officer Rizzer repeats the company name and writes it down in his small spiral notebook and then asks, "Is that locally?" Juan then finds a business card for the company and says, "This is the business card," not knowing that Rizzer is collecting information that he will give to ICE to help them arrest the two of them potentially while at work. Rizzer continues, "So what's your address?" Juan then points with this thumb to Senan and answers Rizzer, "Uh, him?" to which Rizzer responds, "Yeah, Senan, what's your address?" The driver then picks up a folded white piece of paper with writing on it and shows Rizzer that it is his address, and the passenger says it aloud to the officer. "In Birchwood?" Rizzer asks, to which they both respond, "Yeah." "Is there an apartment number or anything?" Rizzer asks. Senan nods and says, "Yeah, 448." Juan then chimes in, "No, it's a house." "What's a good phone number for ya'?" Rizzer then asks. As Senan again holds up the piece of paper with his address and phone number for Rizzer to record in his notebook, the editor of the BWC video uses visual blurring blocks and a long "beep" noise to block out the audio of Senan telling Rizzer the number. Rizzer then asks, "Aan' [and] where you born at? Brazil?" "Yes," Senan responds. "What city in Brazil?" asks Rizzer. Senan looks at Juan, who repeats the question in Spanish, "¿Qué ciudad de Brazil?" Senan then tells him. Rizzer then notes it down and asks him, "Alright, single, married, divorced, anything like that?" Juan says, "Wife," answering for Senan as he nods. Senan holds up the paper again with his wife's name added to the paper, not knowing that Rizzer may share this answer with ICE and that they may target her as well. Rizzer then asks, "Any tattoos?" Juan repeats the question in Spanish for Senan, "¿Tatuajes?" "No."

Rizzer then says in a friendly way, "OK, now the tow guy is comin', so if you guys just want to walk to wherever you gotta go, 'cause you [Juan] don't have a license either, right? So, as long as you just leave a key, he'll lock it up for you, OK?" The two say, "OK." Rizzer continues, "So, you are going to have to call Fibernew to have them get it registered to get it out, OK guys?"

After this short two-and-a-half-minute interaction ended, Officer Rizzer then closes his notepad and turns to walk back to his patrol vehicle, having concluded the traffic stop and allowed Senan and Juan to leave. As he approaches his car, he spits on the ground and opens his driver's side door, sits down in his driver's seat, picks up his phone where the LESC rep had been waiting on the line, and says to him, "Ahaight, sir you there?" The rep says, "Yes, I am." Rizzer continues, "K, his local address is 448, 4-48 West Birch Avenue in Birchwood." After a moment of pause, the LESC rep says, "West . . . Birch, Birchwood, alright, and you got his phone number?" Rizzer responds, "Yeah, he's working for a company called Fibernew." "Is that outta Birchwood? Orrr . . ." asks the LESC rep. "Ahhh, hold on, I'mma see what the registration comes back with," says Rizzer. Then, holding his phone in his left hand, Rizzer uses his right hand to type something into his patrol vehicle laptop. He then says, "Nah, it looks like they're gonna be outta Philadelphia." "OK," responds the rep. "At least that's where the registration comes back to," continues Rizzer. "Yeah, I'll try to Google them and see if I can find anything," the LESC rep tells him before then asking, "Any phone numbers or anything like that?" Rizzer tells the rep his phone number, which has been auditorily covered over by a 14-second "beeeep" sound inserted into the BWC by the agency records custodian to conceal the numbers. The LESC rep then asks him, "Alright, um, now you're set. Are you givin' him a ticket where you're gonna have to appear?" "Yeah, he's gonna have to appear. He's an unlicensed driver, so he's gonna have to appear on the 17th of March," says Rizzer. "If he even shows up," the LESC rep replies, to which Rizzer responds, "Yeah, *exactly*." The LESC rep then, noting the court date, says, "OK, March 2020, and what court?" Rizzer responds, "Birchwood." "Is there a ticket number for that?" Rizzer reaches over and picks up his black clipboard with his ticket pad still attached to the front cover and says, "Aaaahhhh, yeah, it's gonna beeeeee, gimme one sec." He flips through the pad to the first ticket where he wrote "1-9-2-0-3-2" and then flips the pages back down as the LESC rep repeats the number.

Outside of the patrol car, the second officer can be heard telling the truck driver and the passenger in a very positive and friendly manner,

"Alright, thanks, guys," as they walk past Rizzer's patrol vehicle in view of the body camera, away from their vehicle, and leave the site of the traffic stop. Almost at the exact same time that the second officer says this to Senan and Juan, in a sort of poetic synchrony, the LESC rep simultaneously says to Rizzer over the phone, "Alllllright, well, thank you very much for takin' the time and I know you're very busy, I don't want to hold you up any longer." Rizzer then says to the rep, "Nah, I appreciate it, I just didn't know what the process was, so I just wanted to contact you." The rep then says, "Yeah, well, if it's one of our, any of the ones that start with N, it's administrative for us, so . . ." "OK," says Rizzer, who then turns off his body camera, ending the video and audio recording of the interaction while the LESC rep continues to speak to him on the phone.

Introduction

Sanctuary Policing, Force Multiplication, and Force Division

In November 2018, New Jersey Attorney General Gurbir Grewal issued an executive directive called the Immigrant Trust Directive which adopted much of the language from sanctuary state laws of other states such as California's SB54, also known as The California Values Act. The Immigrant Trust Directive prohibited New Jersey's local, county, and state law enforcement officers, including police, sheriff's deputies, parole officers, park police, jail staff, juvenile detention staff, and prosecutors, from stopping, questioning, arresting, searching, or detaining individuals on the basis of their immigration status or suspected violations of civil immigration laws except in certain circumstances outlined in the policy. The directive limited when law enforcement could participate in civil immigration enforcement operations, provide personal information of any individual to federal agencies to enforce civil immigration laws or provide federal agencies access to local law enforcement equipment, office space, databases, or property not available to the general public. Law enforcement could not provide federal immigration enforcement agencies access to interview the people the local agency had detained unless the local agency informed that individual of their right to refuse the interview and had obtained their consent. The directive prohibited local law enforcement from continuing the detention of people in their custody after they would otherwise be eligible for release so that immigration officers could arrive to arrest them. It also prohibited local agencies from providing immigration officers with information about when and where the agency would release individuals to the public. These prohibitions did not apply in certain circumstances, however, what the Attorney General was communicating to law enforcement in New Jersey, to the immigrant public, and to then-US President Donald Trump through issuing the directive was that the law enforcement personnel under his authority would not be dedicating their time and resources to an unimpeded search for undocumented immigrants to deport.

President Donald Trump's immigration enforcement strategies initiated in 2017, and to which Grewal was responding, treated all violations of any law, be they minor local or state infractions or serious felonies, as equal grounds for targeting and deporting the undocumented immigrants arrested. This included individuals with no criminal record and individuals whose charges were dropped or who were found not guilty of the crime for which they were accused. In practice, this was not unlike the approach under the Obama administration, which similarly targeted all immigrants on the basis of their criminal histories and criminal bookings in jails. President Trump, however, introduced a whole new level of mean-spiritedness to the business of immigration control that was less present in the Obama years. While the Obama administration deprioritized deportations for certain categories of immigrants, such as certain children, and had issued a policy memo to instruct immigration agents to refrain from making immigration arrests at schools, hospitals, churches, and other "sensitive locations," the Trump administration retracted these restrictions, essentially giving agents free rein to arrest any deportable immigrant anywhere, and renewed the use of worksite immigration raids as an enforcement tactic. This was done expressly to create widespread fear and panic throughout immigrant communities nationwide and to send the message that no one was safe from deportation. President Trump's gloves-off approach toward immigrants followed a presidential campaign filled with his vociferously anti-immigrant rhetoric, blaming immigrants for crime in America's urban centers and border states.

Given the relatively unrestrained, wide net that this dragnet approach cast, the Trump administration sought the cooperation of local law enforcement who encounter immigrants every day, arrest them, and detain them in their local jails. This approach was not new, but rather, had been developed by previous presidential administrations as far back as that of Ronald Reagan in the 1980s. It is also an approach that extended beyond the borders of the American mainland to other locations throughout the world where US immigration agents sought the partnership of local law enforcement to fight transnational crime and unauthorized migration.

This highly diverse set of law enforcement agencies spread throughout the world, including local police in New Jersey, are increasingly serving as force multipliers within a global network of immigration control agencies seeking to regulate immigration, fight crime, and manage the lives of migrants on the move.

The force multiplier concept was originally developed by US military and security officials and generally referred to any type of instrumental tool or auxiliary partner that greatly increases the capabilities of the military to achieve its mission or objectives that it couldn't achieve on its own.[1] As the concept has been taken up by immigration control officials and their local partners through new joint initiatives targeting immigrants, the term has taken on many new meanings and has made possible new ways of conceptualizing the role of local police in contemporary society. This book not only introduces a wide spectrum of force multipliers in the field of immigration control but pays in-depth attention to a primary force multiplier in the federal government's fight against undocumented immigration—local patrol officers as they conduct surveillance, identification, arrest, detention of, and information sharing about deportable immigrants with the US federal government. Further, it demonstrates how local police in New Jersey assist US Immigration and Customs Enforcement as force multipliers even while also complying with the state's sanctuary policy, the Attorney General's Immigrant Trust Directive.

As we will see, sanctuary policies in New Jersey put forth the public relations façade that police, by and large, do not cooperate with ICE. As with all policing policies, at best, they provide local police officers with a written guidepost for how they *should* interact with immigrants and with ICE in the field. Ideally, they protect police from being compelled to assist ICE in many cases and help them exercise immigrant-friendly policing. In practice, however, sanctuary policies afford police the discretion and ability to elaborate creative new ways to routinely assist ICE anyway. In the end, sanctuary policies paradoxically establish a facially "pro-immigrant" immigration enforcement-assistance policing regime.

This book offers a guide through individual policing incidents that involved local New Jersey police officers, ICE agents, and undocumented immigrants as they were recorded by local police with their police officer body-worn cameras. Through the view of these BWCs, this book undertakes what I call surveillant anthropology, a critical social scientific investigation that is itself a type of surveillance or watching over the police and is conducted through the view of the police's own surveillance technologies, their BWCs. This book provides detailed, immersive narratives created from video analysis of roughly fifty BWC videos following an extensive review of public records documents from 416 New Jersey law enforcement agencies that represent 68 percent of the state's total agencies. These records pertain to local law enforcement's implementation of the New Jersey Immigrant Trust Directive. Through the narratives in this book based on police videos, I aim to provide an "on the ground" portrayal not only of local policing and police interactions with immigrants under sanctuary policies, but also of the manner in which sanctuary policy links police and ICE and *facilitates* immigration enforcement activities. What this book shows is that through this linkage, sanctuary ceases to be solely a form of protection for immigrants from deportation, as is typically assumed of sanctuary policies, and increasingly becomes a style and mode of policing immigrants and the sanctuary spaces in which they live—what I call sanctuary policing.

The term "sanctuary" in the immigration context refers to a vast diversity of ethics, practices, symbolic expressions, social and religious movements, sociocultural governance structures, policies, laws, physical spaces, and geographies over different historical periods.[2] While the term sanctuary may be used to describe these various phenomena, it does not mean that an essential element of each of these phenomena is consistently present across each case where individual and group actors assert that a certain action, activity, humanitarian provision of aid, or protection for immigrants is a form of sanctuary.

The most common referents of the term sanctuary are *practices* that aim to protect individuals subjected to forms of threat, danger, harm, or violence in the context of a pursuit from a harmful pursuer.[3] This is a scenario that might include a variety of roles—there is typically a seeker of sanctuary, a provider of sanctuary that utilizes sanctuary practices, and a provider of past, present, or potential harm. What is provided in this scenario—that is, the object that is exchanged as a gift or through a contract—is sanctuary. Sanctuary here is thought to frustrate, delay, or deny the pursuer from contact with the sanctuary seeker. In the process of exchanging sanctuary with the sanctuary seeker, in return, the sanctuary provider may request from the sanctuary seeker their adherence to rules of cohabitation in a protected sanctuary space, voluntary labor, or providing public testimony, for instance, to media outlets, of the reasons why the sanctuary seeker is seeking sanctuary or why the provision of sanctuary has improved their lives.[4] In accepting and complying with the terms of the exchange relationship between the sanctuary seeker and the sanctuary provider, an asymmetric relationship between the two parties is typically established wherein the provider has a greater degree of power in determining the conditions of the exchange and ongoing relationship than the sanctuary seeker. In the immigration context, this dynamic has been instantiated in a variety of practices that sanctuary providers use to frustrate ICE in its pursuit of undocumented immigrants whom they seek to deport. Deportation may send immigrants to places where they might encounter harm, and the separation of immigrants from their communities through deportation may also create harmful consequences for those who were not deported, such as family members, including financial destitution and emotional trauma in the wake of the deportation.

The sanctuary protection is accomplished through practices of resource provision, acceptance, compliance, rule establishment, rule adherence, dominance, exchange, and denial. What is ideally provided as sanctuary is space free from harm from the pursuer—a physical, legal, spiritual, symbolic, or political barrier that an individual or institution keeps between the sanctuary seeker and the pursuer, life-sustaining resources such as food and health provisions, and time, which acts upon the pursuer to diminish their desire for harming the sanctuary seeker. Another key provision is a chance to obtain a more fair legal hearing, as well as, in some cases, legal representation, which permits the sanctuary seeker to terminally stop the pursuer and publicize their testimony in a manner that might vindicate them from the wrongdoing for which they have been accused. The sanctuary seeker may also be afforded a greater chance to secure the support of various publics so that the seeker might move out of the sanctuary space safely and maintain their lives with less fear. In effect, sanctuary in this form is a practice to enact legal processes or laws to prevent extralegal popular justice—vengeance—or when protective laws ensuring due process for the accused are not being implemented.[5] Insofar as the sanctuary provider is a private actor or private institution such as a church and the pursuer is a government agency such as ICE, some theorists have framed the provision of sanctuary as private sector refusal or resistance to government power or one front of the battle between "church and state."[6]

Well-documented examples of this form of sanctuary have been religious institutions that formally allow individuals who have been accused of committing a crime to enter into and take shelter in their religious buildings so that, provided they abide by the rules of the religious institution, the institution will deny access to the harmful pursuer. In the case of the Hebraic Cities of Refuge described in the Book of Joshua, this form of sanctuary is one that allows someone accused of manslaughter to evade violent retribution from the victim's family members—a "blood feud"— to ensure an emotional cooling down period. This allowed for a more just trial after tensions had settled to determine if the accused individual in sanctuary was actually guilty. This practice of protection was to ensure due process under Hebraic law, after which the individual if found guilty, would be turned over to the family to be killed. If the original death was found to be accidental and the accused sanctuary seeker found to be innocent of intentionally causing that death, they could return to their home without fear of retribution from the aggrieved family.

More contemporary forms of this sanctuary scenario include the activities of social and religious movements that have provided sanctuary to immigrants and refugees across a network of sites, whether in movement members' homes, organizational buildings, or in other private sector spaces such as safe houses that are nonetheless networked as nodes of the movement.[7] According to the Church World Service, by 2018, thirty-seven people had entered into a sanctuary space provided by a church, and by January 2018, more than 1,100 religious institutions and forty coalitions were involved in faith-based forms of providing sanctuary to sanctuary seekers.[8] While this, in many ways, is a provision of many forms of care, certain practices involved in this form of sanctuary also entail the use of methods of surveillance, wherein the provider of sanctuary literally or figuratively watches over the seeker of sanctuary and their pursuers. This might be a paternalist form of watching over a sanctuary seeker to understand *where they geographically are to be rescued*, as is the case of European "search and rescue" organizations that operate surveillance airplanes over the Mediterranean that locate endangered or lost refugee boats and then coordinate via satellite phones with their sea ships to attempt rescue missions.[9]

It may also take the form of a vetting process at the gateways of sanctuary spaces to ensure that prior to agreeing to provide sanctuary, the provider assesses the risk that a sanctuary seeker poses to others in the sanctuary space, as was the case in the US sanctuary movement that provided sanctuary to Central American refugees in the 1980s.[10] Finally, to a certain degree, the sanctuary provider watches over, or at least is attentive to the sanctuary seeker within the sanctuary space to fully understand their ongoing needs, who the sanctuary seeker is as demonstrated in their behavior, and to ensure that they are not violating the terms, spoken or unspoken, of the sanctuary relationship. These practices of sanctuary regulation and soft "watching over" of the sanctuary seeker are part of the provision of private, uninhibited space as well, where sanctuary seekers obtain a sense of internal peace away from even the eyes of sanctuary providers. A key practice of sanctuary providers in many cases is also to occlude external surveillance of sanctuary seekers, as was the case among settled communities of fugitive slaves that composed nodes in the underground railroad in North America. In this case, settled fugitive slaves who provided sanctuary to other slaves on the run occluded the surveillant practices of slave catchers by creatively hiding them from public view and sometimes through creating elaborate theatrical performances that allowed fugitives to escape arrests, including helping them take on other identities, for instance as whites or as a person of another gender.[11]

The etymology of the term sanctuary refers to the physical space of the part of a church immediately surrounding the altar, and more generally, a sacred place where one is given immunity from arrest, an etymology based in religious traditions, including the Hebraic case examined above.[12] Given this history of religious space being used to provide sanctuary, the conceptualization of sanctuary as *space* or territory more generally has been among the most theorized. When sanctuary and hospitality are considered together, the spaces to which the term sanctuary is applied have included those where foreigners may request some form of life-sustaining assistance from others more generally, even in the absence of any proximate harm or pursuer. Such assistance may be provided by "full" members of a society, such as national citizens or by other private individual immigrants and immigrant families.[13]

Hospitality and life-sustaining assistance as sanctuary can also be provided by the community organizations that immigrants have created, and as such scholars have theorized communal self-help for recently arrived immigrants as a form of sanctuary as well.[14] Sanctuary here is conceptualized spatially in terms of making a space, be it an organizational space or a geographical location like a neighborhood or city, where outsiders are welcome, where immigrants work together among themselves to build communal self-sufficiency, minimize immigrant precarity and vulnerability, and amass resources for development internal to the community and among their transnational networks. Rather than a governmentally created space through policy or law, this form of spatial sanctuary aims to foster immigrants *thriving* rather than merely surviving and is more often a grassroots and autonomous form of sanctuary that makes use of private cultural practices of hospitality, balanced reciprocity, ethics, and values of sanctuary. In this type of situation, sanctuary providers and sanctuary receivers are the same people who may alternate between these roles as they mutually work together over time. In this formulation, sanctuary need not be created within the confines of an institutional space into which sanctuary seekers arrive but rather is taken out into the everyday places where vulnerable people need support, accompaniment, and assistance. In this manner, sanctuary extends anywhere that sanctuary people go out and make people's lives better, whether they are immigrants, refugees, or other populations facing oppression and violence.[15] This may include confronting and engaging in activities that aim to abolish systems that reproduce such oppression and violence.[16]

Protagonists of these previously discussed forms of sanctuary may also link with government agencies, public sector executives, and lawmakers, to advocate for policies and laws that transform government operations so that within territorial jurisdictions, they enact new procedures inspired by the values associated with sanctuary explained above. Social movements may work with policymakers and bureaucrats to provide legal and administrative rights to sanctuary seekers; to extend voting rights to immigrants to make decisions about government operations; or to produce policies and procedures to provide governmental services and benefits to sanctuary seekers in ways that do not expose them to harm, including immigration enforcement actions.[17] These policies define when it is appropriate and inappropriate for government employees to play a role in immigration enforcement processes targeting individuals in the jurisdiction they manage and are typically called sanctuary policies, sanctuary laws, and firewall policies in a general sense.[18] Each policy that is labeled with the sanctuary term is different, though some typical characteristics are evident.

Some sanctuary policies prohibit or limit the ability of local government staff to collect information from members of the public in the course of government service provision that could be used to target that person for deportation. Other policies place general prohibitions upon local government staff, disallowing them from using local government resources to voluntarily assist immigration enforcement officers with an immigration enforcement task. Others prohibit police and other law enforcement from initiating contacts or investigations with people to determine their immigration status and to report it to immigration officers; detaining people for immigration officers to make an immigration arrest; or sharing information about when an individual will be released from a local jail to the public so that immigration officers can come and arrest them. Most significant are policies that determine how staff may provide services to members of the public without asking them about their immigration status, in effect rendering national citizenship unnecessary for the operation of these government processes. There are many other types of policies that are rarer, for instance, policies that prohibit harassment of immigrants or housing discrimination on the basis of immigration status, that have been given the label sanctuary as well.

While these types of policies may be created with anti-deportation intentions, they need not be and may merely be administrative policies designed to maintain the efficiency of local services—clarifying how to keep services operational despite a large population of people whose cooperation and trust the local government requires. In the end, the government needs information flowing from all sectors of society, including from communities that include undocumented immigrants, so it can best manage the use of public resources. In this manner, sanctuary may also be thought of as a lever of government resources mediated by a particular sanctuary style management strategy.[19] Sanctuary in this formulation is a style of public administration, or what Susan Coutin and Walter Nichols call "adminigration" management,[20] which creates what Els De Graauw calls a type of local "bureaucratic membership" for immigrants—members of society who may engage local bureaucracies such as schools when the national government will not extend national citizenship to them.[21] Effectively, this is a manner in which to make government services operate in an immigration-status-blind manner. From this, sanctuary as a mode or strategy of public administration, government practices, processes, and benefits have been theorized as sanctuary government services and sanctuary government practices, as the public sector correlates to those life-sustaining provisions of sanctuary provided by private sector or religious and social movement actors.[22]

However, as with private sector sanctuary, governments place conditions upon obtaining sanctuary as a sanctuary government service or benefit. In some cases, government services will be provided to any jurisdictional *resident* regardless of their immigration status, and should they commit a certain type of crime, the jurisdiction may authorize its staff to deny services or work with ICE to detain and transfer custody of the individual for deportation. Reflecting on this, some theorists of sanctuary policies have described them as *neoliberal* policies—policies that draw societal boundaries in a manner to selectively include only immigrants who are law-abiding; who privately take responsibility for their social welfare while living in the shadows; who may not have protections against deportation due to their immigration status; and who are therefore more easily kept in line by managers who can threaten them with calling ICE should they stand up for their rights. Those immigrants who are not permitted to receive sanctuary by policy are those who commit crimes, especially those who threaten property, business, and the well-being of the labor force; and who are not integrated into either the formal or informal economy but rather merely into black markets. In effect, according to this theory, sanctuary government provisions maintain a docile and easily exploitable labor force that is multicultural and, therefore can additionally contribute financially valuable cultural assets—ethnic food, clothing, events, and linguistic capabilities—that can be used to market the jurisdiction as desirable to cosmopolitan-minded working professionals, companies, and investors.[23] These are framed as neoliberal because they generally align with neoliberal conceptions of how economies should work—for instance, by minimizing regulations upon companies that protect workers, minimizing the government's responsibility for the welfare of workers, and placing a greater responsibility upon the workers for taking care of themselves, all toward the minimization of production costs and maximization of profit.

Because sanctuary policies administer governmental operations in territorial space, writers have theorized these in terms of their spatial or territorial *effects* as well. In some cases, scholars have framed sanctuary policies as creating territorial spaces where immigrants are protected by local governments, that is, local sovereigns, from the immigration enforcement agencies of national governments, and in so doing, create spaces outside of national sovereignty where immigrants and refugees who the national government wants to remove from the nation have a better chance to remain present, assert their rights, and influence or make decisions about that society.[24] In this sense, the discourse of private sanctuary as resistance is adapted to frame government sanctuary policy as resistance to the rule of federal law and national sovereignty, despite these policies in most cases passing constitutional legal muster and surviving federal lawsuits seeking to overturn them.[25] Some legal scholars have argued to the contrary, however, that sanctuary policies largely reinforce a sort of legal status quo—that is, they reaffirm constitutional boundaries and state's rights—and push back upon national attempts to overstep its legal powers and *overcontrol* these local and state spaces.[26] In the United States, there are currently eleven states that have passed state policies and laws that have been labeled sanctuary state policies and that apply to all local jurisdictions: California, Colorado, Connecticut, Illinois, Massachusetts, Maryland, New Jersey, Oregon, Rhode Island, Vermont, and Washington.[27] The vast majority of the country's local and county sanctuary policies are implemented in these states; however, there are many other localities with pro-immigrant, sanctuary style policies in Michigan, Minnesota, New Mexico, New York, and Wisconsin as well. All these states, with the exception of Wisconsin, are dominated by Democratic Party leadership in state legislatures.

While the creation of policy or law may be the aim of the protagonists of sanctuary, private and public sector actors—activists, organizations, and policymakers—may also advocate to public sector executives not to make laws but merely to take executive action, be that in the form of executive directives, or single-incident executive decisions that for instance suspend an immigrant or refugee's deportation order and allow them to remain in the territory as a one-time exception to the rule. Scholars have framed such actions as *sanctuary incidents*—essentially an act of nation-state decisionism that accomplishes a variety of outcomes.[28] First, it suspends a bureaucratic decision to deport a person that was made on the basis of law and bureaucratic judgment. As such, it is an assertion of higher state power over subordinate executives and staff and a reaffirmation of the power structure as a whole. Second, it demonstrates a willingness or vulnerability of the state to popular pressure from forces auxiliary to the state—immigrant rights organizations and various public constituents of the executive that makes the decision to suspend deportation. Third, it may remove the immediacy of the deportation but places the targeted individual in a holding pattern where they might not be free from a potential future deportation. If the individual is not granted permanent permission to remain in a territory with full membership rights and a means to financially support themselves, the individual may come to rely on private sector sanctuary providers of various life-sustaining human services—the provision of food, clothing, education, housing, legal services, language services, job training, employment services, and informal employment. In this case, theorists have described such private sector sanctuary practices as serving in an auxiliary role to the state, providing services that the state would otherwise provide citizens with full rights, and easing the experience of indefinite waiting.[29] Private sector sanctuary provision becomes part of a process that encourages immigrants to wait for further government rulings in their immigration cases, thereby keeping them calm during a sort of temporal detention, one where the immigrant is not so agitated as to demand immediate full rights and membership from the state.[30]

Scholars have studied how the various phenomena that are labeled sanctuary largely fail to produce completely safe spaces, sustain vulnerable people in the long term, or allow them to thrive as fully expressed and self-determined people.[31] Other scholars have examined how protagonists and promoters of sanctuary, at the very least, symbolically affect their networks in a variety of ways. Sanctuary providers may publicly declare the spaces and resources that they have to provide as open to sanctuary seekers even if no one takes them up on their offer; that as an individual or organization, they are supportive of sanctuary seekers and that they would defend them if pursuers approached sanctuary seekers, as is the case in "sanctuary restaurants" and "sanctuary universities"; or that they denounce the activities of pursuers or the conditions and circumstances that led sanctuary seekers to initially flee toward finding various forms of sanctuary.

These are communicative expressions that not only convey content about their intentions, but also have an effect on sociopolitical power dynamics in various ways. Such symbolic actions validate these stated positions among other actors in their networks and may aggregate to build forms of creative support for sanctuary seekers, a "culture of sanctuary" and hospitality for sanctuary seekers, as is the case in the "City of Sanctuary" movement in the United Kingdom.[32] Given that new threats are constantly emerging for groups of people who flee and seek sanctuary, anthropologist Rachel Humphris has treated the term sanctuary as a "mobilizing metaphor" that different groups of people interpret through different ideological lenses and input different meanings based on the social group to which they belong, their institutional roles, or governmental processes in which they are engaged.[33] In their disagreements, different groups assert their own interpretations of sanctuary, create new meanings, and are motivated to adapt, expand, reinterpret, and approach new situations through sanctuary logics.

Where governmental sanctuary practices and policies are not implemented quietly without public announcements—what legal scholar Rick Su calls "silent sanctuary"—or when such policies and procedures are not codified in policy—public expressions from government agency superiors that advocate or support the provision of various forms of sanctuary may signal to governmental staff how they want staff to informally treat immigrants.[34] They may also lay the groundwork for public sector leaders to create new alliances with others and influence various initiatives or ancillary policy actions that symbolically and materially distinguish their jurisdictions from those that are hostile to sanctuary seekers.[35]

The study of sanctuary as a set of diverse but seemingly related phenomena has examined sanctuary in the law enforcement context as well. According to the Immigrant Legal Resource Center, which tracks local policies in the United States pertaining to immigration law enforcement, by 2019, more than 700 counties had created policies that were given the sanctuary label and that limit when their local police and jails will hold people for immigration enforcement purposes alone; 196 counties passed policies to stop police and jails from notifying ICE each time they release someone who ICE has identified as a potentially deportable person; 240 counties instituted policies limiting local law enforcement from allowing ICE agents to interrogate individuals who are detained in local custody; more than 160 counties prohibited their local law enforcement officers from asking people about their immigration status; and 176 counties created policies that establish a general prohibition for all local government staff against using local resources to help with immigration enforcement or participate in joint operations with ICE.[36] Additionally, the Immigrant Legal Resource Center found many more counties to have ended local law enforcement data-sharing agreements with ICE, preventing ICE from entering municipal facilities without a federal warrant and reducing arrests and prosecutions by linking local criminal justice and policing reforms.[37]

By and large, the theoretical conceptualization of sanctuary in this law enforcement domain has focused on the legality of policing and jail-focused sanctuary policies with regard to their harmony with federal immigration law and the constitution; the mechanisms of certain procedures affected by such policy, most prominently jail-house transfers to ICE; or the effects of such policy upon crime rates in jurisdictions where law enforcement implement sanctuary policies. Using statistical analyses of crime rates, some studies have found that sanctuary policies lead to no significant increase in crime rates,[38] while others find reductions in certain types of crimes across jurisdictions and over various periods of time. One study examining almost twenty years of crime reporting data from locations across the country also documented that in jurisdictions where sanctuary policies are enacted, Latinx crime *reporting* behavior increases, indicating greater trust in the police in the ethnic group that includes the largest number of undocumented immigrants.[39]

These data, along with the narratives provided in this book, point to the need for an additional theorization of what happens when sanctuary policies, practices, and provisions are enacted in the context of law enforcement. Simply stated, a theorization of sanctuary in law enforcement and *as law enforcement* is needed. This book offers such a theorization and argues that sanctuary is a form of policing, sanctuary policing, with two modes: It is, in some cases, a force multiplier for police and for ICE, and in other cases, it is a force divider. On the one hand, sanctuary in the form of sanctuary policy allows local law enforcement to solicit and obtain the collaboration, support, and cooperation of communities that include undocumented immigrant populations toward crime-fighting and prosecutions—that is, it allows police to treat undocumented immigrants as informants, community policing auxiliaries, and therefore force multipliers or local emissaries for police in immigrant communities. Second, sanctuary policy as in the New Jersey case, one that is comparable to sanctuary policies in other states, formalizes policy provisions that are exceptions to the rule, or carve-outs, and links local police agencies to ICE by clarifying exactly how and in what exceptional circumstances may local law enforcement *assist ICE* in immigration enforcement. In this manner, sanctuary is a mode of policing, policing-with-undocumented-immigrants, and policing-with-ICE.

Sanctuary policies also make possible policing methods, tactics, and strategies that de-link or divide local law enforcement from federal immigration enforcement when sanctuary policy exceptions are not met. When police interact with individuals who may be undocumented and choose not to ask about their immigration status, when they look beyond immigration status as a factor of the incident while continuing to watch over criminal behaviors, they attempt to treat immigrants in a manner similar to that afforded to people who they know are citizens. In this case, sanctuary policing initiates a process of what I call *force division*. Such sanctuary policing keeps police from serving as force multipliers or auxiliary partners from immigration control collaborations *in those incidents but not in general*; simplifies their capacities to a more limited scope; and de-links them from joint operations, joint task forces, and joint missions with ICE. In these incidents, sanctuary policy and practice as force divider need not be an act of heroic pro-immigrant resistance or governmental rebellion but simply a rather mundane act of policing, what I call *sanctuary policing*. While police in these policing incidents achieve the desired effect that immigrant advocates want in general from sanctuary policies—to fully and finally "disentangle local police from federal immigration enforcement"—local police do not fully cut ties with ICE but rather continue their assistance to ICE in other policing incidents as they arise.

Organization of the Book

The following chapters of this book provide a historical and social scientific account of how police implement sanctuary policies in New Jersey and, at the same time, mostly continue to serve as force multipliers for ICE. Chapter 1 provides an overview of the various types of force multipliers that US immigration control agencies work with inside and outside of the country and the manner in which ICE has conceptualized what force multipliers are according to their public discourse. Chapter 2 examines the law enforcement policies in New Jersey, including the Immigrant Trust Directive, that have regulated local police interactions with undocumented immigrants and cooperation activities with ICE.

To demonstrate what immigration control force multiplication looks like on the ground, chapter 3 provides a descriptive narrative of a joint operation carried out by ICE and various New Jersey law enforcement agencies as captured in video by a local police officer's body-worn camera. Chapter 3 also explains how BWCs work, what type of data they capture, and the history of how police have used BWCs. This chapter argues that police serve as force multipliers for immigration control—as auxiliary videographers—when they use BWCs at immigration control events, and that BWCs themselves serve as force multipliers for immigration control by producing "data doubles"—digital representations of immigrants and immigration control events—that may be instrumentalized to identify, capture, and deport immigrants in person.

Chapter 4 provides a descriptive narrative of a policing event in New Jersey in which local police responded to an emergency call from ICE and spent an hour standing in the street, directing traffic, and engaging pedestrians as ICE arrested a man outside of his home. The narrative in chapter 4 is created from a BWC video recorded by one of the two police officers who responded to the immigration enforcement event.

Chapter 5 examines the moral components of the immigration enforcement event presented in chapter 4 and the value systems that inform police officers about how to make improvisational decisions in situations involving undocumented immigrants and ICE that nonetheless remain in compliance with sanctuary policies. Chapter 5 also examines the various force multipliers that ICE used to arrest the targeted immigrant—not only the police officers who provided "scene security" but also the man's son, who they attempted to conscript in their efforts. It also describes how ICE used the idea of a *potential viewer* of the police BWC footage—likely an immigration judge who will view the video showing the man's noncompliance—as a way to convince the man to allow his arrest so that his actions will not be held against him.

Chapter 6 discusses the ways in which the prohibitionary provisions of sanctuary policies and the policing practices they make possible serve as force dividers—forms of policing that de-link local policing processes from immigration enforcement. It also provides a descriptive narrative created from the analysis of a police officer's BWC video of a traffic stop in which the officer obviously *does not* investigate immigration status or any potential immigration law violations when he could have.

Chapter 7 examines the force of and authority in sanctuary policies through an analysis of two texts. The first is a transcription of a video-recorded press event at which Attorney General Gurbir Grewal explained what the Immigrant Trust Directive is and does. The second analysis is of the Immigrant Trust Directive itself. Through a comparison of the two texts, it examines how sanctuary values, when transformed into a type of legal language, roots it in a depersonalized governmental authority—a subject of the policy that I call the *commander in policy*. Police invoke this legal authority in the course of their police duties when investigating and arresting immigrants in New Jersey. The chapter then provides a descriptive narrative of a traffic stop in which police pull over an immigrant man, arrest him for having an imitation firearm—an "airsoft" gun that is modified to look like a real gun—and in the process, discover various personal identity documents and financial documents that the police agency later provides to ICE after the arrest. They do this in hopes of charging the man with attempt to commit fraud. It will also demonstrate how the police refer to and "voice" the provisions of law in the course of their duties with immigrants, that is, how the authority of the commander in policy is present in policing events.

To maintain the anonymity of the individuals and local policing agencies narrativized in each of the chapters, I have used pseudonyms throughout the book. I have additionally changed the place names of the towns, townships, suburbs, and counties, including when they are part of agency names. I have also anonymized the names of federal officers that appear in the narratives but used the real names of the federal agencies they work for.

These chapters are followed by a concluding chapter that returns to the main points of the book, outlining sanctuary policing, force multiplication, and force division. The book also provides an extended appendix discussing the methods used, with a focus on how I created the policing narratives based on video analysis of BWC video footage. It also explains the methodology I have introduced here as surveillant anthropology. This appendix includes an overview of the many creative ways that scholars have studied certain forms of policing that are no longer practiced, intentionally hidden, secret, or rare, as is the case with local immigration enforcement assistance in a sanctuary state.

The ethnographic narratives provided in this book have been chosen not because they represent policing in general in a sanctuary state or because they may somehow reflect each New Jersey agency's practices or policies pertaining to immigrants and ICE. I have chosen them because they are representative of a mode of policing that is activated when a certain style of sanctuary policies is in effect when police interact with immigrants, and they are being pursued by immigration control agencies. In comparison to the vast number of incidents that police are involved in during the course of their day, the activation of this mode of sanctuary policing is presumably infrequent.

The BWC videos and the instances narrativized are mere tokens of various archetypal interactions for which immigrants, immigration advocates, and immigration lawyers throughout the country have provided public testimony in town hall meetings, the media, or in court over the previous fifteen years, during the time that I have been conducting research on the topic of sanctuary cities.[40] Due to their infrequent nature in comparison to the sheer number of other types of policing incidents, they are very difficult to capture by news media cameras, investigative journalists, or even anthropologists who conduct in situ participant observation over long periods of time. There are no reliable statistical metrics or other systematically collectible evidence that account for all instances of police collaboration with ICE in a sanctuary state, and therefore, there is no way to ascertain the degree to which these forms of police assistance to immigration agencies are common.

While the Attorney General Immigrant Trust Directive requires law enforcement agencies to report any instance of such collaboration, researchers have found in some cases that police have not reported instances of collaboration with ICE to the Attorney General that *are* reflected in the agency's internal records, such as police incident reports.[41] Police collaborations with ICE in the course of everyday policing activities in a state with a sanctuary policy may be conducted covertly or may not be considered to even be "immigration enforcement assistance" by the involved police and so may go unreported to the Attorney General. The onus for documenting instances of collaboration between police and ICE in sanctuary jurisdictions has largely fallen on immigrants who have been targeted and who must be able to come forward and publicly describe the instances. However, what makes this type of public testimony rare is that immigrants may not even be aware that the police helped ICE to target them, they may be removed from the country and not able to make a public statement, may not want the public attention, may find it difficult to connect with advocates of their case in the United States, or may not believe that their efforts will have any positive effect for their lives or the lives of other immigrants still in the United States.

Therefore, this book adds an ethnographic account, albeit in vigilant, surveillant detail, of cases that substantiate what immigrants and their advocates throughout the country have described in public testimonies—police traffic stops that turned into immigration arrests; joint operations involving police and ICE with the objective of fighting crime but that end up targeting "collateral" undocumented individuals; and instances when police provide backup and scene security to ICE in the course of an administrative immigration arrest at a home. The account of immigrant- and immigration control–related policing provided in this book aims therefore to provide a fine-grained empirical and interpretive entry point into the phenomena and a theoretical launching pad to create an outline of force multiplication, force division, immigration control assistance, and sanctuary policing in contemporary America.

1

Immigration Control's Force Multipliers

Unlike many countries around the world where police are national-level employees and enforce all laws, from traffic laws and criminal laws to immigration and customs laws, local law enforcement agencies in the United States are an entirely separate entity from federal LEAs, including the two immigration enforcement agencies, US Immigration and Customs Enforcement (ICE) and US Customs and Border Protection (CBP). Local police are paid for and managed by town and city officials and are legally and organizationally independent entities that nonetheless extend help to and maintain cooperative affinities with LEAs at all jurisdictional levels throughout the country. While local police enforce local, state, and federal laws, they are not required to enforce *civil* immigration laws. The enforcement of civil immigration laws, which are federal laws, is the domain of the federal government, and the federal government has the exclusive authority to decide who may enter and remain in the country.[1] Investigations can overlap, however, where an individual or criminal organization may violate multiple laws in the course of a criminal enterprise, such as the creation of fake passports and human trafficking, which may include violating certain criminal laws that local police enforce, such as fraud *and* civil and criminal immigration laws, that ICE or CBP also enforce.[2] In these cases, the different agencies may work together to find and arrest the individuals involved unless there are local laws preventing such cooperation.

With regard to the enforcement of *civil* immigration law, this separation of enforcement duties does not mean that local or state law enforcement is prohibited by federal law from helping ICE or CBP enforce these laws if they voluntarily choose to and if there is otherwise no state- or local-level sanctuary law prohibiting them from doing so. Indeed, ICE and CBP routinely attempt to conscript local law enforcement, including in jurisdictions with sanctuary policies, to voluntarily help them locate people who are potentially deportable. The simple fact is that local police around the country are more likely than ICE agents to interact with deportable people in everyday encounters such as routine traffic stops, arrests, interviews with witnesses to crimes, and when people come into police stations to, for instance, pick up a police-impounded vehicle. There are roughly 1.2 million local and state law enforcement officers that operate throughout the country, by far more than the 60,000 CBP officers and 20,000 ICE officers. Local, state, and federal law enforcement agencies carry out their work in the same geographic spaces.[3] That includes law enforcement activities in sanctuary jurisdictions.

Despite ICE having one of the largest budgets of all policing, detention, and investigatory agencies in the United States, standing at $8.5 billion in fiscal year 2023, to meet its goals for arresting and deporting people each year, it turns to local jails and police to find more people than it can find on its own.[4] Rather than having their field officers doing more investigative work to locate suspected undocumented people or people who have removal orders and go to their homes to attempt an arrest, it's easier for them to go to a local jail to gain custody of someone who is already locked up and who did not have a profile in federal identity databases. In 2008, President George W. Bush initiated a program called Secure Communities, where local law enforcement in every jurisdiction in the country uses fingerprinting technology and sends digital copies of the fingerprints of everyone booked for a crime first to the Federal Bureau of Investigation (FBI) for a criminal background check, and then automatically from the FBI to ICE for an immigration status background check.[5] If the person was known to the federal government as being deportable, or if the person was not known at all, ICE generated a "detainer," a faxed form requesting the voluntary assistance of the local law enforcement agency to hold the person in custody up to forty-eight hours beyond when they would otherwise be released so that ICE could come to the facility, interview them, and potentially take custody prior to deporting them.

Secure Communities, what the immigrant rights community referred to as S-COMM, was interpreted by local law enforcement across the country largely as a mandate to help ICE primarily because law enforcement couldn't opt out of using fingerprinting technology, and law enforcement thought they were complying with what ICE called ICE warrants that ICE agents issued rather than judges and that local officials believed had some legal force although they did not.[6] Through this systematic nationwide cooperation with ICE, jails became the primary source where ICE found people to deport, and deportations skyrocketed under the late Bush and first Obama administrations. Refocusing jails as hubs of deportable people and using police and sheriff's deputies as the finders and preliminary detainers of these deportable people turned local LEAs into what immigrant rights organizations characterized as paramilitary extensions of ICE. ICE began to explicitly refer to local, county, and state law enforcement that did this work as force multipliers for ICE.[7] That is, they considered local police as integral partners, boots on the ground *for ICE* that did much of the finding, arresting, and detaining of people prior to their transfer to ICE custody and therefore were multiplying ICE forces in the enforcement of immigration law.

With the onset of Secure Communities in 2008, the immigrant rights movement around the country immediately began, first, to demand that states opt out of the contracts that they signed to initiate their participation in the program.[8] Then, when ICE responded that the contracts are no longer necessary because the program is mandatory, the immigrant rights movement began to educate law enforcement throughout the country that ICE cannot legally mandate them to enforce immigration law. The states have the right to control how their local resources, including law enforcement resources, are used, and the federal government cannot require them to use those resources to enforce immigration law.[9] Further, the immigrant rights movement, primarily its advocate attorneys, undermined the legitimacy of the "detainers" sent to local law enforcement. They informed local law enforcement that the detainers were not warrants signed by a judge and did not confer legal authority to the local agency to hold someone after they were releasable on the infractions or crimes they had been arrested for. To do so would be to expose the local agency to lawsuits from the person held on the basis that the agency infringed their habeas corpus rights—the individual was being imprisoned unlawfully.

The immigrant rights movement then also began to draft and provide LEAs with policies that clearly stated when they would and would not respond to a detainer request from ICE. These policies came to be known as "detainer policies." The policies were written under the same guiding logic and values as more general "sanctuary" policies, which had been in existence since the 1980s and which prohibited the use of local resources in many ways for enforcing immigration law. As local agencies and even entire states like California adopted detainer policies and sanctuary policies to reduce their participation in Secure Communities and in immigration policing more generally, deportations that result from agencies responding to detainers dropped dramatically. In 2015, the Obama administration, with the wind taken out of its Secure Communities sails, addressed the legal liability element on which it had assumed LEAs were adopting detainer policies. The administration began *not* to ask LEAs to hold people after they'd otherwise be released but rather to inform ICE in advance of when the person, whom they suspected was deportable, would be released. They continued to issue detainers, but the forms had been modified so that ICE requested this release information rather than requesting extended detention. ICE officers could use the requested information to show up at the release and make an immediate arrest. The administration called this new approach the Priority Enforcement Program; the immigrant rights community named it PEP-COMM to show it as a continuation of Secure Communities using a slightly different tactic.[10]

Agencies throughout the country responded in a variety of ways to this move. Some agencies flat out posted all of the release information for everyone in their custody on their websites so that ICE could simply look up the information on their own and show up whenever they wanted to upon a person's release to arrest them.[11] This type of arrest would not be considered a custody transfer because the arrest would take place officially post-release, albeit on the agency's property. In some cases, such "arrests" might occur in a locked corridor that in no way would be considered a public place, where the person had not been free to leave on their own and therefore should arguably be considered a pre-release transfer. In other cases, agencies would *not* post release information online for the public but they would put the information on the new detainer form and send it back to ICE, while others would make more direct communication with ICE by, for instance, calling them and telling them the release information.[12] The immigrant rights movement, on the other hand, began drafting policies and providing them to local agencies and legislatures to limit the circumstances not only of when agencies would hold people for ICE to pick up but also when agencies could provide release information to ICE. These policies did not grant LEAs new authority but rather asserted the authority LEAs already had to decline ICE's voluntary requests.

During the Trump administration's management of ICE and its efforts to terrorize immigrants, they returned the Secure Communities program to its former practices of requesting agencies to hold people, but also requested that agencies provide release information.[13] Despite his "tough on immigrants" approach, however, Trump never could return the program's deportation numbers under Secure Communities to their highs under the Obama administration, likely because so many agencies throughout the country, including in highly immigrant-populated states like California, already had laws in place to require noncooperation or limited cooperation with ICE in responding to their detainer requests.

Force Multiplier, a Military Concept

While ICE's use of the term force multiplier to refer to their local police partners may have seemed like it arose in the context of Secure Communities and ICE's immigration enforcement goals, this was actually an appropriation of a concept from the world of military strategy more generally. Anthropologist Maximilian Forte has charted the genealogy of the "emic" concept "force multiplier" as it was born in the heart of twentieth-century US military strategy and expanded dramatically over the following three decades.[14] Forte tells us that the term refers to "friends and allies, partners and protégés, extensions and proxies," multiples of US imperialist power that leverage networks of partners, collaborators, and proxies in an expanding network in a manner through which the US, in particular, the military, retains centralized control.[15] For the military, effectively anything can serve as a force multiplier— "cultural systems, social relationships, and material production can become force multipliers for imperialism."[16]

While now applied in the sphere of geopolitics and military domination throughout the world, it was adapted from a quasi-scientific realm of military strategy, Forte tells us, in which the term referred to "machines which allow a small effort to move a larger load. . . . a crowbar, wheelbarrow, nutcracker, and bottle opener. . . . The number of times a machine multiplies the effort is called its mechanical advantage. The mechanical advantage of a machine is the number of times the load moved is greater than the effort used."[17] However, when appropriated by the US Department of Defense to mobilize resources to extend its reach throughout the world without overextending itself, Forte points our attention to its definition: "A capability that, when added to and employed by a combat force, significantly increases the combat potential of that force and thus enhances the probability of successful mission accomplishment."[18]

The force multiplier for the US military is not merely a technological device or technique but also a social or cultural factor that, if understood, mastered, manipulated, controlled, or utilized, may allow for more effective control of a society. It may take the form of the tactic of framing oppressive gender relations or oppression against sexual minorities as a justification for humanitarian military intervention. Humanitarian aid provided by the military through third-party nongovernmental organizations in war zones may be utilized to win the hearts and minds of the local population. It may take the form of entertainment or spokespeople who strategically influence news discourse to gain the support of populations for a military occupation that needs justification and acceptance.[19] Force multipliers may also be "mechanisms, processes, and institutions: trade treaties, military education, or the rule of law."[20]

A key to the force multiplication concept is the development of sociopolitical networks with various auxiliary actors—anti-government protesters who may be supported in overthrowing their governments, pro-US leaders and social classes who desire a US way of life in those countries, or armed rebels.[21] Support may be public communication and endorsement for local actions, military aid, training, or financing. The force multiplication effect here is accomplished through the combination of resource provision and the people, infrastructure, and programs locally situated.[22] As Forte points out, such networks also extend through US universities, among professional associations, philanthropies, and corporations playing the roles of training and educating pro-US leaders, providing aid or funding for aid, or donating "democratizing" technologies—computers and internet connectivity—in enemy states.

Force multipliers according to Forte enable the imperial power and its external collaborators, allowing it to maintain its projection in scale rather than, as Forte says, scaling back to "small effort, small load, or no effort, no load."[23] The primary force of the US military is thus recognized as "insufficient on its own and thus requires extensions, that is, *multiples of itself*."[24] As the "load bearing hands of US empire recede into the background, those of its local collaborators stand out on the front line. This shifts struggles for power from the international arena, between states, to the domestic arena within states."[25] This shifting of action to the local also allows the central power to shift responsibility to the force multipliers—to those who carry out much of the work on the ground within the auxiliary network of imperial power.

This language also signals that power is fragile, that the use of such technologies belies an inability of the institutions of control that use them to deploy their own forces and resources directly without sacrificing their hold in the centers of power or to achieve their expanding projects. It thus publicly acknowledges an imperial project's limits. Force multiplication entails a certain economizing, or at least the presentation of an attempt to economize in an era of neoliberal budget cutting, rising costs, increased debt burdens, and privatization of government institutions and public functions, including military functions that may be outsourced to private contractors.[26]

Forte notes that ultimately, force multiplication as elaborated in military thinking is a form of extraction, that is capital accumulation,[27] wherein the military reduces energy expended, expressed in terms of cost, by passing the costs onto others who subsidize the US intervention. This may take the form of expending resources, taking on risks that the US military does not take on, or "doing the leg work."[28] Here power is not so much multiplied from the center outward, spread abroad, or shared with collaborators, but rather power is extracted from them.[29] It is "using humans as strategic resources, and by using more of them and at the least possible expense," instrumentalizing partners and "using cultural means—'shared values'—to win allegiance, acceptance, and acquiescence."[30]

ICE's Force Multiplication Mechanisms

Kansas Attorney General Kris Kobach, a former attorney for the Federation for American Immigration Reform and later immigration advisor to then-US President Donald Trump, who earlier had served as Professor of Law at the University of Missouri Kansas City, argued that domestic police officers are not only an existent foundation of order in the modern nation state—a pillar of society in its own right—but also that they should be considered the "quintessential force multiplier" for immigration enforcement.[31] Kobach, applying the US Department of Defense's definition of force multiplier, argued that the nearly 800,000 police officers nationwide could provide ICE with assistance on an "occasional, passive, voluntary" basis and "pursued during the course of normal law enforcement activity."[32] Kobach reasoned that

> the net that is cast daily by local law enforcement during routine encounters with members of the public is so immense that it is inevitable illegal aliens will be identified. When a local police officer establishes probable cause to believe that an alien is in violation of U.S. immigration law, he may contact the ICE Law Enforcement Support Center in Williston, Vermont, to confirm that ICE wishes to take custody of the alien.[33]

Laying out the legal argument for involving local and state police in immigration enforcement, specifically as force multipliers, Kobach argued that various congressional legislative actions have shown intent for state police to have the inherent power to make inquiries about immigration status and immigration arrests and to share immigration information with the federal government; he also argued that various courts have reaffirmed this in related judicial rulings and that in 2002 US Attorney General John Ashcroft issued a legal opinion that stated "arresting aliens who have violated criminal provisions of the INA or civil provisions that render an alien deportable . . . is within the inherent authority of the states," including state and local police officers.[34] This opinion expanded upon existent laws authorizing the Attorney General to enter into memoranda of understanding with state and local authorities to enforce immigration laws.[35] Kobach focused on missed opportunities for local and state police to detain four of the 9/11 terrorists when they encountered them during routine traffic stops in the two years prior to when they hijacked the planes that were used in the attacks on the World Trade Center and the Pentagon.

Kobach argued that had the federal government disseminated immigration violation information in the National Crime Information Center (NCIC) database available to police via laptops in police patrol cars, the local officers could have seen that the individuals had overstayed their tourist visas—*civil* rather than criminal violations—detained them, and turned them over to immigration authorities, and the attacks may have been averted. More importantly, Kobach argued, such traffic stops or encounters based on the breaking of laws required to plan terrorist activities may be *the only* opportunities to apprehend an immigration law violator before they engage in a terrorist act.[36] As such, Kobach conceived of local police as force multipliers for immigration enforcement as well as for national security.

However, an additional effect was made possible when police were capacitated with immigration enforcement authorization—the officer, who otherwise "would possess no legal basis to make the arrest," is given "a powerful tool that the local police officer can use when necessary to protect the public."[37] In this sense, local police could use immigration enforcement, its legal authority, its databases, and its infrastructure reciprocally as a force multiplier for achieving local public safety. Looked at this way, it cannot be assumed that federal agents simply asymmetrically and instrumentally utilize police as force multipliers. Those who are considered force multipliers are not passive tools but are themselves subjects who in turn utilize their federal partners, appropriating their capacities as well, again not as bare instrumentalities but as collaborators. Force multiplication—the collaborative linking of these partners and their resources—constructs surveillant assemblages, new techniques, and socio-technical amalgamations that allow each agency to achieve forms of policing that would be impossible if each was working in isolation from the other.[38]

For Kobach, this mutually beneficial arrangement—local police force multipliers for ICE that in turn use federal force multipliers for local police—wasn't only applicable to the targeting of the relatively small population of potential terrorists but to any of the almost half million immigrants who have disobeyed final orders of removal from immigration courts and whose names have been placed in the NCIC for arrest.[39] Though immigrants commit crimes at a lower rate than the general US population, Kobach argued that local officers could use immigration-related information in the NCIC to target immigrants who have committed crimes, who are involved in gangs or in a case of human trafficking and smuggling far from the border.

Cross-Designation in the Homeland and Abroad: 287(g) and Title 19

While ICE's Secure Communities program beginning in 2008 fundamentally transformed local police and jails across the country into force multipliers for immigration control as was explained above, ICE did not first apply the term to police in the context of that program. Rather, that same year, ICE began to refer only to its collaborations with federal, state, and local partner agencies as part of a "force multiplier approach to investigations" wherein ICE, under Title 19 of US Code 1401, formally and legally cross-designated officers from these partner agencies to investigate and enforce *customs* laws.[40] Title 19 is a provision of federal law that outlines the duties of federal customs officers, and the definition of customs officer includes "any agent or other person, including foreign law enforcement officers, authorized by law or designated by the Secretary of the Treasury to perform any duties of an officer of the Customs Service."[41]

This cross-designation was similar to the deputization of local police and jail staff in the United States to enforce civil *immigration* laws under 287(g) agreements first made possible in the mid-1990s but that few agencies implemented until after September 11, 2001.[42] The 287(g) agreements deputize local jail officers to legally act as federal agents empowered to interrogate jail inmates about their immigration status and issue their own ICE detainers—formal requests that are normally faxed from ICE to a local agency to request that the LEA detain an individual or provide ICE information for immigration enforcement purposes. LEAs using this 287(g) Jail Enforcement Model may also be authorized to transfer custody of individuals to other wings of their local jails where immigration arrestees are held in ICE custody or to external ICE detention centers. Other forms of 287(g) agreements in the 2000s deputized officers, including police, who were working in the field to enforce immigration law by asking about immigration status, advising other officers in their department on immigration enforcement issues, and working in joint task forces with ICE. This latter model was known as the 287(g) Task Force Model and was discontinued in 2012. Today, the jail enforcement model remains, as does a Warrant Service Officer model in which local jail staff are authorized to execute ICE's administrative warrants.

A report by the US Government Accountability Office (GAO) examining how ICE can further enhance its planning and oversight of state and local 287(g) agreements identified that when ICE considers entering into 287(g) agreements with a particular LEA, it focuses on three main factors: (1) availability of ICE and LEA resources; (2) the LEA's record on civil rights and civil liberties; and (3) the "LEA's capability *to act as an ICE force multiplier*."[43] To assess the ability to serve as a force multiplier in a 287(g) capacity entails ICE

> reviewing data that indicate the LEA's likelihood of encountering individuals who are potentially removable from the United States. For example, ICE collects and reviews historical data on the number of encounters and detainers lodged by ICE in the LEA jurisdiction as an indication of the approximate number of potentially removable individuals the LEA could identify and arrest per year. Among other things, ICE also reviews the estimated average number of foreign-born individuals arrested by the LEA per month, information that [Jail Enforcement Model] applicants provide in their needs assessment. ICE 287(g) program officials from one of the five field offices we met with said they also consider whether an ICE field office needs additional help with immigration enforcement activities.[44]

The needs assessment that LEAs provide to ICE for their evaluation of the LEA's force multiplication capacities includes

> information on the LEA's governance structure (such as the political entities that are required to approve the joining of the program), booking and intake capabilities, other operational agreements with ICE, and data on the estimated number of foreign nationals without lawful immigration status in the LEA's jurisdiction.[45]

The GAO's ICE interviewees also indicated that ICE sees 287(g) cross-designated officers in local jails as a force multiplier for ICE field offices because they "provide additional opportunities for ICE to identify and process potentially removable individuals, which allows ICE to reallocate resources towards conducting other enforcement actions such as identification and arrest, transportation, detention, case management, and removals."[46] In addition, they told GAO interviewers that 287(g) force multipliers "also help reduce the number of ICE deportation officers that ERO [Enforcement and Removal Operations] field offices need to assign to certain areas and may help with immigration enforcement activities in areas where ICE ERO resources are not located."[47]

While 287(g) authority was extended only to local law enforcement agencies in the United States, cross-designation authority under Title 19 of US Code 1401 was also extended to foreign law enforcement partners for cases that cross international boundaries. Title 19 cross-designation, according to ICE, "enhances ICE's ability to work more closely with these counterparts, fostering secure relationships and cooperation between the U.S. and other countries."[48] Federal, state, local, and foreign officers who received Title 19 customs officer authority "supplement the ICE investigative mission and participate on task forces throughout the United States and abroad" that target narcotics smuggling, money laundering, human smuggling and trafficking, and fraud. The US Secretary of the Treasury authorized the cross-designated officers to execute and serve search and arrest warrants, subpoenas, and summonses, conduct customs searches at the border, effect seizures and arrests of people in violation of customs laws, and carry firearms in compliance with ICE firearms policy. ICE's Panama City, Florida Resident Agent in Charge Scott Springer would comment years later about the Title 19 cross-designation program: "We save ourselves a world of gasoline and time by training our partners to identify potential criminal violations," rendering force multiplication a solution "in a world of limited resources."[49]

ICE's Two Agencies: HSI and ERO

The agency that ceremonially carried out these Title 19 cross-designations is ICE's Homeland Security Investigations (HSI). HSI is one of ICE's two independent federal law enforcement agencies, along with ICE's Enforcement and Removal Operations (ERO). In the interior of the country, ERO carries out most of the federal government's immigration arrests and administrative removals, while HSI is responsible for investigating transnational crimes such as human smuggling and trafficking and threats involving criminal organizations that "exploit the global infrastructure through which international trade, travel, and finance move."[50] With more than 6,000 criminal investigators known as "special agents" and more than 8,700 total employees, HSI is the country's second-largest investigative service behind the FBI. HSI operates in 237 American cities and ninety-three overseas locations in fifty-six countries and is the Department of Homeland Security's largest investigative law enforcement presence outside of the United States.[51] In the process of conducting investigations into transnational crimes, HSI has the authority to enforce federal customs laws and the Immigration and Nationality Act (INA) and to make arrests of individuals who have solely violated civil immigration laws—people who have merely entered the United States in an uninspected, unauthorized manner.

HSI partners with ERO and local, county, and state law enforcement officers in the United States to target people who can be charged with violations of state and federal crimes and civil immigration violations as a result of a joint operation. Theoretically, local and state police focus on the criminal aspects of the operation, while HSI officers focus on federal crimes and immigration violations. However, the roles that each partner plays are mutually supporting. In some cases, when only a small number of the targeted individuals wanted for federal crimes are located, the operations may result in far greater numbers of collateral civil immigration arrests of other individuals present at the arrest site.[52] As the targeted criminal offenders of the joint operations are determined to be higher priorities for criminal prosecution and deportation due to the perceived or real threat to public safety that they pose, such cooperation is permitted by local and state law enforcement officials even in jurisdictions governed by sanctuary laws that generally prohibit their law enforcement officers from assisting ICE in enforcing civil immigration laws.

Many of the country's most restrictive sanctuary state policies, including the New Jersey Attorney General Immigrant Trust Directive,[53] grant local and state law enforcement the ability to participate in joint task forces with federal agencies where the enforcement of civil immigration law is not the primary purpose, but rather just a secondary one. These permissive exceptions to sanctuary policies allow agencies to actively participate with HSI in criminal/immigration raids that blur the lines distinguishing criminal control from immigration control, local law enforcement officers from federal immigration agents, and the criminal from the immigrant.

Among local police officers who would eventually be cross-designated were the Puerto Rico Police Department's twenty-six officers in the United Forces of Rapid Action who received their credentials from both ICE HSI San Juan's Special Agent in Charge and Puerto Rico Police Department's Superintendent for Field Operations during a ceremony at the Caribe Hilton Hotel.[54] This cross-designation was conducted to enhance HSI's abilities in cases that cross international boundaries and enhance HSI's abilities to "work more closely with these counterparts, fostering secure relationships and cooperation between the United States and other countries."[55] HSI Special Agent in Charge Angel Melendez commented that this formal linking of the authoritative capacities of local Puerto Rican police and HSI would "complement our missions and serve as a force multiplier. The maritime domain represents the most commonly exploited venue by transnational criminal organizations to introduce contraband, particularly narcotics in Puerto Rico."[56] In addressing the newly designated officers, Melendez referred to the cross-designation as "a unique tool, which equates to an additional authority to counter these activities in collaboration and support of HSI and the Department of Homeland Security's partners."[57]

Targeting "Criminal Aliens" and Fugitives

ICE extended the use of the force multiplier concept in 2008 when elaborating on its Operation Community Shield Initiative objectives. As part of this initiative, ICE partners with federal, state, and local law enforcement "combining resources, authorities and expertise in an effort to target members of violent street gangs . . . to develop a 'force multiplier' effect in investigations and other law enforcement actions against gangs."[58] ICE Special Agent in Charge of the ICE Office of Investigations in Newark, New Jersey, stated that the agency "has unique customs law enforcement authorities [capacities] which complement the authorities of our federal, state, and local partners. ICE removes dangerous gang members and their associates from our streets, making our communities a safer place to work and live."[59]

ICE also began to refer to its Fugitive Operation Support Center, which used technology and partnerships with local law enforcement agencies, as a force multiplier for the National Fugitive Operations

Program, a program in which ICE Fugitive Operation Teams "identify, locate, arrest, and remove criminal aliens, fugitives who had ignored orders of removal and went into hiding, and other immigration violators from the United States."[60] The Center reviewed and updated fugitive cases, developed leads for and provided assistance to Fugitive Operations Teams, assisted in developing national fugitive field operations, and supported national ICE initiatives. In this sense, ICE used the notion of force multiplication to refer to an internal, centralized administrative technique of data collection, analysis, and sharing that served as a bridge within ICE between ICE branches and external, local law enforcement agencies.

Within two years, ICE continued to refer to local law enforcement as force multipliers, albeit newly recognized in operations with ICE's Enforcement Removal Operations and its Joint Criminal Alien Removal Taskforce, also known as JCART. ERO, JCART, and their law enforcement partners targeted "criminal aliens," who were removable sex offenders, drug distributors, and others engaged in illegal entry, embezzlement, forgery, and document fraud.[61] Dorothy Herrera-Niles, Acting Field Office Director of ICE-ERO in El Paso, Texas, stated that "working in a collaborative effort with our DHS [Department of Homeland Security] partners is a force multiplier that has proven to be highly effective."[62] In these portrayals, ICE additionally framed the force multiplier as the *collaborative effort, the relation or connection* between the agencies, rather than either of the agencies or the individual capacities of the agencies themselves.

As the Secure Communities program was rolled out state by state, and local law enforcement began to adopt the programs' biometric data-sharing technology as part of their booking processes, allowing for locally booked individuals to be checked against the Department of Homeland Security's Automated Biometric Identification System also known as IDENT, local law enforcement began to adopt the discourse of the force multiplier as well. By 2011, Secure Communities had been implemented in 1,049 jurisdictions in thirty-nine states.[63] In Georgia, Walton County Sheriff Joe Chapman expressed, "I am excited to partner with ICE along with my fellow sheriffs in Newton and Barrow counties to combat the illegal immigration problem. The *expertise of ICE* in this area is a definite force multiplier."[64] Affirming Kobach's argument, not only did local law enforcement serve as force multipliers for ICE, but ICE expertise was a force multiplier for local sheriffs, helping remove unwanted immigrants who make it to their local jails.

Customs and Border Protection (CBP), ICE's immigration enforcement counterpart at ports of entry and the country's borders, also adopted the language of force multiplication to describe its joint operations with ICE and local law enforcement. Specifically, CBP used the term force multiplier to refer to joint operations that aimed to detect and arrest attempts to import illegal counterfeit merchandise, thereby protecting the branding of American companies. In 2011, two men were arrested for attempting to import $2 million in counterfeit collectible Disney pins from China, which they intended to sell over the internet.[65] They were caught when CBP intercepted a parcel at Los Angeles International Airport containing more than 150 pounds of the pins. After HSI and Anaheim Police collaborated with CBP to arrest the two men involved, CBP's Acting Director of Field Operations in Los Angeles commented,

> Collaboration with agencies such as ICE, the Anaheim Police Department and the Orange County District Attorney is essential to combat crimes involving counterfeiting and piratical goods. Our cooperative efforts serve as a force multiplier in thwarting the attempts of those who try to enter illegal goods into the commerce of the United States. Through these partnerships, we work to protect America's innovation-based economy and the health and safety of its consumers.[66]

To further combat brand theft and merchandise counterfeiting, ICE's National Intellectual Property Rights Coordination Center (the IPR Center) hosted an all-day symposium at the Ohio Bureau of Criminal Investigation's police academy in Richfield. The IPR Center is an ICE "task force" that "uses the expertise of its 21 member agencies to share information, develop initiatives, coordinate enforcement actions, and conduct investigations related to intellectual property (IP) theft."[67] The symposium focused on actions taken by the US government and by the intellectual property industry to combat counterfeit merchandise, and ICE organized presentations from corporate brand holders, including Amber Lilly, Deer and Company, maker of John Deere–branded products; Underwriter Laboratories, and other brand holders. Breakout sessions discussed current trends in counterfeiting and emerging threats, as well as detection methods and best practices in enforcement, and HSI officers linked intellectual property theft with other criminal activities.[68] Brand protection officers from several corporations contributed information on "threat detection and other investigative techniques," demonstrating how the state is not merely a protector of the economy but in the reverse, companies might infuse state agencies like ICE—the federal government's lead agency investigating intellectual property theft—with policing capacities in such an exchange.[69]

In addition to the utilization of a state police academy facility to hold the event, ICE HSI's Special Agent in Charge of Michigan and Ohio Brian M. Moskowitz described the event itself as a force multiplication activity: "Events like these are a key element in the overall strategy to protect American brands and jobs. Educating the public and industry is an important force multiplier in the effort to fight intellectual property rights theft."[70] In this sense, echoing Walton County Sheriff Joe Chapman's formulation of ICE *expertise* as a force multiplier for local law enforcement, ICE, in the context of its IP partnerships, expressed that not only are external partners and the relationships that ICE maintains with them force multipliers for ICE's objectives, but the *activities* in which ICE invests expertise in those partners and from which they obtain corporate investigatory expertise from those partners are force multipliers as well.

ICE Operations in Foreign Countries: TCIUs and Global Network Building

ICE also cultivated force multiplication mechanisms transnationally in the form of collaborative investigative units based in foreign countries. In November 2022, ICE collaborated with the US Department of State Bureau of International Narcotics and Law Enforcement Affairs and the Colombian National Police to hold a conference—"Fighting Networks with Networks through Interregional Partnerships"—to "promote the exchange of knowledge and skills in support of joint international efforts to combat transnational criminal organizations," which included a three-day seminar titled "2011 Transnational Crimes, Global Threats, and Illicit Pathways."[71] This conference supported HSI's Transnational

Criminal Investigative Units (TCIUs), which are special host country police units that assist ICE with investigations in source and transit countries.[72] ICE describes TCIUs as

> multi-disciplined units that work with domestic and international ICE HSI offices to disrupt, dismantle, and prosecute the entire spectrum of criminal smuggling, trafficking, gangs, cybercrime, money laundering and terrorist organizations that pose a national security threat to the United States. ICE HSI TCIUs act as a force multiplier by building on existing partnerships to foster the exchange of real-time intelligence and information necessary to collaborate on joint investigations.[73]

TCIUs identify targets, gather evidence, share investigative intelligence, and conduct joint investigative activities with ICE so that ICE can "target the criminal network, not just the portion operating in the United States."[74]

More than a hundred participants attended the conference. This included foreign officials working in HSI TCIUs from countries in the Western Hemisphere and the Middle East, HSI attachés and assistant attachés, and US Department of State representatives. Keynote speakers included the Deputy Director of ICE, the US Department of State International Narcotics and Law Enforcement Affairs Director for Anti-Crime Programs, the Director General of the Colombian National Police General, the US Ambassador to Argentina, and the US Deputy Chief of Mission Embassy Bogotá. While the ICE Deputy Director commented on how TCIUs serve "as a model for all police forces worldwide" that face a common threat from transnational criminal organizations, US Department of State International Narcotics and Law Enforcement Affairs Director for Anti-Crime Programs David Luna commented on the force multiplication aspects of the TCIUs: "By leveraging our collective capacities, expertise, and will to combat transnational organized crime and dismantle transnational illicit networks, we can shut down illicit markets in order to strengthen our own markets, protect our communities, bolster our economies, and preserve the stability of our nations."[75] Under this same model, ICE would create a permanent presence in Haiti in 2022 and a TCIU with host country law enforcement and customs organizations to combat gang-related violence.[76]

A similar convening was held in the Philippines, and partnerships forged bore fruit two years later when HSI special agents in Manila assisted the Philippine National Police and the nongovernmental organization International Justice Mission in the arrest in Balibago, Angeles City of two Filipino nationals for human trafficking of twenty-one sex workers, eleven of whom were minors.[77] The agencies executed two search and arrest warrants in a sex tourism hotspot on two commercial sex establishments that provided children for sexual acts to foreign customers, including customers from the United States. The arrested pimps were charged with violations of Philippine laws against trafficking in persons and child abuse and exploitation, leading to convictions of life in Philippine prison. According to ICE, its HSI agents

> played a dual role in this investigation primarily to identify threats to the United States by attempting to determine potential involvement of transnational organized criminal elements or other nefarious actors. HSI's secondary role was acting as a force multiplier to foreign counterparts including lending subject matter expertise, organizational support by bringing together multiple entities including non-governmental organizations, after-care services, foreign and U.S. law enforcement as well as logistics, operational planning and surveillance.[78]

In this sense, the force multiplication mechanism that ICE performed was that of a joiner of disparate elements, informer, informant, educator, care provider, logistics coordinator, covert watcher, and planner, and explicitly as a force multiplier *for others*, a resource that is willing to be used. What is also of note here is that force multiplication incorporated the capacities of a nongovernmental agency so as to focus not only on law enforcement but on provisioning services to survivors of sexual violence and exploitation. Such forms of care are not an afterthought to force multiplication projects but anchor them in global policing mentalities guided by humanitarian principles.[79] Such humanitarian forms of governance, as they appear in policing strategy, are carried out in no small part, as anthropologist Didier Fassin tells us, to "manage, regulate and support the existence of human beings"—they govern "precarious lives . . . threatened and forgotten lives that humanitarian government brings into existence by protecting and revealing them."[80]

Force Multipliers at the US-Mexico Border: ACT Teams and BEST Forces

Prostitution rings have also been targeted inside of US domestic territory by the ICE-initiated task force, the El Paso Anti-Trafficking Coordination Team, or ACT Team. The ACT Team is a human trafficking task force that ICE considers a force multiplier and that is composed of HSI and FBI special agents and the US Department of Labor (DOL).[81] In 2015, the task force targeted and arrested a middle-aged couple that "knowingly persuaded or attempted to persuade" five women to travel from Ciudad Juarez, Mexico to the US border city El Paso, Texas to engage in sexual activity for financial gain.[82] HSI El Paso Special Agent in Charge Tom Hernandez described the task force as an "effective and efficient law enforcement force multiplier for us to identify, arrest, and prosecute criminals involved in luring and prostituting young women. This team of professionals help us place these criminal networks on our radar that operate in our region."[83] ACT Teams were created to streamline coordination of human trafficking investigations and prosecutions and enhance collaboration between

> frontline enforcement efforts and national human trafficking subject matter experts in the Justice Department's Human Trafficking Prosecution Unit, Executive Office of U.S. Attorneys and FBI Civil Rights Unit, DHS's Immigration and Customs Enforcement's Homeland Security Investigations, DOL's Wage and Hour Division and the Office of the Inspector General.[84]

ICE not only considered the ACT Teams that had been set up in El Paso, Atlanta, Kansas City, Los Angeles, Memphis, and Miami as force multipliers in their cooperative structure but averred that they made possible a "force-multiplier effect of *interagency commitment* to implementing coordinated, joint anti-trafficking strategies . . . due to advanced training, expertise and operational support."[85]

Nonetheless, ICE's force multiplier mechanisms have not been restricted to the operations of official task forces, be they domestic or transnational or cross-designating or deputizing programs. ICE more generally referred to any collaborative efforts in which it participated with non-ICE law enforcement agencies that emerged ad hoc to target criminal activity or that might pertain to their areas of law enforcement focus as involving force multipliers. For instance, in 2012, when a local man in Pecos, Texas, a West Texas town roughly two hours by car from the border, threatened online to kill local police officers in the police departments of Fort Stockton, Pecos, Big Spring, and Midland, as well as deputies in Midland County Sheriff's Office, and their family members, ICE's HSI agents, who monitor cybercrimes, threats to national security, and other crimes the man threatened to commit became involved.[86] Working with the FBI, police departments in Stockton, Pecos, and Midland, and the sheriff's offices of Ector and Midland, HSI arrested the man. HSI El Paso Special Agent in Charge Dennis A. Ulrich commented that HSI special agents in West Texas "worked cooperatively and vigorously with our local, state, and federal law enforcement partners. This arrest exemplifies the efficiency and force-multiplying effect of law enforcement agencies working together."[87] In a very real sense, in this case, ICE served as a resource, a force multiplier for local law enforcement, providing its online surveillance capabilities to root out a criminal threat and as a *protector* of local law enforcement officers and their families.

While the preceding examples demonstrate ICE's force multiplication mechanisms as focused primarily on criminal investigations domestically and across vast international territories, ICE also cultivates force multiplication through joint task forces that engage in a mix of criminal investigations and border enforcement, as is the case with the Border Enforcement Security Task Force (BEST). BEST is an ICE-led initiative that operates along the US-Mexico border and has thirty-two units with locations around the United States and Mexico.[88] ICE uses BEST units to combat transnational criminal organizations by "employing the full range of federal, state, local, tribal and international law enforcement authorities and resources," creating a comprehensive response to "the growing threat to border security, public safety, and national security."[89] Through BEST, ICE has created a model to "eliminate the barriers between federal and local investigations (access to both federal and state prosecutors) and close the gap with international partners in multinational criminal investigations."[90] BEST units incorporate personnel from ICE's HSI and ERO, CBP Offices of Field Operations, Border Patrol, and CBP Air and Marine, the US Coast Guard, and US Secret Service; the US Drug Enforcement Administration, Bureau of

Alcohol and Tobacco Firearms and Explosives, FBI and US Attorney's Offices; the US Department of Defense, the Internal Revenue Service's Criminal Investigations; and by 2024, it involved more than one hundred state, local, and tribal law enforcement agencies as well as international law enforcement agencies.[91]

Following the investigation of a heroin trafficker who was also a member of a prison gang in Albuquerque, New Mexico, HSI agents in ICE's BEST unit worked with the Albuquerque Police Department to execute a search warrant and arrest of the man at a local motel after buying heroin from him as part of an undercover investigation. The charges brought against him were for illegal possession of a firearm and ammunition, as well as possession with intent to distribute heroin.[92] Referring to HSI's partnerships with the Albuquerque police and other law enforcement agencies as a force multiplier, Special Agent in Charge for HSI in El Paso Ulrich commented that "these joint investigations help ensure the safety of New Mexico citizens," stressing the local law enforcement, public safety capacities that such force multiplication makes possible.[93]

Citizen Academies, Awareness Campaigns, and the Branding of Immigration Enforcement

Similar to the forging of force multipliers from collaborations with corporate security in the sphere of intellectual property rights protections mentioned earlier, ICE has also cultivated force multipliers through Citizen Academies that bring together community leaders in US states and foreign nations where ICE HSI is conducting investigations.[94] The community to which ICE refers should not be mistaken for local communities or grassroots communities. For instance, in 2015, ICE HSI agents selected thirteen leaders in San Juan, Puerto Rico, "representing government and the bank, security, and media industries" who participated in a program designed by HSI San Juan special agents to provide "members of the general public" with an "inside look at HSI and how the agency enforces immigration and customs laws."[95] Hardly members of the general public, the members included Assistant US Attorneys; a representative from the Puerto Rico Department of Justice; Commissioner for Security of the Puerto Rico Department of Education; a Compliance Officer for Scotiabank, Senior Asset Protection for First

Bank, and a representative from Doral Bank Security; Director of Corporate Security at AT&T, a producer with Telemundo, and others—each strategically well-positioned to support ICE in its mission. ICE stated that the Citizens Academy would "enhance agency and community relations . . . identify the agency with the community it serves and protects while allowing the community to interact and learn from actual special agents."[96]

Interestingly, a new force multiplication mechanism ICE attributed to the Academy was that it would "*brand* the agency [ICE] *with the community* while serving as a force multiplier by creating awareness of HSI's mission and developing an information network."[97] This forging of informant networks among strategically situated public and private sector "community" actors in covert policing is not new, but rather a core component of secret police globally as has been thoroughly documented by historians, anthropologists, and sociologists. Katherine Verdery provides perhaps the most personal and compelling account of how police use informant networks following two decades of ethnographic fieldwork during which she was personally targeted by Romanian Secret Police.[98] Verdery describes how in the 1970s and 1980s, the Romanian Secret Police not only sought to turn her closest companions and professional contacts into informants, but it sought to *induce* or forge an informant network around her, inserting informants in her life who could influence her and intervene to prevent her from what they thought she was doing—serving as a spy and painting a negative picture of Romania in her scholarship. One aim of their work was to influence Verdery to love Romania and write a positive portrayal of it in Western scholarly literature, to brand soviet Romania as good in the minds of anti-communist Americans.

Participants of ICE HSI's Citizens Academy in Puerto Rico had been selected to undergo a ten-week program that met once weekly for two hours each session and included classroom and field training exercises. Participants visited the HSI San Juan Computer Forensics Laboratory to learn "how HSI special agents retrieve information and evidence from electronic/digital devices and conduct child exploitation investigations."[99] Participants also received training in firearms at the HSI firing range and learned how HSI conducts a variety of investigations "ranging from drug trafficking to human smuggling and trafficking to financial crimes and fraud cases."[100] While it is uncertain the degree to which these citizens would come to play a role in ICE HSI activities, Melendez, in announcing the academy, expressed that this marked for them "the first step to become part of our legacy, to become the best emissaries of our agency's values of honor, service and integrity."[101]

Around the same period in 2015, the ICE HSI Identity and Benefit Fraud Unit (IBFU) initiated another national network of informants as force multipliers for ICE among state government Department of Motor Vehicles (DMV) offices throughout the United States.[102] ICE HSI sought to "create awareness among DMV employees, law enforcement, and the public" to promote accountability and vigilance regarding DMV employees "exploiting their positions by selling DMV-issued identification documents for financial gain."[103] ICE conducted a national awareness campaign so that DMV stakeholders would be on the lookout for DMV employees who might use the tools and technologies of their DMV offices to produce identity documents that criminals could use to "mask their identities and commit crimes ranging from narcotics trafficking, firearms distribution, and murder to even terrorist acts."[104] ICE created posters that said, "HSI and DMV—A Partnership that Works" and outreach materials that provided guidance to DMV employees. HSI agents from the IBFU disseminated their materials, made public presentations, and fortified connections with DMV stakeholders at regional and international DMV conferences, training sessions, and working groups. ICE also leveraged the position of the American Association of Motor Vehicle Administrators, an association that represents members throughout the United States and Canada who administer and enforce motor vehicle laws.[105] Through this administrators association, ICE was afforded easier access to directly speak with DMV administrators with whom ICE fostered a message of partnership and "an emphasis on joint investigations," and as a result, ICE's outreach materials were sent to every state DMV at the request of the administrators, giving them greater legitimacy among state DMV offices. As a result of this work, DMVs transformed their approach to one of zero tolerance, taking on a more proactive role in the investigation and policing of license fraud. This initiative therefore instilled a *will to police* license fraud in DMVs that served a force multiplication function in addition to creating a partnership network where HSI, DMVs, and state and local law enforcement agencies contributed resources.

Intensifying the Focus on Transnational Gangs and Public Safety

In 2017, during the first year of Donald Trump's presidency, ICE continued its work cultivating force multipliers among local and state law enforcement partners not only through detention-focused models like the Secure Communities program but also in joint field operations. Transnational gangs like MS-13, which Trump utilized as an icon of fear in his campaign speeches and political advertisements that was a key to linking immigrants with criminals in the minds of conservative voters, became the focus of joint local-federal policing partnerships that materialized in well-known sanctuary cities like New York City. Prior to this period, ICE-HSI, as early as 2004, had worked with the San Francisco Police Department's Gang Task Force to conduct a four-year joint operation known as Operation Devil Horns despite the city having some of the most wide-reaching sanctuary policies prohibiting local police from participating in immigration enforcement operations.[106] For ICE's HSI, working with the local Gang Task Force officers was critical owing to their intimate knowledge of the gangs and personal relationships with many local gang members that they used as informants in the course of the operation. HSI for its part could use the threat of immigration enforcement to turn reluctant undocumented gang members into informants about the gang's criminal activities. Operation Devil Horns led to the conviction of thirty-seven gang members on racketeering charges.

Building from this work, HSI's National Gang Unit, which develops intelligence on gang membership, associates, activities, and international movements, initiated Operation Raging Bull and Operation Matador to target MS-13 in 2017. HSI's National Gang Unit "develops strategic domestic and foreign law enforcement partnerships and utilizes those partnerships, along with all of its unique legal authorities, to target gangs, to suppress violence and prosecute criminal enterprises."[107] Operation Raging Bull incorporated the resources, infrastructures, networks, and capacities of not only HSI, but also ICE's ERO, CBP, US Citizenship and Immigration Services (USCIS), the US Department of Justice, US Department of Treasury and unnamed international law enforcement partners.[108] The operation targeted not only gang members in MS-13 but also others providing financial support to gang leadership in El Salvador. Emphasizing that such a law enforcement operation can only be accomplished through use of force multiplication mechanisms, ICE HSI New York Assistant Special Agent in Charge Jason Molina explained, "The problems posed by transnational gangs cannot be tackled by one agency alone. It requires multiple agencies working together in a coordinated effort."[109] The operation was initiated due to the rising gang violence and a realization that local "law enforcement was not going to be able to arrest their way out of the problem."[110]

Through Operation Matador, ICE HSI worked with the Suffolk County Police Department, Nassau County Police Department, and the New York City Police Department to target MS-13 on Long Island, New York, and netted 342 people, 183 of whom were MS-13 members and associates, with the remaining being "collateral" arrests, many of them undocumented immigrants. Local law enforcement involved provided "actionable intelligence which is critical in the targeting of gangs and their membership for enforcement actions."[111] ICE HSI's Molina commented, "That raw intelligence from the boots on the ground is key to our investigations in Nassau and Suffolk Counties. Our local law enforcement partners are the key force multiplier. They have ears to the ground and know the communities that they're policing."[112] From the local law enforcement perspective, as represented by Suffolk County Police Commissioner Timothy D. Sini,

> The Suffolk County Police Department is committed to eradicating MS-13 from our communities, and that would not be possible without close collaboration with our law enforcement partners in HSI. Through strategic targeting of gang members, focusing on known hot-spot locations frequented by gang members, and sharing intelligence with our fellow law enforcement agencies, we have continued our successful efforts to remove MS-13 members from our streets.[113]

Molina called upon local law enforcement officials to serve as force multipliers for ICE in yet another way—as local quasi-ambassadors of HSI to the community, to "remain engaged with the community in which they serve. That includes letting them know who HSI is and why the special agents are there."[114] This representational activity would be what would allow "the collaboration to continue to be successful."[115] Nassau Commissioner of Police Patrick Ryder committed to "continue to work toward this common goal with continuous exchanges of resources and intelligence to keep our communities, residents, and our children safe."[116] ICE also called upon the community as an essential informant network of force multipliers, stating that "outreach in schools and community centers, along with educating the local communities on who they can report to if they're approached by MS-13, helps law enforcement personnel at all levels fight these criminal enterprises." Recognizing the limitations of ICE and the police departments, ICE's Molina noted, "The federal agents and police departments can't do it alone. Yes, we need each other, but we also need the community."[117]

ICE's ERO also led its own multi-agency field operations that incorporate state and local law enforcement as force multipliers. In June 2017, in Newark, New Jersey, ERO's Fugitive Operations officers worked with US Customs and Border Protection's New Jersey Field Office, the New Jersey State Parole Office, and ICE's HSI to conduct arrests of 113 deportable immigrants from all over the world with criminal records.[118] Adopting the language of force multiplication while commenting on the operation, James T. Plousis, Chairman of the New Jersey State Parole Board, said,

> The State Parole Board is pleased to have been able to take part in this very successful fugitive operation. Cooperative efforts with other state and federal agencies serve as a force multiplier resulting in a significant public safety benefit. We are proud of the efforts of our parole officers and all that took part in the operation.[119]

ICE has long relied on the impromptu notifications of local and state law enforcement officers who have no cross-deputization, are not responding to an ICE detainer, and are not working in a formal joint task force with ICE, or in a joint investigation and operation, but rather encounter individuals in the course of their work investigating violations of state laws and reach out to ICE to provide them information while still at the point of contact or arrest of the individual. In some cases, ICE develops more sustained working relationships with local police agencies and dedicates officers to working as participants of cross-agency teams coordinated by local police departments to respond to instances of local crimes. For instance, HSI's Douglas Office in Arizona has assigned an agent to work in the Sierra Vista Police Department Community Response Team to provide assistance with certain crime scenes and interviews.[120]

Following the drive-by shooting and murder of an eighteen-year-old driver in Sierra Vista in September 2020, the Sierra Vista Police Department arrested a local area man after he surrendered himself the following afternoon. Through the conduit of the Community Response Team and the participating HSI agent, an ad hoc multi-agency team consisting of HSI's Douglas Office, the US Border Patrol, the Cochise County Sheriff's Office, and the Sierra Vista Police Department conducted a joint investigation of the shooter and the murder. Describing the multi-agency effort as a force multiplier, and framing ICE as the supporting partner rather than the primary actor, Scott Brown, Special Agent in Charge of HSI Phoenix, said, "HSI is a proud partner of the Sierra Vista Police Department and is committed to *working alongside* local law enforcement to keep our communities safe," echoing the reciprocal, additive quality of force multiplication that ICE exercises in these types of situations.[121]

Centers of Force Multiplication: The JIOCC

Under the Biden administration, ICE continued to use the abovementioned force multipliers domestically and internationally, as well as serving in a force multiplier capacity for other partners. In addition, beginning in June 2022, leaders from ICE's HSI, the US Coast Guard in the Houston-Galveston, Texas sector, Houston's CBP office, and the Transportation Security Administration Houston—all federal agencies— jointly established the Joint Intelligence and Operations Coordination Center (JIOCC).[122] This Center, housed by the Coast Guard and staffed by members of each agency together with a full-time counterdrug analyst from the Texas National Guard, supports "regional efforts to combat maritime threats along the Gulf Coast" by acting as a "unified control center and to coordinate operations . . . to bolster interoperability and deconflict where an agency's operations may overlap with others."[123] The Center serves as a "ready-made event command post in the event of a natural disaster or other emergency, such as a strong hurricane."[124]

Agencies shared intelligence and created unified responses not only to natural disasters but also to combat transnational criminal activity in the maritime domain by "leveraging each agency's unique strengths, authorities and capabilities . . . to protect the ports and waterways of Southeast Texas and Southwest Louisiana."[125] CBP Port Director Roderick Hudson, who is a Center partner, commented on the force multiplication functions of the center: "Using a multi-agency approach committed to sharing intelligence and resources to support operations developed within the JIOCC positions the group to provide a unified, agile and encyclopedic response to maritime threats. The varied experiences, assets, and abilities will serve as a force multiplier, enhancing our ability to provide a *scalable* security presence along the Gulf Coast.[126] The center, then, demonstrates how force multiplication, in this case, entails the conglomeration of authorities and capacities, a flow of consistent communication, a centralized location from which operations already in place can be quickly mobilized (not scaled) throughout the region through heterogeneous analysis, coordination, and deployment, institutionalized through partnership and enshrined in a physical infrastructural node—the Center.

Industry Surveillance Partners and the Collection of Data

One final mention should be made of the powerful service-based technology companies that ICE contracts to help them find undocumented immigrants to arrest. Among these companies, Palantir and Vigilant Solutions stand out. Palantir is a data-mining firm that provides various forms of software that collects and assesses "big data" and allows ICE to map social relations and the locations of immigrants through millions of data points online. ICE loads Palantir software on ICE officer cell phones and uses its data to make mass arrests, including planning and carrying out workplace and home raids.[127] Vigilant Solutions is a private company that provides a network of stationary license plate reader cameras typically mounted on light poles in various public and private locations. These cameras automatically take photographs of license plates on automobiles as they drive in and out of certain areas. Local law enforcement and ICE subscribe as members of the Vigilant Solutions system from which they receive automated alerts if the system detects someone who ICE has included on lists of people they are looking for. From an analytical perspective, we might assume that ICE would consider these ancillary services to be force multipliers; ICE has not referred to them as such—rather, they refer to Palantir services as "mission critical." This disuse may mean that for ICE, a force multiplier, as this section has pointed out, is not simply an instrumental tool that can be purchased, subscribed to, or one that ICE pays for, but rather is a collaborative partner that offers up their own resources to mutually get something beyond payment from the process as well.

* * *

As we have seen, the concept of force multiplier was created within the context of warfare strategy and taken up and adopted by federal agencies such as the US Immigration and Customs Enforcement and US Customs and Border Protection and their partners at the state and local levels. As the term has been applied in new contexts, it has taken on many new meanings and has facilitated new kinds of professional relationships and new, collectively constructed objectives.

Force multipliers take the form of the NCIC database; local police and jail booking processes linked to ICE through the Secure Communities fingerprint sharing program; cross-agency coordinating centers; local police officers in the street investigating immigration status; joint task forces between ICE, CBP, and local agencies; ERO's Joint Criminal Alien Removal Task Force; ERO-led multi-agency task forces; HSI transnational crime and gang task forces; Anti-Trafficking Coordination Teams working with local police around the continental United States; Border Enforcement Security Task Force units along the US-Mexico border; Department of Motor Vehicles administrators and staff who police identity document fraud; 287(g) officers in local jails and Title 19 cross-deputized officers in external territories of the United States and foreign countries; HSI Transnational Criminal Investigative Units in local law enforcement agencies throughout the world; transnational networks of policing officials, immigration officials, and corporate security heads brought together in regional conferences; and citizens' academies and the well-positioned bank officials, government officials, and television producers who brand ICE positively in the minds of locals in foreign countries.

At an abstract level, force multipliers are not merely strategically placed *people* who collaborate with ICE but also forms of information, cultural practices, technologies, and strategic *techniques* forged in relationships. They link ICE capacities, authorities, and positions to that of many others to render new, increasingly efficient, and effective policing of crime, migration, and transnational social order. However, force multipliers are not perfect multiples of ICE officers. Force multipliers do not consist of what Anna Tsing calls the "*nonsoels*" of modernity— "non-social landscape elements," elements or units designed for interchangeability, extension, or "expansion without change,"[128] which are autonomous, detachable, isolated from social relations, and not dependent upon the contingencies of the contexts in which they are situated. Tsing calls our attention to nonsoels such as the plantation, the slave, and the sugarcane, where native entanglements have been extinguished, and each is mediated by machine-like alienated relations. Force multiplication in law enforcement processes amalgamates, appropriates, and contributes nonscalable policing resources—those agents that are locally particular—unique local police forces, units, capacities, infrastructures, social networks, and powers—that differ from ICE's but may nonetheless complement them. Contributing nonscalable resources, capacities, and authorities allows local policing units to function toward a broader regional, statewide, national, or transnational goal that neither these contingent, local policing forces nor contingent ICE can expand enough to meet on their own.

The force multiplication of highly differentiated, segmented, and competitive national security, immigration control, and local public safety actors forms a global network of policing, one that targets certain populations of people on the move—immigrants, refugees, subversives, and criminals, as well as their organizations and circuits of movement.[129] Force multiplication is the linking and repurposing activity of these nonscalable policing actors, capacities, authorities, and resources that had been designed first to serve locally contingent purposes in certain segments of the global policing network. If these local actors and their agencies can be thought of as siloed data collectors and repositories within surveillant assemblages, linking them through force multiplication is a way that they work together, aspiring to soak up *all* data by breaking down the firewalls that heretofore have made unimpeded interoperability impossible.

Force multiplication can also be thought of as a process that compounds the effects of nonscalable local capacities, authorities, and resources so that they simultaneously solve multiple additional policing problems beyond the jurisdictions and segments they were designed for. The quotidian activities of force multipliers need not change, and local police, for instance, need not expend more energy, investigate more people, issue more tickets, or make more arrests. Rather, simple, local investigations, traffic stops, pedestrian engagements, social networking activities, and local arrests, when carried out by force multipliers, double as immigration policing when local police officers share information gleaned from these activities with ICE through various methods.

However, local police officers also conduct the activities of immigration enforcement surveillance agents and informants; culture brokers, local representatives, ambassadors, and networkers; and identifiers, arresters, detainers, and jailers of immigrants. Through these activities, they add to their policing toolbox a set of immigration control practices that make them force multipliers for ICE. Most local, American police—those who are not cross-designated or in special immigration-related units—are not constantly involved in these activities, but rather they enact force multiplication in mere slices of their workday, on only certain workdays, or in certain periods of an operation. Furthermore, only certain officers rather than others in the same local police force might serve as force multipliers for ICE. Force multiplication is therefore the primary linking mechanism by which local policing *stays the same*, is augmented, and becomes connected with partners throughout the world like ICE to make transnational and global policing possible.

Through mutual exchange, each partner in force multiplication contributes toward the force multiplier effect that is produced in the partnership—for instance, in the joint operation, joint mission, ad hoc initiative, coordinated enforcement action, or joint task force. Only through the force multiplier "effect" produced by this contemporary law enforcement Frankenstein may the various partners together disrupt, dismantle, and prosecute the *entire* threat. Only through force multiplication can the spectrum of criminal organizations spread out over networks of vast distances and domains or throughout the complete circuit of undocumented migration and unauthorized entries within and outside of securitized borders be addressed. Such lofty goals could not be possible without force multipliers, be they Puerto Rican police units or global anti-trafficking nongovernmental organizations working together with ICE. ICE and their partners in force multiplication therefore play central roles in forming each other's institutions and legacies.

Such collaborations and the assemblages they make do not always persist as institutionally consistent entities such as task forces, however. They may also arise in an impromptu manner and dissipate as soon as a single operation or arrest concludes. They may also arise with aspirations to create a fully comprehensive solution to a social order problem without ever truly achieving such a goal. Thus, force multipliers and their collaborations, when they exist, are always in a state of becoming.[130]

Force multiplication both empowers local police as subjects of immigration control and objectifies police as resources to be used by immigration agencies. It allows police agencies to offer up their legal authorities and their resources for use by ICE and others in a quasi-instrumental way in order to achieve their own local policing goals. It also allows local police to strategically use ICE resources and authorities toward local ends. In some cases, ICE imposes its will upon its force multipliers, as in the imposition of the Secure Communities program upon local police and jails. In other instances, it partners with them when their goals are compatible, including, as we will see, in sanctuary cities and states. It is toward this cooperation in a sanctuary state, New Jersey, to which we now turn.

2

Force Multiplication in a Sanctuary State

The relationship of New Jersey's local and state law enforcement agencies with federal immigration agencies has followed a slightly different trajectory than the general, national rollout of the 287(g) program, cross-designation of officers, Secure Communities, and the creation of sanctuary policies to limit local participation in federal immigration enforcement. This chapter provides a brief overview of the two key state law enforcement policies that have regulated how and under what conditions local and state law enforcement may assist ICE in enforcing immigration laws and participate with the agency in joint task forces. In particular, it examines New Jersey Attorney General Anne Milgram's 2007 Law Enforcement Directive 2007-3 and Attorney General Gurbir Grewal's 2018 Immigrant Trust Directive. It demonstrates that while Milgram's policy was intended to facilitate a maximal amount of local immigration cooperation and Grewal's policy, a sanctuary policy, intended to limit this cooperation, given the rather broadly defined allowances written as carve-outs or exceptions to the policy's general prohibitions, even Grewal's Immigrant Trust Directive offers up local and state law enforcement resources as force multipliers for ICE in a very open-ended but still seemingly "pro-immigrant" manner. In effect, Attorney General Grewal's sanctuary policy is itself a force multiplier for immigration control, one that codifies a formal set of procedures that links local police and ICE and facilitates local police participation in immigration activities in both old, direct and new, indirect ways.

* * *

In 2007, then-New Jersey Attorney General Anne Milgram, a Democrat who from 2021 to 2025 served as Administrator of the US Drug Enforcement Administration, issued Attorney General Law Enforcement Directive No. 2007-3, which stated:

While enforcement of immigration laws is primarily a federal responsibility, State, county, and local law enforcement agencies necessarily and appropriately should inquire about a person's immigration status under certain circumstances. Specifically, after an individual has been arrested for a serious violation of State criminal law, the individual's immigration status is relevant to his or her ties to the community, the likelihood that he or she will appear at future court proceedings to answer State law charges, and the interest of the federal government in considering immigration enforcement proceedings against an individual whom the State has arrested for commission of a serious criminal offense. When there is reason to believe that the arrestee may be an undocumented immigrant, the arresting agency is responsible for alerting federal immigration officials, the prosecuting agency, and the judiciary.[1]

Directive No. 2007-3, though issued as an executive decree by the Attorney General, the highest law enforcement official in the state, had the force of law to regulate the work of 36,000 law enforcement personnel in all 600-plus local, county, regional, and state LEAs, including prosecutor's offices throughout New Jersey. Milgram's directive also supported local agencies signing 287(g) agreements with ICE.

Monmouth County and Hudson County correctional facilities in New Jersey both implemented 287(g) agreements with ICE. ICE's Enforcement and Removal Operations (ERO) later publicly recognized the Monmouth and Hudson deputies "cross-trained as immigration officers in a correctional setting" as a "force multiplier, allowing ICE officers to engage in other enforcement operations in support of national security, public safety and border security."[2] Through each of the county's 287(g) programs, designated officers according to ERO "worked to assist ICE by vetting the individuals at the jails and initiating removal proceedings for criminal aliens who fall within the ICE priorities."[3] ICE ERO saw these arrangements as a collaborative program whereby ERO and local officers worked together and pooled resources to "accomplish their respective public safety goals."[4]

New Jersey Attorney General Milgram's 2007 executive directive on immigration enforcement assistance conceptually connected immigration law enforcement to other policing activities by stating that local law enforcement officers should, whether a 287(g) agreement is in place or not, exercise federal immigration enforcement authority in a manner consistent with ensuring public safety in New Jersey communities. In very practical provisions, Milgram's directive required that when a local, county, or state law enforcement officer made an arrest for "any indictable crime, or for driving while intoxicated," the arresting officer or a designated officer, as a part of the booking process

> *shall* [is required to] inquire about the arrestee's citizenship, nationality and immigration status. If the officer has reason to believe that the person may not be lawfully present in the United States, the officer *shall* notify Immigration and Customs Enforcement (ICE) during the arrest booking process. The only exception to this requirement shall be if the County Prosecutor or the Director of the Division of Criminal Justice determines, in writing, that good cause exists to refrain from notifying ICE during the arrest booking process.[5]

In effect, this directive rendered 287(g) agreements unnecessary. Rather, the directive required all booking personnel in local police stations and jails to serve in the same kind of capacity as a 287(g) detention model officer would, albeit without requiring that ICE provide each agency with training and a supervisor to oversee this work. Notifications to ICE could be made by telephone, fax, or by other means "as ICE may provide." Local officers needed to document when and by what means notification to ICE was made and the factual basis for believing that the person may be an undocumented immigrant. The local officer would also need to notify the county prosecutor handling the case as well as any court officer setting bail or conditions on pretrial release that the officer had notified ICE, for instance, so they wouldn't release them before ICE got to the local jail to arrest them before the trial.

In Milgram's approval to local agencies to enter into 287(g) agreements, the Attorney General clarified in the policy text that local officers operating under such an agreement could only exercise their immigration authority when a person had been arrested for one of the aforementioned offenses. Officers were also required to report any instance when they inquired into the immigration status of an individual under these provisions and to provide them to the county prosecutor. The policy also stated that if local law enforcement were already assigned to work full-time with a federal law enforcement agency, for instance, in a joint task force, this directive didn't limit them in any way if they were acting under the authority of federal law.

Victims, witnesses, potential witnesses, or people requesting police assistance could not be questioned about their immigration status, however, unless the county prosecutor granted the local officer permission or if the person had been arrested for any of the offenses already mentioned. County prosecutors needed to collect information from the local agencies to report to the Division of Criminal Justice of the Attorney General's office so that the office could file the information into a report that was then published on the office's website.

Milgram's directive was effective immediately upon signing on August 22, 2007, and wasn't repealed until March 15, 2019, the day that a new directive called the Immigrant Trust Directive, signed by the subsequent Attorney General Gurbir Grewal, became effective. Grewal's directive was hailed as a new direction for law enforcement in the state akin to sanctuary state policies elsewhere. A sanctuary policy, law, or directive in the United States, as noted earlier, is merely an institutionally codified set of rules that defines for local, county, or state government staff, management, and executives under what conditions and how they can assist federal immigration authorities in collecting information, locating and holding people, and turning them over to federal custody.[6] While many policies like this have been passed at the local level, when one is passed or issued by an executive law enforcement official at the state level, it becomes effective in all jurisdictions and law enforcement agencies in a state.

This definition of a sanctuary policy as one that facilitates immigration assistance may seem odd to people who think of sanctuary policies as those that prohibit local cooperation with such agencies as US Immigration and Customs Enforcement (ICE) and US Customs and Border Protection (CBP). But sanctuary policies allow subfederal employees to assist these federal agencies, albeit in a conditioned manner, and they do prohibit some types of cooperation as defined in the particular sanctuary policy.[7] In this sense, they can be considered pro-immigrant immigration enforcement assistance policies; that is, immigration enforcement policies that are shot through with values of protecting certain immigrants and deporting other types of immigrants. Similar to sanctuary policies elsewhere, Grewal's directive didn't change local law enforcement officers' status as force multipliers for ICE. Instead, the new directive merely reined in their immigration enforcement assistance powers and rebranded them as pro-immigrant.

Under Grewal's new directive, no representative of local, county, or state LEAs in New Jersey could stop, question, arrest, search, or detain any individual based *solely* on actual or suspected citizenship or immigration status or actual or suspected violations of federal civil immigration law.[8] However, with the inclusion of the word *solely* in this prohibition, law enforcement could still use immigration status as an initiating factor of stopping, arresting, searching, or detaining an individual if another reason also existed for initiating the activity.

Law enforcement officers generally were also prohibited from inquiring about the immigration status of an individual, but they could do so if they subjectively deemed it "necessary to the ongoing investigation of an indictable offense by that individual" and in cases when it was "relevant to the offense under investigation." Given that no further guidance was available to law enforcement to explain why immigration might be necessary to an investigation or which offenses it might be relevant to, this gap largely allowed law enforcement to inquire about immigration status in a broad number of situations that the police, on their own, thought might be relevant or necessary. For instance, is immigration status relevant in the course of a traffic stop of an unlicensed driver driving someone else's car? A police officer might deem it relevant if trying to ascertain whether the driver even has a license and can't provide any other form of identification. An immigration status check in federal databases may arguably then be allowed by the directive for purposes of identifying the individual despite the underlying spirit of the directive, which purports to minimize immigration status in law enforcement interactions. In fact, to bolster this particular activity of inquiring about immigration status information, the directive includes an explicit exception allowing for immigration enforcement assistance in the course of "requesting proof of identity from an individual during the course of an arrest or when legally justified during an investigative stop or detention," effectively rendering the prohibition on asking about immigration status ineffective in every instance.

Grewal's Directive's main thrust for policy change from Milgram's Directive came in the form of provisions that sought to limit law enforcement assistance with ICE in enforcing federal *civil* immigration law; that is, law that is primarily administrative. The directive prohibited New Jersey law enforcement officers from participating in civil immigration enforcement operations, such as an ICE arrest of an individual subject to a removal order from an ICE judge at their home when the individual was not considered a public safety threat or who was known to be unarmed. As with the inclusion of the word *solely* in the example above, here too, this prohibition from participation in civil immigration enforcement operations included the phrase "when the sole purpose of that assistance is to enforce federal civil immigration law," therefore allowing law enforcement to participate in these types of operations when the sole purpose of that assistance was *not* just to enforce federal civil immigration law. This language, then, would potentially allow law enforcement to participate in a house arrest if they could provide a non-immigration enforcement reason to participate. For instance, the police could claim they were enforcing some other type of law—traffic law, right of way law, or criminal law—and justify their actions as merely maintaining the orderly flow of traffic in front of the home or keeping neighbors safe from potential violence at an ICE arrest.

The directive also generally prohibited officers from providing nonpublic, personally identifying information regarding an individual to ICE; law enforcement equipment such as office space, databases, and property not available to the general public to ICE; ICE access to a detained individual; and notice of a detained individual's upcoming release, including information about when and where ICE could arrest the individual. The directive also prohibited continuing the detention of the individual beyond the time they would be released to the public so that ICE could arrest them. However, again, local and state officers were only prohibited from taking these steps if enforcement of civil immigration law was the sole purpose. If law enforcement could find other public safety reasons within their purview for participating in these activities, they could do so under the exceptional language.

In the case of two of the prohibited activities—providing notice to ICE of the release of an individual from local custody so ICE could arrest them and continuing the detention of an individual past their release time so ICE could come to interview them and potentially obtain custody of them—further language was added so that New Jersey law enforcement could always carry out these assistance practices if the targeted person had a particular criminal record. To be more specific, regardless of the reasons for cooperating, that is, whether or not immigration status and enforcement of civil immigration law was the sole reason for the cooperation, law enforcement could *always*, should they so choose, notify ICE or detain people past their release time if that person

(a) is currently charged with, has ever been convicted of, has ever been adjudicated delinquent for, or has ever been found not guilty by reason of insanity of, a violent or serious offense as that term is defined in Appendix A.[9]

The directive's Appendix A lists all the specific crimes policy drafters delineated as crimes committed by people they wanted to help deport. This includes any first- or second-degree offense in New Jersey Statutes (NJSA) 2C:43-1 and any indictable domestic violence offense defined in NJSA 2C:25-19 and in NJSA 2C:25-19A(2). The list of offenses also included the drafters' chart of the limited number of Violent and Serious Offenses, including assault; knowingly leaving the scene of a motor vehicle accident involving serious bodily injury; stalking; throwing bodily fluid at officers; criminal sexual assault; exposing genitals to minors under the age of thirteen and other vulnerable populations; bias intimidation; arson; causing widespread injury or damage; burglary of a dwelling; endangering the welfare of children; witness tampering and retaliation; eluding a law enforcement officer; hindering apprehension or prosecution; criminal contempt (violation of restraining orders, domestic violence orders, etc.); manufacture, transportation, or possession of weapons; and aggravated hazing. Law enforcement could also notify ICE or detain people for ICE if the individual, "in the past five years, has been convicted of an indictable crime other than a violent or serious offense," or "is subject to a Final Order of Removal that has been signed by a federal judge and lodged with the county jail or state prison where the detainee is being held."[10]

New Jersey law enforcement officers were also allowed to participate with ICE and CBP in joint law enforcement task forces as long as the *pri-*

mary purpose was unrelated to federal civil immigration enforcement. Notably, in a public memoir written by the pseudonymous Michael Santini, a decorated ICE-HSI operations manager who collaborated with the San Francisco Police Department's Gang Task Force to dismantle the local branch of the transnational gang MS-13, HSI officers always keep immigration enforcement action as a tool to use in joint task force operations.[11] The fact that immigration enforcement is not the primary purpose of such a task force focused on a gang does not mean that it is not an integral part of the operations that local New Jersey police may then participate in. With the directive's permissive language on task forces with ICE and CBP, local law enforcement may be able to partake in civil immigration enforcement action as long as there may also be another aspect, such as the enforcement of criminal laws that they are enforcing.

New Jersey law enforcement could also provide ICE and CBP with information that is already publicly available or merely "readily available to the public" such that the public can obtain it. This language not only allows local police to post information on release dates and times on their website so that ICE can access it without having to file requests on detainer forms but also, if the information that they can provide isn't already publicly posted, it merely needs to be "readily available to the public." This means that essentially any internal information that the local law enforcement agency has that could be released to the public could be given to ICE.

Last, local police are allowed "when required by exigent circumstances" to provide "federal immigration authorities with aid or assistance, including access to non-public information, equipment, or resources." This permissive language may lead New Jersey law enforcement to interpret it as allowing them to respond to an ICE officer calling 911 and asking for police backup at a civil immigration enforcement operation when someone has injured an ICE agent or merely if a person is threatening ICE and members of the public, or when ICE very publicly and dramatically portrays an immigrant to be a potential threat.

Accordingly, this sanctuary policy–style directive, with its exceptional language, would allow for local law enforcement to continue to cooperate in the activities of asking about immigration status, participating in civil immigration enforcement operations, stopping, questioning, arresting, searching, and detaining individuals based in part on their immigration status, providing nonpublic personally identifying information regarding an individual to ICE, providing law enforcement equipment, ICE access to a detained individual, ICE notice of a detained individual's upcoming release with information about when and where they could arrest the individual, and continuing the detention of the individual past the time they would be released to the public so that ICE could arrest them. The trick was that in *limiting* these force multiplier activities somewhat, the directive rebranded them as if they would be the exception to the rule, though they were still allowable if either good arguments could be made to show that the officers undertaking them weren't doing so *only* to enforce civil immigration law, or if the individual they were targeting either was charged with the right crime or had been found guilty of that crime in the right period of time. Such a qualification of these activities as reasonable branded them as acceptable in sanctuary policy, allowing law enforcement to continue to do them—that is, to continue to be force multipliers for ICE even as they were rebranded throughout the state as law enforcement officers who immigrants could trust.

The directive included a specific provision for all New Jersey agencies before the effective date of March 15, 2019, to "adopt and/or revise their existing policies and practices, consistent with this Directive, either by rule, regulation, or standard operating procedure."[12] From 2020 to 2022, this author co-led a research team in conducting a statewide public records investigation that received records on the implementation of the directive in more than 400 law enforcement agencies in New Jersey. We found that only 221 agencies or just over half (53%) of the agencies studied, changed their internal policies to comply with the Immigrant Trust Directive.[13] The study found that among those that did adopt their own directive-related policy, a large number adopted policies that weren't fully compliant with the directive because they didn't adopt all the prohibitions on immigration assistance, or they created language similar to that in the directive but less prohibitive. One hundred and thirty agencies used a template policy purchased from a third-party contractor with whom they had a subscription service, and *that* policy had added permissions for agencies to cooperate with ICE in instances that the Immigrant Trust Directive did not. For example, the template policies allowed law enforcement officers to ask about immigration status in the course of collecting information to notify a foreign consulate that their citizen was in New Jersey LEA custody, something not called for by the directive or the laws governing that notification process.

Thus, the two different directives—Milgram's and Grewal's—in effect are simultaneously each in their own half of the state. It should be noted, however, given the policy language of Grewal's sanctuary directive, immigration control assistance was still allowable, and therefore the two directives should not be seen in opposition to each other. Rather, they can be characterized as two different brandings and approaches to the same type of allowable immigration enforcement assistance, the same type of force multiplication with ICE; one that explicitly champions an ethic of cooperation with ICE and CBP, and the other that embraces the immigrant community while still cooperating with ICE and CBP, albeit in a slightly more qualified and limited manner.

In popular, political, legislative, judicial and scholarly discourse, sanctuary values, sanctuary movements, and most of all sanctuary policies have been conceptualized as the quintessential comportment, value system, and policy and legal mechanism by which to ontologically transform local law enforcement from immigration control assistance force multipliers for ICE, into just local police, or to reestablish the traditional division of policing powers that sociologist and legal scholar Trevor Gardner calls "the old normal" of police federalism.[14] However, when sanctuary policies that seek to merely limit only much of or only some of local law enforcement's force multiplier capacities for ICE and not outright discontinue *all* of them, as the analysis above demonstrates, sanctuary policies end up institutionalizing immigration enforcement assistance protocols, making them routine, automatic, and acceptable in everyday policing. In this sense, sanctuary policies function as part of a force multiplication process that facilitates deportations in no small number of cases if one accounts even only for arrests that ICE makes at local jails as part of the Secure Communities program. In the three years prior to the Immigrant Trust Directive becoming active, 2016–2018, under Milgram's directive, ICE made, respectively, 409, 596, and 1,015 immigration arrests at local jails through the Secure Communities program.[15] In the first year and a half of the Immigrant Trust Directive for which data exist, 2019–July 2020, wherein limitations were placed on jail staff's immigration enforcement assistance, ICE made 711 and 382 (from January to July 2020) immigration arrests and removals through the Secure Communities program.[16] These instances of immigration assistance from jails, which are typically operated by sheriff's departments, don't account for the instances when local police and other forms of law enforcement cooperated with ICE in their respective policing environments under the Immigrant Trust Directive.

This has seemed from the outset to mean that attempts by law enforcement officials in sanctuary states have failed in their mission to protect immigrants from deportation, that perhaps they have duped immigrant rights advocates who have called for full protections, or that they are failing to safeguard their resources for local uses. But these interpretations fail to consider how thoroughly police have integrated themselves as force multipliers into broader policing networks and force multiplication processes that include partnerships with federal agencies like ICE *to achieve their own local goals*. That is, it fails to take seriously how local public safety prerogatives now hinge upon force multiplication. It should not be surprising that when police departments are required to adopt sanctuary policies, they will likely try to reconcile them with their locally specific understandings and approaches to force multiplication in their jurisdiction.

Aside from the Immigrant Trust Directive's broad permissiveness—its open-ended exceptions to its general prohibitions on immigration enforcement assistance—the type of force multiplication that police have been involved in with ICE has been a two-way street, so to speak. Not only has ICE, under Milgram's policy, used local law enforcement as boots on the ground for immigration control, but also local law enforcement has used ICE as a force multiplier to assist them in their criminal law enforcement pursuits. Force multiplication has not totally subordinated police as instruments to a dominating authority—ICE. Police have forged and maintained collegial relationships with officers in their region, joining their authorities, capacities, and resources in order to achieve something identified in the force multiplication process itself. Sanctuary policies, as permissively written, are grafted into this existing professional relationship, modifying it but not ending it. Sanctuary policies serve the force multiplication processes that link local police, ICE, and law enforcement executives like the Attorney General with humanitarian organizations, immigrant rights groups, and undocumented immigrants *who serve as eyes on the ground, witnesses, and informants to police in immigrant communities.*[17]

Sanctuary values, ethics, and activities in other contexts—private spaces and organizations—may actually motivate sanctuary providers to protect individuals from removal when they are fleeing violence. However, when sanctuary discourse is adapted in the law enforcement environment, it not only becomes a resource that combines with national security discourses,[18] it also serves as a discursive force multiplier in the form of policy—as guidelines for adaptive policing in emergent scenarios. Sanctuary policing policy is in turn embodied through functional training, yielding police behaviors, which in turn are reflected upon and further honed, disciplined, chastised, applauded, and internalized. In some cases, when sanctuary policy with policy exceptions is transformed into policing practice, it leads to the opposite policing outcomes than were desired by immigrant advocates and sanctuary policy makers. However, before we explore the ethnography of sanctuary policing, policing immigrants, and working with ICE under sanctuary policy in New Jersey, the next chapter turns to an ethnographic portrayal of a joint operation conducted between local police, local sheriff's deputies, state law enforcement, and ICE during a period governed by Attorney General Anne Milgram's pro-immigration control directive, 2007-3. The following chapter also explains how local police body-worn cameras play a role in immigration and crime control force multiplication processes that span the local and the international.

3

Capturing Migrants with Police Body-Worn Cameras

In early November 2018, in the weeks before New Jersey Attorney General Gurbir Grewal issued the Immigrant Trust Directive, the Freeman Township Police, Mason County Prosecutor's Office, Mason County Sheriff's Office, and the New Jersey State Police participated with US Immigration and Customs Enforcement–Homeland Security Investigations (HSI) in a coordinated raid. This raid targeted an international human trafficking, sex trafficking, prostitution, money laundering, and worker exploitation ring at multiple residences and businesses in a suburban New Jersey town I will call Freeman Township. This chapter introduces ICE's HSI officers and some of the local and state law enforcement officers it works with in New Jersey through a detailed narrative of the joint operation. It also provides a history and overview of the technology that was used to video-record the interrogation and arrests of the immigrant workers: police officer body-worn cameras.

Much of HSI's work is publicized by ICE's communications department in press releases that highlight arrest or conviction success stories and through triumphant reports framed to legitimize the work of ICE in saving and safeguarding victims of transnational criminal organizations.[1] This informational image and branding work has played a role in justifying the ever-increasing infrastructure and budgetary development of ICE within the context of the global war on terror, illegal immigration crises, and public calls to abolish ICE. To this end, ICE must not only capture criminals and immigrants, put them in federal prisons or immigration detention centers, and deport them, but must also capture the work of its field officers in representational forms that can be utilized to gain political support and secure increased funding.

To thwart immigration detentions and deportations, and to advocate for pro-immigrant policies, including sanctuary policies at the local and state levels, immigrants, their advocates, and their lawyers have engaged in a form of "sousveillance"—watching the surveillant watchers from below—looking back at the state, mainly by capturing policing and immigration control through personal cell phone camera videos.[2] Immigrant sousveillance of ICE—oppositional "alter-captures" of immigration enforcement—are positioned toward and against immigration officers and express a certain view of ICE that may simulate the onlooker perspective or the targeted immigrant's perspective. News media outlets such as CNN have circulated these cell phone videos, and separately, immigrants themselves have given first-hand testimonial accounts of how they were targeted by ICE in press releases, town hall meetings, policymaking sessions, immigration court removal hearings, and at public demonstrations.

The camera view of local law enforcement being with and on the side of ICE in immigration control operations has also been captured digitally from the view of police officer BWCs, as they follow, collaborate with, and augment the sight lines of ICE. Police BWC also records the evidentiary details of joint arrest operations and format them as digital video files that state and federal prosecutors may use when seeking prosecutions and other judicial orders in court. Until the spring of 2023, ICE agents, including those in HSI, did not use body-worn cameras. In the context of police-ICE force multiplication operations, however, police have assisted ICE by serving as cameramen, digitally documenting their actions; capturing migrants on film, including details related to their identities, legal statuses, behavior, and living and working conditions; and afforded ICE the ability to copy, share, and replay the videos of the event for an unknown number of remote viewers and purposes. In these cases, not only do police serve as force multipliers for ICE, but so do their body-worn cameras. When police capture migrants on video with BWCs in joint criminal/immigration operations these actions do not merely support the immediate crime/immigration control efforts, but also produce digital video representations of migrants and immigration law enforcement officers as ready-to-hand, storable, and quickly accessible digital resources available for police, ICE, and other law enforcement agencies to use.

Body-worn cameras are small, visible video recorders mounted on the outside of a law enforcement officer's uniform, most often on their chest. In New Jersey, local and state law enforcement officers are required by state Attorney General policy to activate the cameras and initiate recording when responding to calls for service and during interactions with members of the public, including victims, witnesses, and perpetrators.[3] Police may, however, turn off the cameras during arrest events to conduct private strategy conversations with other officers. Law enforcement officers are thus able to make discretionary decisions about when to activate and deactivate the BWC and when to mute the audio recording.

Contemporary BWC technology first became available to American police in 2009.[4] The rapid proliferation of BWCs among US police agencies occurred as a result of rising police visibility due to an increase in civilian cell phone recordings of the police killings of Black and Brown US citizens and mass mobilizations to stop such police violence.[5] In 2015, to restore greater public trust in the police and render their work more transparent, the Obama administration pledged $20 million annually from 2015 to 2018 to purchase 50,000 BWCs for law enforcement.[6] In 2015, 95 percent of the seventy largest law enforcement agencies and half of all police agencies throughout the United States reported that they had implemented or were soon to implement BWC programs, many with expressed intent to provide greater police accountability and transparency.[7] By 2022, all 650 law enforcement agencies in New Jersey were required to implement BWCs in frontline activities and were eligible to seek newly available state funding to finance purchase of the equipment needed.[8] In response to a funding announcement from the New Jersey Attorney General's Office in 2021, 490 agencies throughout the state applied for $57,500,132 to purchase 28,214 BWCs at an average price of $2,038 per camera. Four hundred seventeen agencies asked for fewer than 100 cameras each, 53 agencies requested up to 199 cameras, and 17 asked for up to 1,300 cameras.[9] The most cameras requested were by the New Jersey State Police (1,300 cameras), Jersey City Police (1,120), Newark Department of Public Safety (500), New Jersey State Parole Board (460), and Camden County (401).[10]

BWCs were incorporated into an existing "securityscape" that includes,[11] among many other ambient policing surveillance technologies, automobile mounted "dashcams" and closed-circuit cameras (CCTV).[12] Unlike CCTV, which are fixed in their position, for instance, on lampposts and the sides of buildings, and are thus fixed in their range of view and necessitate that people come within that range, BWC cameras are mobile and thus are with the officers wherever they go.[13] This includes spaces considered public such as city streets, sidewalks, and parks, as well as spaces considered private such as the interiors of residential homes. As Benjamin Goold has pointed out, data capture of these spaces in digital video creates them anew as digital state spaces that are "on the record" and normalized as places where police may go, and allows remote viewers a virtual, repeatable reentry to the spaces when reviewing the videos.[14]

The BWC may be the quintessential example of what Giorgio Agamben, following Michel Foucault, refers to, theoretically, as an "apparatus." In the 1970s, Foucault had provided a rather broad explanation of the term "dispositif," translated as "apparatus," that he used in his genealogies of the prison and clinic—to paraphrase, it was an ad hoc strategic formation of various material, institutional, rational, discursive, moral, and scientific elements, pulled together in a networked relation for societal governance purposes to strategically address urgent needs of society, including new forms of management of until-then uncontrolled societal problems.[15] Once fully operational, the apparatus manipulated and guided or blocked (according to its strategies) the relations of forces—of all of these types of elements composing the apparatus and the power games between individuals and collectivities upon which it relied. This includes the subjectification of individuals as certain types of subjects and a certain type of ordering of elements in the social landscape.

Agamben, departing from Foucault's work, in his essay "Che cose un dispositivo?" (What is an apparatus?),[16] offers a new definition of apparatuses—"literally anything that has in some way the capacity to capture, orient, determine, intercept, model, control, or secure the gestures, behaviors, opinions, or discourses of living beings."[17] While Foucault focused on prisons, madhouses, the panopticon, military institutions, and schools, Agamben's definition allows him to argue that apparatuses of capture also exist at what we might treat as a more basic level—"the pen, writing, literature, philosophy, agriculture, cigarettes, navigation, computers, cellular phones"—anything that we allow ourselves to be captured by "without realizing the consequences" we will face as a result of being captured by that apparatus.[18] For Agamben, the site of the struggle between people and apparatuses is also the site of subjectification of individuals, where the lives of people are "modelled, contaminated or controlled."[19]

BWCs are apparatuses in the theoretical sense of the term used by Agamben in addition to a more popularly understood technological sense. They not only capture video and audio images, but they also make law enforcement activity possible during operations, in this sense steering law enforcement officers in certain ways. When recording, they serve as a data-absorbing net, widely capturing ambient lines of sight that may align with that of the officer, but which fail to capture the officer's full range of peripheral views. BWCs additionally capture temporal data, locational and spatial arrangement data, and information about people's identities, bodies, and relationships between subjects and objects in a scene.[20]

BWCs are one type of force multiplier that allows policing agencies all over the world to access distant lands and past policing incidents because they capture—that is, produce, separate, and make possible the distribution of—"data doubles," abstract signifiers or digital video representations of people, places, and things that in some contexts even stand in for those living people and things they represent.[21] The result of this surveillance technology–facilitated data duplication, as Kevin Haggerty and Richard Ericson explain, is a "decorporealized body, a data double of pure virtuality" comprised purely of information.[22] Rather than being a pure multiple of oneself or one that accurately represents oneself, the data double serves as a sort of "additional self" that affords, limits, directs, and manages the digitally captured individual in new ways.[23] For instance, data doubles represent us in airport terminals in the computer systems of various gatekeepers to our flights, in stores where our shopping history profile is used to suggest new items to buy, and in policing patrol car laptops where our criminal histories and digital mug shots are pulled up when we are pulled over in our cars. Catching immigrants on BWC video produces data doubles for the purpose of scrutinizing, targeting, arresting, and prosecuting immigrants, which policing agencies increasingly treat as a sort of "flesh-technology-information amalgam."[24] BWC capture of immigrant data doubles is contiguous to what Simone Browne calls "digital epidermalization"—the rendering of bodies as digitized code, the possibilities of identification that are said to come with certain biometric information technologies, where algorithms are the computational means through which the body, or more specifically parts, pieces, and, increasingly, performances of the body are mathematically coded as data, making for unique templates for computers to then sort by relying on a searchable database, or to verify the identity of the bearer of the document within which the unique biometric is encoded.[25]

BWC technology not only captures moving digital representations of human bodies, or pieces of them, but captures video representations of policing bodies, be they individual police officers, ICE officers, entire police units, or an HSI team. BWC truly captures all sorts of "*extended bodies*"—homes, streets, trees, cars, clouds, sounds, steam, and their spatial arrangements. Most importantly, it captures data doubles of policing *processes and scenes* in which these bodies operate and interact.

At first glance, the BWC seems to capture everything, including what Simone Browne calls "dark matter" in biometrics technologies as well—those bodies that trouble biometric technologies, like dark irises or cameras that "can't see black people."[26] Biometrics are technologies that Browne explains are guided by

> standard algorithms that function under a logic of prototypical whiteness. This is a logic that privileges users, in this case, in relation or proximity to blackness. Prototypical whiteness . . . is the cultural logic that informs much of biometrics information technology. It sees whiteness, or lightness, as privileged in enrollment, measurement, and recognition processes . . . prototypical whiteness is reliant upon dark matter for its own meaning.[27]

Dark matter is that which troubles algorithms, that which cameras cannot see based on their technological design and implicitly programmed biases that take whiteness as the norm, allow whiteness and white people to pass through relatively unabated while triggering alerts, stops, and searches of those people composed of dark skin and dark matter. As BWCs capture image, sound, and spatial arrangement, it appears as if there is no filtering process, no identifying, sorting, or alerting officers to dangerous bodies—just a digital dragnet soaking up everything. The

BWC seems to capture all, light and dark matter, wherever it is pointed. It sees the light that can be identified and measured, as well as that which cannot under contemporary prototypical categories, that which is "dark," though not entirely without discrimination. As with the analysis of biometrics, new companies like Polis Solutions and Truleo play the roles of sorter, identifier, and alerter. These companies can provide police departments with software tools powered by artificial intelligence to automatically scan thousands of hours of police BWC videos for various elements, including police officer violations of department policy, use of force incidents, use of unprofessional officer language, and aggressive interruptions, among other things.

It would appear that the BWC on its own, then, provides only "raw unbiased data." However, upon closer examination, dark matter is implicitly *absent* in BWC recordings themselves as well, as that which lays just outside of the video capture, those bits of communication that are unintelligible to the viewer, those that the officer mutes to deny the observer the ability to hear them, and that part of the video capture that *can be seen* but that contradicts the stories the officer intends to tell in the summarized police arrest or incident reports. This is the dark matter that does not support the officer's in situ judgments and decisions to use force or to identify criminal charges, the information that confounds the police officer's own algorithm.

Therefore, the police officer is not in full control of the operation of BWC as might be assumed. The perspective of the BWC in some ways escapes the officer's attempts to make it see or hear what the officer wants it to.[28] For instance, the camera may not be pointed at what the officer believes it to be or may not be within auditory reach of what the officer wants it to capture. Though the camera maintains a persistent focus different from that of the officer who uses it, the viewer of BWC ends up experiencing the footage as if it were the point of view of the police officer, as they carry out routine policing behavior, interpret unfolding events, improvise in emerging policing scenarios, and perform for the camera. As Richard Jones has described it, BWC is an "expert system" offering a way of seeing what the individual officer sees in a way that dis-embeds the experience so that it no longer belongs to the officer's memory alone, offering it as a stabilized, realist representation.[29] This representation can then be shared with remotely located viewers and circulated throughout the criminal justice system and its court processes, or through the sociocultural system via nightly news and social media platforms.

BWC is also broadly appreciated as a facilitator of police transparency that the public can use to counter incorrect, misleading, or deceitful police accounts of violent events. It may provide an alternative account from the police officer that appears closer to what really transpired.[30] While it is true that the video capture escapes the control of the officer and presents a view independent of and, in some cases, contradictory to officer accounts, scholars have also pointed out how officers using BWC to record events take artistic license in choosing when, what, and who to record, where to point the camera and also, importantly, what to point away from or to mute.[31] That is, officers maintain a great degree of control in the productive process and record with certain aims in mind that pertain to law enforcement objectives. BWC videos represent those objectives first and foremost and arresting officers utilize the videos to produce incident and arrest reports and, if needed, submit the videos to a court as evidence, part of the prosecution of the individuals.

Returning to the case of the joint operation introduced at the outset of this chapter in Freeman Township in November 2018, local police used body-worn cameras to document the force multiplication activities involving New Jersey law enforcement agencies and ICE's Homeland Security Investigations. In the early morning, "breach teams" simultaneously entered a trafficking ring's Asian fusion restaurant in a Freeman Township strip mall; a residential house that served as a dormitory for restaurant workers; a massage parlor; a home where a trafficked sex worker who worked at the massage parlor rented a room; and an apartment owned by one of the restaurant owners where the crime ring's administrative and financial files were kept. The following is an ethnographic transcription of the BWC footage of three videos that were recorded by one Freeman Township police officer who participated in the arrests at the restaurant worker dormitory.

* * *

Freeman Township Police Officer Chris Donello turns on his body-worn camera while standing in the street in a tree-filled residential neighborhood. He stands in front of a 1950s ranch-style, pale yellow, single-story, single-family house; it is early morning, and the sun is still low in the sky. To his left on the street walks an Asian male law enforcement officer in his thirties, roughly five feet tall with black crew cut hair, wearing a dark blue, short-sleeve polo shirt, black dress pants, and a holstered handgun. This officer, from the New Jersey State Police, is serving as the Mandarin translator for all the law enforcement agencies participating in today's operation. Up past the curb in front of the State Police officer stands a female ICE-HSI officer with long brown hair pulled back in a ponytail, roughly five feet tall, wearing sunglasses on top of her head, a grey hooded sweatshirt, and a tactical armor carrier—a type of bulletproof vest with compartments for ammunition and other tools.

The ICE-HSI officer's vest has "Police" written in small white letters on the front top right, and there's a small badge next to it, making it more likely for members of the public and targeted immigrants to mistake her for a local plainclothes police officer. Such use of this iconic law enforcement sign is a form of "passing" that allows ICE to pass as local police and evade the sousveillant gaze of members of the public who may otherwise try to intervene and stop a deportation activity; or who perhaps may call news media outlets to come and cover the event. Passing as local police also visually brands the event as one of a solely criminal nature and not one that merely targets removable immigrants or refugees. Passing-as-local-police is thus a force multiplication tactic that renders immigration control more effective. For ICE, passing in terms of jurisdiction and passing in terms of authority to use force—that is, passing in terms of having the right to *be there as the local police*—all play a role in passing into the homes and lives of removable people to affect arrests and deportations. Passing here is not a freedom practice that disrupts surveillance, as Simone Browne has described acts of Black slaves passing as whites to flee slavery,[32] but rather, it is a symbolic practice that links and aggregates local, state, federal, and transnational surveillant policing systems, while operationally retaining their differences—a force multiplier par excellence.

The ICE officer is looking at Officer Donello while holding a packet of white paper at her side in her straight left arm. To her immediate right stands a Sheriff's deputy, a tall, muscular white man in a navy blue sweatshirt, bulletproof vest, khaki pants, and black athletic shoes. The word "Police" is printed on the front of his vest in yellow, and on the back, "Sheriff." Sheriff's deputies are county-level law enforcement officers who detain and jail people within a particular county of the state and are directly accountable to a Sheriff. Like the police, they also operate under the authority of the state Attorney General, the highest law enforcement official of the state.

The Sheriff's deputy is holding a cell phone horizontally with both hands, pointing it directly at a group of eleven immigrant workers sitting on the lawn in two rows that extend from the sidewalk in front of Donello roughly five meters to the front entrance of the house. They include one woman and ten men in their thirties, forties, and fifties; nine are Chinese, one is Cambodian, and one is Mexican, and their hands are zip-tied behind their backs. Some are wearing slippers, others are barefooted, and they are all in pajamas or other sleepwear. The detainees had been woken up by officers from the various agencies involved in the raid in the early morning hours while they were still in bed sleeping and were taken out of the house and told to sit down in this lined formation along the lawn. It appears that the Sheriff's deputy is taking multiple still digital photographs of the detainees.

Officer Donello has arrived at the scene after the initial entrance to the home. To the left of the seated group is a driveway on which there are two parked vehicles—closest to the street is one unmarked white van and in front of it is a silver sports utility vehicle parked in front of the home's opened garage door. As Donello walks forward, the ICE officer smiles at him as Donello says, "We're *live* on just so you know." Donello was telling the ICE officer, Sheriff's deputy, and the State Police translator that he is recording the scene with his BWC. The ICE officer and the Sheriff's deputy don't say anything and casually turn to look at the individuals detained in the grass. Donello takes a couple of steps forward and stands still, capturing the detained immigrants with his camera in a clear shot, a digital representation of them to be eventually archived in their police department's body-camera video cloud server, operated by the private company Axon, with whom the local agency has a subscription contract. The video will be used later, if needed, to render a more complete police report of the immigration enforcement and human trafficking arrest and may be digitally copied and shared with the Sheriff's Office, the Prosecutor's Office, and ICE. These other agencies may use it to justify the arrest and bolster their legal cases in state and federal criminal courts and in federal immigration court when seeking removals of some of the immigrants.

None of the ICE officers or other New Jersey law enforcement officers at the arrest are wearing BWCs. Donello's presence at the event then is not merely to police state and federal crimes, but also to serve as a cameraman, an evidence-gathering videographer for a transnationally situated immigration control agency—ICE's HSI. Donello's use of the BWC to film the event, as well as standing guard over detained undocumented immigrants who are not themselves accused of any crimes, therefore expands his role as well: from a local public safety officer to a transnational immigration control assistant with multi-scalar capacities.

At the end of the two rows of seated detainees appears a second white, bald, tall police officer wearing a bulletproof vest that also reads "Police" on the front and back in yellow letters, a navy sweatshirt, khaki pants, and black gloves. The Sheriff's deputy, who is taking pictures, walks past the group of detainees to the house and walks inside the front door. The seated group remains silent.

Donello takes a few steps toward the rear passenger side of the white van and turns toward the group of seated detainees, capturing video shots of them from new views. From this angle, we can see that the second man in the left row does not have a shirt on, while others have t-shirts, sweatshirts, and jackets. One man is wearing shorts. No one is protesting, all are remaining quiet and calm, and they all have straight faces expressing nothing but mildly inquisitive interest in the happenings of the scene. The detainees move their focus each in their own sequence from the grass next to their folded legs, to the officers, to each other, to the unmarked law enforcement cars in the street and back down to the grass while they wait for the next step in the immigration enforcement process.

In addition to documenting the scene, Donello, the Sheriff's deputy, and the ICE officer are all standing guard over the detainees, keeping them in place. Most of the detainees are immigrant workers that ICE considers trafficked from Asia and exploited in a criminal trafficking ring, and they are not among those for whom ICE, the police, the prosecutor, and Sheriff were attempting to carry out a criminal warrant to arrest. Those who are accused of initiating, organizing, or carrying out crimes are all absent from this arrest site. The detainees on the lawn are considered victims and witnesses, despite being handcuffed. However, one of the men was not considered to be trafficked, but he entered the country in an unauthorized manner at the US-Mexico border and is merely working at the ring's restaurant without federal work authorization.

The Sheriff's deputy, who had been photographing the detainees, walks in front of Donello, and one of the detainees, who is wearing only a shirt and pajama pants, tells him that he is cold. The Sheriff's deputy nods his head and walks inside of the house. The man then looks up at Donello and says, "I'm cold," with a Chinese accent indicating that he speaks English as a second language. Donello responds, "He's gonna go get somethin'," referring to the Sheriff's deputy. "Oh, OK, alright," says the seated, zip-tied man.

Another tall, overweight ICE officer with a five o'clock shadow, shaved head, mustache, and a black tactical armor carrier vest that reads "Police" comes out the front door. He looks over at Donello, uses his right hand to point to his own chest, and says, "We *live*?" to ask if Donello is recording with his body-worn camera. Donello does not respond verbally, but the ICE officer steps down from the patio quickly as if he got confirmation from Donello, perhaps in the form of a head nod outside of the view of Donello's BWC. The mustached ICE officer then looks down at the black, mobile, wireless, digital fingerprint scanner slightly larger than a cell phone that he is holding.

He walks over to the first seated detainee, taps him on his left shoulder, steps immediately next to the man's left leg, leans over him, and says, "You speak English?" The man says with a Latin American Spanish accent, "A little bit." "A little bit? OK." The ICE officer motions to the man with his fingers to stand up and says in poorly pronounced Spanish, "Ven aquí." (Come here.) The ICE officer takes the man's left arm from behind to pull him up to standing and says, "¿Cómo se llama?" (What is your name?) "Gabriel," the man says as the ponytailed ICE officer walks over to Gabriel and the mustached ICE officer. "¿Gabriel qué?" (Gabriel what?) says the mustached ICE officer. "Gabriel Antonio Machado," the man says, getting to his feet. "¿Dónde es tu dirección?" (Where do you live/what is your address?)

The mustached ICE officer walks Gabriel over to the brick front porch and asks him to sit down on the second step, which he does. They are slightly out of reach of Donello's BWC microphone and Gabriel's response is not captured. Donello walks closer to the front porch, into audible range.

The bald police officer standing above Gabriel to his immediate left reaches down with his right, black-gloved hand and pats the left side of Gabriel's thigh, searching for something hidden in the interior of his pants. Feeling nothing, the police officer stands back up.

The ponytailed ICE officer has walked over to the left side of her colleague as he is engaging Gabriel. He hands her something, and she begins writing on the top piece of paper of the packet she has been holding. "¿Cuánto tiempo dura aquí?" (How long have you been here?) the mustached ICE officer asks Gabriel. "¿No, solo tengo como . . . seis meses." (No, only like . . . six months.) "¿Seis meses?" (Six months?) responds the ICE officer. "Mmhmm," says Gabriel. "¿Por qué vives aquí?" (Why do you live here?) asks the officer. "¿Ah, pues trabajo en el restaurante con él," (Ah, well, I work in a restaurant with him) Gabriel says, nodding to one of the other detainees sitting on the grass. "¿Dónde?" (Where?) asks the officer. "Aquí cerca en la plaza Cruz."(Nearby here in Cruz Square.) "¿Qué es el nombre del restaurante?" (What is the name of the restaurant?) the ICE officer asks. "Ah, es el Fusion Wok," he responds. Fusion Wok is a restaurant located only a few blocks away from the worker house in a large strip mall-style shopping center.

Donello repositions himself to the right of the porch, where he can more directly record the questioning. From this angle, he can capture the faces of the ICE officer and Gabriel. The ICE officer stares down at his hands—in his left, at a digital fingerprint scanner, and in his right, at his smartphone, both of which are at waist level. While looking at these two mobile devices, he continues to ask Gabriel questions. The ICE officer is attempting to pair the devices over Bluetooth so that he may scan the fingerprints of the detainees there on site and relay them via the mobile data network through a series of federal digital fingerprint databases operated by the FBI and ICE. Additionally, it cross-checks fingerprints with a transnational database—the Biometric Identification Transnational Migration Alert Program (BITMAP).[33] This will initiate a national and international criminal background check and immigration status background check for each detainee, again, who are only considered victims and witnesses. The detainee merely needs to press each finger on a touchpad located on the front face of the fingerprint scanner for roughly 10 seconds, held in place by the ICE officer. The networked system then sends responsive criminal background and immigration status information, including current and expired visa information, to the ICE agent's cell phone in a matter of seconds.

This digital fingerprinting technology, named EDDIE, does not just facilitate a matching process—to retrieve information connected to digital fingerprints already on file in federal and transnational databases. It also allows an ICE agent to *produce* new digital fingerprints and submit them along with photographs of the individual's face and GPS coordinates of the scanning location for storage in the databases.[34] Previously, digital fingerprints were only produced during immigration status adjustment application processes, at a port of entry like an airport customs booth, and in custodial environments like police department booking and intake rooms, in county jails, state and federal prisons, and in ICE detention centers. ICE's use of this networked mobile digital fingerprint device expands the sites where the fingerprints and faces of deportable people may be digitized in a capillary manner anywhere ICE agents go. This means that now, anywhere that ICE goes, a digital migrant can be identified. At this point in the arrest, however, the HSI agent's devices are not pairing.

"¿Qué clase trabajar [*sic*]?" (What is your job?) the ICE officer asks Gabriel. Not understanding what he is asking, Gabriel momentarily pauses before the officer repeats himself: "¿Qué clase trabajar?" "O! Yo soy preparador," (Oh! I am a food preparer/cook) says Gabriel. "¿Preparador? ¿En la cocina?" (Preparer? In the kitchen?) asks the ICE agent. "Sí, en la cocina," (Yes, in the kitchen) Gabriel responds. The ICE officer then looks up from the fingerprint scanner he had been staring at and says, "Yo soy oficial de migración. ¿Entiendo [*sic*]?" (I am an immigration agent. Do I understand?—intending to ask, "Do *you* understand?") "Mmhmm," responds Gabriel. The ICE officer looks back down at his mobile devices and asks, "¿Tiene papeles de migración aquí?" (Do you have migration papers here?), inviting Gabriel to volunteer his immigration status. "No," responds Gabriel. "No, no. ¿Tiene papeles en los estados unidos? ¿Carta de residencia, una visa, TPS [Temporary Protected Status], nada?" (No, no. Do you have papers in the United States? Residence card, a visa, temporary protected status, anything?) the ICE agent says after looking up from his device. "No, no, no," says Gabriel. "No tiene arrestado antes [sic]?" (Have you been arrested before?) the ICE officer asks. Gabriel shakes his head to communicate he has not and then he looks to his left at the bald, black-gloved police officer and two plainclothes county Prosecutor's Office agents coming out of the home.

The two Prosecutor's agents are followed by a third Sheriff's deputy who is wearing a black ski mask, a green tactical armor carrier that displays the word "Police," matching green cargo pants, a holstered handgun, a black hooded sweatshirt, and black gloves. He was part of the original breach team that first entered the home. At this point in the arrest, his role is to photograph all the evidentiary items inside of the residence, including any documents about the human trafficking ring.

"Next stop," the first plainclothes Prosecutor's agent says to the bald police officer, indicating that they had seen what they needed to from this home and that they would go to one of the other operation arrest sites that were targeted that morning.

As they walk past, the State Police Mandarin translator who had been observing Gabriel's porch-side questioning turns to the group of detainees in the grass and begins to speak to them in Mandarin to find out who is the driver of the white van parked beside them and who has the key. This is the van that is used to bring the workers to and from the restaurant where they work with Gabriel. When the agent finds out, he turns to the two ICE agents and while pointing to one of the detainees says, "He has the key."

A third ICE officer walks out from the open garage and stands behind the other two. He is a white man in his fifties wearing a black bulletproof vest with the words "Police—HSI" printed on the front in white letters next to an ICE badge, a tan t-shirt, khaki pants, and brown shoes.

The mustached ICE officer questioning Gabriel puts down the mobile fingerprint scanner on the brick porch and picks up Gabriel's passport which another officer had removed from Gabriel's pocket and placed next to him. The ICE officer opens it to the photo page and takes a photograph of it with the smart phone he is holding in his right hand. The bald police officer then hands the mustached ICE officer a wallet, and the ICE officer places the passport and wallet into a single, clear zip-top bag and sets it down on the porch next to Gabriel. It is in these minute cooperative gestures of small assistance, the passing of a wallet from police hands to ICE hands during immigration enforcement–related questioning, when local policing and transnational immigration control become indistinguishable.

The ICE officer tells Gabriel to stand up, and with wire cutters, he cuts off the plastic zip-tie handcuffs from Gabriel's wrists. Gabriel sits back down on the porch. The ICE officer picks up the mobile fingerprint scanner and his cell phone and continues attempting to get them to connect over the mobile data network. Each of the detainees will be questioned by ICE and fingerprinted, as well as having a frontal cell phone photograph taken of their faces.

A white male Freeman Township police sergeant in his late fifties, with authority over Donello, walks over to the State Police Mandarin translator and says, "So we need to take him [the van driver], get the keys, and then get the keys over there [to the restaurant]." The State Police translator then explains to the detained driver in Mandarin what is about to happen, and he and Donello each take an arm of the seated driver to lift him up to standing while his hands are still zip-tied. "You're still on, right?" the sergeant asks Donello to make sure his body-worn camera is still recording. "Yes, want me to go in wit' [them]?" Donello asks his sergeant. "Yes, jus' go in with him," the sergeant responds. "Ah'aight." Donello and the interpreter walk the man up the steps of the porch and into the house, where Donello video-records the interior of the worker home's entryway and the driver's living space.

It is a one-by-three-meter space in the living room, partitioned with thin curtains. Inside the space, there are two large windows facing out to the front lawn, and they are both covered by fabric sheets. In the dark room, Donello turns on his small gun flashlight, which illuminates a single mattress covered in bags under a shattered, frosted glass pane dividing the worker's living space from the front foyer. One of the members of the breach team had broken it when they first entered the home. On the wall above the bed hangs a pair of pants on a nail. The worker tells the State Police translator that the keys are in the right pocket of the pants, and the agent takes them out. The Freeman Township police sergeant has followed them in, sees the State Police translator holding the keys, and says, "That's for the van and the restaurant?" The State Police translator asks the worker, who looks at them and nods his head. "Beautiful!" says the sergeant. "OK, so we'll keep the key for the car," continues the sergeant. The worker asks the State Police translator to ask Donello if he can put some clothes on. The sergeant dips his head back into view of Donello's BWC, gets a jacket for the man, and Donello checks the pockets before draping it over the man's shoulders, leaving the man restrained in the zip ties. The State Police translator checks the man's pants pockets as well.

Upon going back outside, Donello provides the restaurant key to a Sheriff's official supervising the other deputies and tells him that it looks like a key to a padlock. The Sheriff's lieutenant tells him that the driver mentioned that the restaurant was secured with a thick chain.

The ski-masked Sheriff's deputy from the breach team, in all green, then approaches the porch and Donello escorts him back into the driver's living space so that he can take still photographs of the space where they retrieved the van key and restaurant key. Donello reminds the ski-masked deputy that he already recorded body-camera video of the area and asks if the deputy still wants to take the photos, which he does.

When Donello and the Sheriff's deputy go back outside to the front porch, the three ICE officers are questioning a Chinese detainee on the porch steps next to Gabriel. The mustached ICE officer has finally linked his fingerprint scanner with his phone, connected to the mobile data network, and is scanning digital fingerprints of the man.

"That's the coolest thing I've ever seen—I've never seen that. It's *super* cool—the little fingerprint thing. I've never seen one," Donello says. The ICE officer takes a photograph of the Chinese man's face from a front angle with his cell phone to submit with the prints through EDDIE. He then helps Gabriel and the second detainee up and brings them back to the lawn to sit down. The mustached ICE officer asks the State Police translator, "Do me a favor; tell them that some of us here are with Immigration [ICE]. Whoever here does not have immigration status—green card [authorization to work], not a citizen, not on a visa, speak up now, so we can talk to them first. Everybody's gonna get fingerprinted. This guy says he doesn't have anything, so we already know. If anybody else wants to admit that they don't have any papers [legal immigration status], we'll talk to them first."

The translator tells Donello that one man admitted to having an expired visa. Donello then takes the man by the arm, lifts him up, and sends him over to the ICE agents to be interviewed and fingerprinted for a criminal background and deportability check. The detainee, who did not have his shirt on, tells the interpreter that he is Cambodian and that he has an expired green card, a card that one receives when they have been given work authorization from the federal government. Donello tells the interpreter to ask the detainees if they at least have some form of identification, to which one man responds that he is in the process of gaining immigration status and only has a New York identification card.

While the mustached ICE officer continues to question the detainees and submit their digital fingerprints and photographs to federal and transnational databases, Donello follows the ski-masked Sheriff's deputy and an agent from the Economic Crime Unit of the county Prosecutor's Office into the house. His job will be to film their inspection of the house's various partitioned dorm rooms. The BWC footage will be a valuable resource for the Economic Crime agent that she may watch when preparing her office's legal strategy for prosecuting the trafficking ring's leaders in criminal court.

When the Sheriff's deputy asks the Economic Crime agent if she'd like body-camera footage to document the house, she says, "Yeah, beautiful. It's one thing to see their pictures, but to see it in video, it's a huge difference."

Donello and the Economic Crime agent enter each of the spaces, many created with walls made of thin plywood sheets nailed to 2- × 4-inch beams with space between the top of the sheet at the ceiling, forestalling any privacy. On some of the walls, clothes hang from nails. Some areas are bedrooms with multiple twin beds at the base of disassembled bunks on which hang clothes hangers. Some rooms fit two or three people, and they are divided by Japanese folding room dividers. One room contains buckets of fresh water, and in another is a spray can of bed bug killer.

Donello and the agent discuss various elements of the living conditions—they note how each space has a hot plate on which each of the workers cooks their own instant ramen noodle soup, that the living setups violate many fire codes, that the electrical switches for the lights in some of the rooms are exposed and not to be turned on; and that the biggest room in the basement belonged to one of the managers of the trafficking ring, a man named Chen who was not present in the home at the time of the raid and was not apprehended. Chen also serves as a master chef in the kitchen at the restaurant where the detainees work. The home and the van used to transport the workers are owned by the restaurant owner, who is later visually identified by the van driver based on a photo that the police sergeant shows to him on the sergeant's smartphone during the arrest.

Following their examination and video documentation of the living quarters, Donello and the Economic Crime agent move outside to the backyard to investigate the interior of a free-standing utility shed. When viewing it, the Economic Crime agent notes, "Musty, but there's no kids, so that's good," referring to the possibility of children being held captive there. Donello responds, "Yeahsss, I guess what's really sad is this . . . to us this [the living condition of the home] is better for, in some degree, better than what they were in [in their home countries], for some . . . it's crazy."

The Economic Crime agent then looks at Donello and says, "Alright, thanks fer comin' through." Donello responds, "No problem. It's all ah . . . captured."

* * *

When local police use body-worn cameras as force multipliers during joint operations with ICE's HSI or ERO that target immigrants for criminal prosecution and deportation, they achieve a new form of capture of immigrant life that augments transnational immigration control, making immigration control more digitally effective. The capture of immigrants, their living conditions, and their arrests by federal immigration agencies in BWC video produce immigrants and immigration control as digital video representations, lifelike digital stand-ins that permeate private law enforcement cloud servers, cell phone networks, and national and transnational law enforcement databases. Capturing the digital selves of immigrants, immigration control officers, forms of local, state, and federal policing operations, and the environments in which they circulate creates in BWC footage a representational form so lifelike that it may even stand in for or contest the summary narratives of their human counterparts found in police reports and potentially oral statements provided by immigrants. BWC video versions of immigrants and immigration officers, in other words, may be used to render "a more accurate account" of immigration control than live testimony of the immigrant, police officer, and immigration agent. The facts that police record for ICE in BWC footage of a criminal/immigration event far outweigh those based on human memory, notes alone, or even still photographs. The body-worn camera footage and the digital immigrant or immigration officer captured on film may speak differently, move in different directions, or act with different discernible intentions than recalled by the living immigrants, immigration officers, or interpreters after the fact.

As such, the local police, integrating themselves and their body-worn cameras in joint criminal/immigration control operations, lend a hand to transnational migration control by augmenting it with copyable and sharable digital video migrants, law enforcement officers, and immigration control scenes. These representations caught on body-worn camera footage may also be accessed and possessed by members of the public. The digital file, the bodycam video, is therefore itself a point of convergence of a wide variety of actors, a battlefield of sorts, and a launching pad through which they attempt to represent and formulate *the real*, including legal truth, scientific knowledge, and the embodied perception of law enforcement anew.

What the BWC footage of this particular event also shows is that when local law enforcement works in joint operations with ICE to enforce criminal laws and immigration laws together, local police—in even such minor forms of assistance as cooperatively passing ICE agents an immigrant's wallet, standing over and watching detainees as ICE officers complete other tasks, or frisking an immigrant's leg while ICE questions them about their immigration status—play a role beyond mere criminal enforcement. When they combine and offer up these local law enforcement capacities and tasks as force multipliers for ICE, they assist in the immigration enforcement process as well. These small acts of assistance, cooperation, and collaboration form the basis of mutual projects, professional kinship, and the achievement of joint goals that are only possible when force multipliers link their agencies together. As a result, immigration assistance that police provide should not solely be thought of as "the obvious actions"—police identifying a deportable immigrant, arresting them, or detaining them only for immigration purposes—the typical activities prohibited by sanctuary policies. More fundamentally, police in joint operations and in situations where they come to the aid of ICE perform countless minute, silent acts of lending a crime-fighting hand, which are offered up and qualitatively transformed in the immigration enforcement process.

These minor forms of assistance may seem insignificant if we only focus on a particular event like this one in New Jersey, and we could rightly conclude that if police had not been present, it would not have significantly impacted the immigration enforcement process. ICE may, and still does, conduct these operations on its own. However, when considering police assistance to ICE at immigration enforcement events nationwide in the aggregate, when local agencies send five to ten officers to an immigration enforcement event, it can significantly reduce the cost burdens for ICE of sending their own additional five to ten personnel to get the job done. To carry out as many enforcement actions as are called for across the nation by the federal administration therefore local police are called upon to shore up ICE's resource shortages and make dragnet immigration policing possible.

Such articulations of local law enforcement, crime-fighting, immigration control, and transnational policing made possible by state policies such as Attorney General Anne Milgram's executive directive 2007-3 are not disarticulated or divided by sanctuary policies such as Gurbir Grewal's Immigrant Trust Directive. They are merely modified in practice and branding. The following chapter explores a case of force multiplication under the Immigrant Trust Directive in which local police continued to provide their minute forms of assistance to ICE, albeit in a sanctuary style form.

4

Parking and Standing in the Street for ICE

In mid-November 2019, after the Immigrant Trust Directive had been active for eight and a half months, two officers from the Benjamin Township Police Department provided "scene security" for ICE when ICE attempted an arrest of a man who had locked himself in his car on the way to taking his teenage son to his son's workplace.[1]

According to department records, Benjamin Township police dispatch received a call from ICE at 6 am the day of the ICE action, notifying the department that ICE would be making a "noncriminal" administrative arrest at a location in Benjamin Township and that ICE wasn't requesting backup.[2] Later, at around 7:30 am, ICE called back mid-arrest to request backup assistance because, as the dispatch log noted, the "subject is inside a vehicle, no weapons on scene, but will not get out of the car. Specifically requesting a sergeant and additional unit to aid them." A minute later, Sergeant Thomas Madigan and Sergeant Steven Sunom were dispatched to the location of the ICE arrest. The following is an ethnographic narrative created from the BWC video produced by Sergeant Madigan. The narrative demonstrates how police, when implementing the prohibitions against immigration control assistance in sanctuary policies, nonetheless act as immigration control force multipliers not by directly laying hands upon targeted immigrants, making immigration arrests, or sharing information but rather by working on the environment immediately surrounding an arrest to ensure that ICE can accomplish it more efficiently. It shows that local policing of traffic and pedestrians and the manner in which local police park their vehicles and merely stand in relation to the immigration enforcement arrest zone are offered up as a local resource to be utilized as a force multiplier for ICE.

* * *

Sergeant Madigan is driving in his patrol vehicle along a tree-filled street at 7:27 am with his sirens sounding. The body-worn camera video has been edited to visually blur the space where the officer's patrol vehicle laptop console would be—a redaction added to the video by the agency's records custodian. As Madigan revs the vehicle's engine, the vehicle speeds down the street. Within 10 seconds, Madigan quickly parks his car and opens his driver's side door to get out. In front of him is a row of two-story, middle-class homes with lawns covered in fallen, dried leaves. In the near proximity can be heard an ICE agent standing on a lawn to Officer Madigan's right. The ICE agent is shouting loudly at a driver, a 37-year-old Mexican man, inside of his parked car in front of the ICE agent, "There is no other way outta here. You're getting arrested!"

As a neighbor walks his dog on the left side of the street, coming toward Officer Madigan, Madigan walks toward the middle of the street where a second ICE officer is standing on the other side of the target's car. This ICE officer is wearing tennis shoes, tan cargo pants, a grey hoodie, black sunglasses, a black winter hat, and a black Kevlar vest that says merely "Police." "So, what's goin' on?" asks Madigan. Responding as if answering a question about why the police were called, the ICE agent says, "For scene safety, just in case the family comes out. We got a guy who's barricaded himself in the car with the kid. I mean, eventually, we're gonna break the window [of the car] if we have to. We just want you here in case neighbors start comin' out, or. . . ." It should be noted that the driver's refusal to open his door to the ICE agents was framed as "barricading himself" in as if he had constructed a major barrier between himself and the ICE agents. In fact, all that separated the man from ICE was a thin pane of car window glass, something very easily broken with the approval of an ICE supervisor.

As the ICE officer was explaining this to Madigan, the ICE officer who had been yelling at the driver through the crack in his driver's side window, trying to get him to come out of the car, says, "I'm just trying to make it easy." A third ICE agent walks from the driver's side of the car back behind the car over to the passenger side where the man's son is sitting, leans on the car right in front of the window, and just stares into the window as the other agent continues yelling, "You are the only person we want here. Come out so you can let your wife take your child to work. We won't let other people get involved."

The second officer at the kid's window calmly says to the kid, "Do you speak English?" to which he responds, "Yes." "Tell your dad to get some sense. It's a lot easier if he does this the easy way. He gets a bond, he comes home, come out and talk to us." The ICE officer is providing the son with information that indirectly presents his father as being unreasonable so as to conscript the son's cooperation with ICE against his father to get him to come out of the car and allow his own arrest. In a sense, this is a tactic of force multiplication wherein ICE utilizes intimates—especially family members—as force multipliers for arrests where they are manipulatively transformed into collaborators who might turn on the target and pursue their own interests, for instance, keeping one's father present in family life and one's status as secure child intact. The child is turned into a force multiplier here if ICE can successfully create a smoke screen whereby the child believes that his unique interests as a child and son are aligned momentarily with the interests of ICE rather than with his father.

At this point, Officer Madigan asks the ICE officer who had been telling him about the situation, "So is this a criminal thing?" to which the ICE officer responds, "Administrative warrant. He's got a couple criminal arrests, some immigration charges, and doesn't want to come out. And we will break a window. " Officer Madigan then tells them, "Alright well, we'll just hang back and let you do your thing then." The ICE officer responds, "Thanks, man," and Madigan responds, "No prob, Bro." In the BWC video, as Madigan turns back to walk toward his patrol vehicle, a black and white SUV, we can see that he has parked alongside one of the ICE agents' small green vehicles, which has boxed in the target's parked car, which is parallel parked on the curb in front of the lawn of his house. One of the other ICE agent's vehicles, a truck, is running with its headlights flashing and is parked immediately behind the target's car, making it impossible for the target to drive away. Madigan's vehicle buttresses one of the ICE vehicles should the target attempt to slam into the ICE vehicle and attempt to drive away. Madigan's vehicle also disallows any other car traffic to pass and drive down the street in front of the site of the arrest.

Madigan walks back to his vehicle and rests his right arm on the side-view mirror as he turns again to watch the situation unfold. Painted on the side of his vehicle, just to the left of the hood, is the word "Supervisor." All of the officers involved, including Madigan, are white. At that point, the ICE officer shouts, "What are you trying to wait for?" After a few seconds, he says, "Your lawyer? Your lawyer is not going to answer the phone. Your private lawyer? K, gah head [go ahead]. I wanna talk to him too." A flock of geese is heard nearby but not seen by the BWC.

Madigan gets in his patrol vehicle and re-parks it, this time behind the ICE vehicle that he had previously parked beside, as well as behind a second ICE vehicle that was parked behind that one, making it even less likely that the target could escape if he were to attempt to ram the ICE vehicles and drive away. This also allows for a lane of traffic to pass along the street alongside the cars, which are all parked on the right side of the street. Madigan then walks back up to the same area where he had previously been standing, down and across the street from the arrest.

The ICE officer, still yelling, then says, "I don't know who you are talking to. Listen, explain to your lawyer that the window is gonna get smashed, and you're gonna get taken outta the car." Madigan walks halfway back to his patrol vehicle and stops to the side of one of the ICE vehicles. After five minutes of being at the scene and with the street totally empty of any people aside from those involved in the arrest, a second Benjamin Township Police officer drives up—Officer Sunom. As Sunom walks up to Madigan, Madigan tells him, "They're at a standoff with him in the vehicle. Sounds like it is a civil order. Um, we're not gonna take any action until he commits a crime, so if he assaults them or something like that, then we go in but until then, we're just here for immediate backup."

This approach is the product of the New Jersey Attorney General's Immigrant Trust Directive's new procedures intended to disallow local police from involving themselves directly in immigration arrests. The Immigrant Trust Directive does, however, permit officers in "exigent circumstances" to respond to ICE and provide them backup. It does not define what "exigent circumstances" are, and so, arguably, ICE's call through the emergency line to dispatch to provide scene security in a situation wherein their target is being noncompliant in a public space inside of a vehicle that he could use to forcefully drive away could meet the vague idea of an exigent circumstance. It does appear, however, that ICE engineered the arrest in this manner. ICE did not attempt the arrest while the man was inside his home, but strategically, once he entered his car, they drove their vehicles up to his car to pen his in. In this manner, ICE seems to have been ensuring that the man didn't lock himself in his home and refuse to come out—a common tactic that immigration advocates train immigrants to do when ICE comes looking for them—taking advantage of the Immigrant Trust Directive's exceptional language so they could still call upon the police as force multipliers to contain the exigent circumstance that ICE created.

At this point, Sunom asks Madigan, "So are they just serving him?" "Yeah, it sounds like they're doing their best to be diplomatic with him to get him to voluntarily come out, but I think they're going to want to bust a window to make him. . . . he's got a kid in the passenger seat. Maybe fifteen years old. . . . they did say he had prior criminal arrests. But whatever they are doing today, it isn't criminal related." Sunom says, "Does he have the window cracked?" "Ah, I think a little bit so they can communicate," says Madigan.

The two stand in silence for about a minute, watching the scene, accompanied by the low humming of the engines of the multiple parked-but-still-running, unmarked ICE vehicles, along with the sight of steam coming from each of the cars' exhaust pipes on this chilly morning. "I think it's time for the beanie," says Sunom, referring to his need for his hat. Sunom is a white man, seemingly in his late thirties, with a buzzed haircut, and he's wearing a black Benjamin Township Police jacket with the agency's patch on his left jacket sleeve at the shoulder over his uniform. He's also wearing Oakley sunglasses. "I think mine's in the car," says Madigan. "I have it in the bag," says Sunom. "If it ever gets cold, I just plunk it in here," says Sunom while motioning to a pocket in his uniform. They continue to stand, watching in silence from afar. The yelling ICE officer seems to have stopped yelling after the past 10 minutes of continual loud commands, questions, and banter. Madigan looks up and down the street—still no one in sight. Looking at the vehicles, some with internal, flashing police lights, Sunom tries to assess which ones are ICE's vehicles and says, "Pickup?" Madigan responds, "A little bit of everything," given that there was an ICE SUV, ICE truck, and an ICE two-door sedan, all unmarked, but with their headlights and internal lights flashing like police vehicle emergency lights.

Madigan then puts on a pair of black gloves, and Sunom goes to his patrol vehicle to get his hat. As Sunom returns, a pedestrian stops to watch the unfolding scene. Madigan asks the pedestrian, "Are you involved in this?" to which the pedestrian says, "no." The pedestrian then asks, "Is everyone OK?" and Madigan responds, "Yep, everybody's good." After the pedestrian leaves, Madigan says to Sunom, ridiculing the pedestrian pretending to be him, "I see a bunch of cops standing around a car, and a bunch of unmarkeds have him penned in; I'm gonna walk over and see what's goin' on."

Sunom, looking at Madigan's gloves, says, "Those are no joke. They're ah." "For mechanics, they don't scrape up your knuckles or anything," responds Madigan. "Remember when Sanchez, he had the ones that almost had like a quarter ounce of sand in 'em across the knuckle there?" "Mmhm," responds Sunom. "You get those on Amazon?" Sunom asks. "Yeah, I think I did." "Are they uh," says Sunom while making a cutting motion as if he had a knife in his right hand and was cutting his left hand. "Cut and slice resistant, yeah," says Madigan. "These aren't, but I like 'em," Sunom says, referring to his own gloves.

A passing red pickup truck turns the corner behind the two officers and drives away from the scene. Sunom, asking for assistance on how to pronounce the targeted man's name, then says, "Ay-bell? Ah-bel?" to which Madigan says, "Ah-bel, A-B-E-L." The two stand in silence as ICE officers continue trying to convince the man to get out of his car. Sunom then says to Madigan, "He don't realize that we're not going anywhere?" and they both chuckle. The ICE officer then loudly repeats through the car window to the man, "I don't know, I don't know who you are talkin' to," referring to the man talking to someone on his cell phone from inside his car. "I could call him," says the ICE officer loudly.

Sunom then says to Madigan, "Tow the car?" and they both laugh, considering the idea of towing the vehicle with the man and child inside. Madigan then says, "Did you see that protest video? I wanna say it was DC; someone parked a van in the middle of the street, and they jumped on top of it, and they were protesting. So, DC has their own police tow truck wirrr, wirrr [he makes the sound of a police siren], hooked it in, they start driving it away. They [protesters] start yellin', 'Hey, that's dangerous. There's a person on top!' It's like, 'dangerous?!' she parked her car in the middle of the street and got on top of it. We're getting her out of the street. We're making her safe now [chuckles]. Good for them." It seems that Madigan gets some relief from examples like this. When police are otherwise constrained and cannot act, as in the current immigration arrest of the man in the car, they sometimes act in simple accord with public safety laws, such as right of ways laws, in ways that might endanger people like the protester, in an attempt to break through the constraints that otherwise tie their hands, and potentially hurt bothersome people in a way that could be justified with a narrative of keeping those same people safe.

The ICE officer then says to the driver, "No matter what your lawyer tells you, you're under arrest . . . you've been arrested before? For what? You've been arrested for murder before, right?"

Madigan overhearing this says, "Oooooh kay." The ICE officer then says, "If we have the wrong person then I'm going to need to see some ID . . . I said, 'murder.'" Madigan continues, "Hmmm, hence why he's being deported I guess." "That'll do it," says Sunom. "I think that's probably valid right [a deportation], " says Madigan. "Gets you every time," says Sunom, and they both laugh. "Jeeeze."

It is noteworthy that despite the immigration arrest not taking place due to a criminal law violation, as the ICE officer clarified when Madigan arrived on the scene, ICE invoked the man's criminal history as part of the administrative arrest as if that previous criminal arrest was somehow present. He presented it as carrying weight and as an appropriate factor in this immigration arrest. It is also notable that this line of conversation between the ICE officer and the driver influenced Madigan's and Sunom's assessment of the man's deservingness of deportation, even after ICE had told Madigan that this was just an administrative arrest and not criminal in nature. This loud, verbal invocation of a past arrest, which notably was not a conviction of murder, therefore can be said to have what sociolinguists and linguistic anthropologists call "illocutionary force." By merely saying that the driver had been previously arrested for murder, the ICE officer effected a change, perhaps minimal but significant, in the power dynamic of the situation. In the minds of the local police, as can be seen in their response, it granted them a greater sense of purpose in participating and justified their staying there. At some time in the past, the driver had been arrested for murder, and while the police couldn't participate formally in making the immigration arrest under the dictates of the Immigrant Trust Directive, Madigan and Sunom found it appropriate to at least provide perimeter security as force multipliers to help ICE nab a person who had been accused in the past of a serious crime and who could potentially be dangerous today.

The ICE officer then says to Madigan and Sunom, "You guys on?" referring to their BWCs. "Good," the ICE officer says. The ICE officer could use the police body cams indirectly to reinforce his tactics of intimidating the driver to amplify his efforts, and he could use the video after the arrest as documented evidence to submit to an immigration judge as part of immigration court proceedings against the driver.

Madigan says to Sunom, "Yeah, they should definitely give those guys body cams." "Mmmhmm," responds Sunom. This calls attention to the fact that while advocates of victims of police force might argue for body cams to illuminate practices of the police that previously might have been conducted without witnesses, law enforcement themselves, ICE and local police included, see them as assets to use for effecting an arrest or to bolster their court cases against an individual.

The ICE officer then loudly says to the driver, "I'll call him right now, what's his number?" referring to the man's lawyer, whom they have been talking about through the car window. "What's the number?" he demands.

After a minute of quiet, Madigan and Sunom make jokes about how to keep themselves warmer in the cold and the ICE officer then yells at the driver after having called the number that he had provided them, "That's not a lawyer, I hung up on them. She is in Guatemala somewhere! You shoulda told me she's outta the country! She's not your representative; she's not a lawyer."

Sunom then asks Madigan, "Kid goin' to school?" "Yeah, I think he's takin' the kid to school. At least he looks like a school-aged kid. It'd be about that right time, right?" Madigan responds. "Mmmhmm," says Sunom. The ICE officer then continues to talk to the man, though it is inaudible to Madigan's bodycam mic. Sunom asks, "Which house is it?" and Madigan responds while pointing at a house to the right with a lawn leading out to the street where the man and his son are locked in their car, "That little grey one right there. I think there's a wife still in the house. I think they asked if there was any other kids or anybody else in the house but the wife, but I don't think he'd talk to 'em."

After two and a half minutes of inaudible conversation between ICE and the man in the car, Madigan goes to his SUV patrol vehicle to get his jacket, and for the first time in the video, we get the chance to see Madigan's face in the reflection of his patrol vehicle passenger rear window.

He is a fit white man in his forties with a brown crew cut and is wearing sports sunglasses and a police uniform. As he walks back to the area where Sunom is standing, we can also see a side street of two-story houses, some white, some grey, and others tan, all with lawns, bushes, and trees, some without any leaves, others with brown leaves, and in the distance some pines. Madigan walks past Sunom's sedan patrol vehicle, and as he arrives at where Sunom is standing, he says, "Much more better," after putting his jacket on, which completely covers the view of the body camera and muffles its audio recording. Madigan opens his jacket back up to allow the body cam to view the scene.

After the police officers had been at the ICE arrest site for roughly 24 minutes, the ICE officer who had been yelling at the man in the car comes walking over to Madigan and Sunom and says in an entirely different tone and degree of friendliness, "Sorry to keep you guys out here," to which Madigan responds, "No problem." The ICE officer continues, "Hopefully, just a couple more minutes, either somebody from the legal team will show up, or he'll come to his senses and . . ." "So, the legal team will hopefully be able to talk him outta the car?" Madigan asks. "Yeah, or my bosses will gimme the green light, and we'll . . . [break the window]," responds the ICE officer. "I was curious about that—you gotta get the green light from those supervisors to do that?" asks Madigan. "And you've heard what he has been arrested for, " the ICE officer emphasizes in response. "Yeah, yeah," says Madigan. "That is the scariest part," says the ICE officer. Madigan chimes in, "Hence why ah, he's gotta lotta potential U-S-L." The author is not familiar with the meaning of "USL" as a law enforcement acronym or jargon but it seems to be an indicator of the reason for prioritizing him as a deportation target. The ICE officer nods and says, "And that is why you all were notified *the night before*," as he turns to walk back to the targeted man's car. "Yap, yap," says Madigan, affirming that he understood.

The fact that ICE contacted Benjamin Township Police the night before about the operation is information that was not included in the police incident report or the Benjamin Township Police call log. The Immigrant Trust Directive allows in certain "exigent circumstances" for local law enforcement to respond to an ICE request for backup assistance and, as noted earlier, some agencies have interpreted this to mean, for instance, if an ICE officer has been shot by a suspect during the course of an ICE administrative arrest or raid. But as we have seen, the directive does not precisely define "exigent circumstances."

Benjamin Township Police records include notes that ICE called the department at 6 am to notify them of the impending arrest and then again at almost 7:30 am after the targeted man was in his car. It is possible that the ICE officer was incorrect in saying the "night before" and that the call he was referring to was really the 6 am call that morning to dispatch. Madigan's acknowledgment of the statement may have been a mere affirmation of ICE having previously called Benjamin Township Police prior to the 7:30 am call for backup assistance. However, if we are to take the ICE agent's statement at face value as true and Madigan's affirmation of the statement as true, the significance of this new information revealed verbally by the ICE officer may indicate that having the police at the operation was preplanned or anticipated and that the police response was not such an "exigent" or "emergency" scenario after all.

In fact, it is hard to argue that a call for backup assistance for mere scene security around a man locked in his car with his child, blocked in a parked position by three ICE vehicles, amounted to a truly dangerous situation for the public or of a truly emerging "exigent scenario" that police should respond to. It shows that the standard for meeting the exigent circumstances clause in the Immigrant Trust Directive is being defined by police in their actions—local police are setting the standard for what is an exigent circumstance in responding to this ICE arrest. Furthermore, the standard by which they may respond to an ICE request for backup is so low that there truly is no stopping ICE from calling emergency dispatch and obtaining police assistance to stand by doing relatively nothing but talking to pedestrians for *any of ICE's field operations* where they carry out administrative arrests on unarmed civilians. In effect, ICE and police, together as partners and force multipliers, are defining what sanctuary policy is, at the very least with relation to the exigent circumstances clause, in the streets of Benjamin Township.

Madigan then asks the ICE officer, "Hey, any concern about weapons? Is there any concern about him being armed?" The ICE officer says, "We always have and that's why we keep having those hands off." Madigan then says, "But I mean, no specific intel?" to which the ICE officer says, "Nah, ah, social media posts have weapons but not in a few years." "OK," responds Madigan. "We're hoping this is it," finishes the ICE officer before walking to the man's car.

Sunom then looks to Madigan and says, "If we gotta pop it [break the car window], it's still all their [ICE's] stuff? We're just gonna . . ." "Yeah, yeah," says Madigan, "unless, and I know this sounds stupid, but we gotta wait for him to commit a crime before we do anything." "Yeah," says Sunom, "but if they're gonna pop it and yank him out, it's still . . ." "That's still them, yep," says Madigan indicating it is ICE's duty to search the man's vehicle and take items into custody as part of the proof of the arrest. "I mean if he starts fightin' with them, or if he jumps in a car and rams through a car, or somethin' stupid like that, then, " says Madigan. "Yeah," says Sunom. "then we'll take action, but right now we're just scene security, makin' sure nobody who's not supposed to be here, no kids walkin' by, somethin' like that," says Madigan. This shows that because of the Immigrant Trust Directive's requirements, the local police are still offering their services as force multipliers to ICE, not as active participants in the immigration arrest but rather as a sort of on-hand, ready-to-act, sentry force that could, if needed minimize the collateral effects of immigration control.

The ICE officer then returns to talking with the man in his car about his lawyer, telling him, "Your lawyer's not helping. He's not a lawyer. He's a, an advocate!" A second ICE officer says, "He's also gonna give you bad advice. Keep your hands up!"

Two minutes after talking about their role as scene security, Madigan turns to look at a car driving up to the scene from a side street behind Sunom and Madigan. Madigan says, "Who's this? Comin' and zippin' in." Sunom says, "Prolly lives over here." A man outside of the view of the body cam then says, "Morning." "Mornin'," responds Madigan. The man, walking toward the officers, comes into view and is white, seemingly in his late fifties, wearing blue jeans, a grey t-shirt, and a sky-blue jacket. Madigan says, "Are you involved with this thing here?" probably trying to assess if the man is the driver's immigrant rights advocate. The man says, "I'm a neighbor," as it becomes clear that he is recording the interaction with his cell phone. "OK," says Madigan. "How are you?" says the man, greeting Sunom. "Do you own this property?" says Madigan. "I'm a neighbor," says the man as he walks on the lawn next to Madigan. "Don't walk past here," says Madigan as the man continues to walk. "Why's that?" asks the man. "Don't walk past here 'cause there's an active scene; it's for your own safety," says Madigan. "Am I interrupting with an active scene?" says the man. "Yes, don't walk past here. It's for your own safety," says Madigan as he moves from the street where he had been standing up onto the lawn in front of the man to keep him from walking in the direction of the arrest scene on the opposite side of the street. "Who says?" asks the man, "What's your name?" "Sergeant Madigan from Benjamin Township Police." "OK," says the man, "I'm going to go this way," and the man gestures toward the house of the lawn on which they are standing, and he defiantly continues to move down the street toward the arrest scene but closer to each of the houses along the way. Madigan doesn't attempt to stop him but tells him, "You have to stay outta the street."

Madigan then turns to watch the man walk toward the scene and an ICE officer then verbally engages the man, who continues to film with his phone from near the houses he is walking past. The ICE officer who is standing on the street near the curb of the lawn tells him, "Give us a wide berth?" "Excuse me?" says the man. "Give us a wide berth," repeats the ICE officer, motioning for the man to stand far away from the car in which the driver and his son are sitting. The man then holds up his hand and yells toward the car of the targeted driver in which he is now in view, "Do you know your rights?! Do you speak English?! We're here to help. They have to have a judicial warrant to let you in." One of the ICE officers then walks over to the curb in front of the man who now has shown himself in his yelling to be an immigrant advocate and says, "Don't make it worse, sir." The advocate continues yelling toward the driver, "A mere administrative warrant, it is not legal." The man then continues walking further down the street, just past the car, and steps slightly into the street.

As he does this, a second man walks up the side street behind Madigan and Sunom and asks Madigan from a distance, "What did he do?" Madigan responds, "I don't know, we're not part of whatever that is."

"They called us out here for scene safety." The advocate who is attempting to inform the driver of his rights then can be heard from a distance saying to the ICE officers, "Do you have a judicial warrant?"

The spectator then asks Madigan, "Homeland Security doesn't do this directly?" "Do what?" asks Madigan. "Ah, take immigrants," says the spectator. "I . . ." stumbles Madigan. "It's an ICE raid, isn't it?" asks the spectator. "I don't know. We just got a call that they had somebody barricaded in their car," responds Madigan in a dismissive manner.

The advocate then walks back toward Madigan and Sunom, away from the arrest, and down the street. "Is there a Benjaminville Police officer here?" asks the advocate. "Yes, two of us," Madigan responds. "Who said that?" asks the advocate, still filming with his cell phone, "You are Benjaminville?" "Yes," responds Madigan. "Why are you participating in this?" asks the advocate. "We are not participating in it. They called us for help because they have someone barricaded in a vehicle. We are just here for scene safety to keep people away. The school's right there, we've had people walk down the street; because we don't want a kid to come walk past the street," says Madigan.

It should be noted that it is unclear why ICE would need Benjamin Township Police to do this kind of street-side safety when Madigan did not, in fact, stop the advocate from approaching the scene and two other ICE officers involved in the arrest were able to engage the advocate and attempt to stop him from approaching the arrest. This fact demonstrated that such police scene safety was ineffective and unnecessary as ICE had enough agents to take care of scene safety themselves.

The advocate continued, "You are aware of the Attorney General's [Immigrant Trust Directive]." "Yes, that is why we are not participating in their actual event; we are just here to keep people safe." This reply illuminates that for Madigan, "participating in the event" pertained only to three activities of the event—talking to the targeted man in his car; eventually breaking the car window if that were to happen; and taking the driver into custody by placing him in handcuffs and putting him in an ICE vehicle. The police were, however, participating in other aspects of the arrest event as force multipliers if we can broaden the parameters of the "event" to also include clearing a space so that an ICE arrest can occur without other people's involvement; documenting the event through body cams and making the driver aware of that fact so that he would start being more compliant with ICE commands; parking their vehicles in a manner that further penned in the driver; and attempting to dissuade the advocate from approaching the driver and informing him of his rights, which could potentially make the arrest impossible in the case that the driver refused to exit his vehicle until ICE left the scene.

It is in these small supportive actions that we may begin to see what sanctuary style policing is, that is, what providing sanctuary *as policing* is, and that it, too, is a type of force multiplication for ICE.

"We are not actively participating in any part of the Homeland Security operation. They just called us for help because they have somebody barricaded in the vehicle. We are well aware of the Attorney General guidelines," finished Madigan. Madigan's framing of the Immigrant Trust Directive as "guidelines" rather than as *his* department's policy with the force of law, which it is, is illuminating, showing that he does not consider the directive as something that must be strictly adhered to. The advocate then asks, "Is there a reason why he has to be barricaded in the vehicle?" changing the framing of barricading from the action of the man locking himself in the car to the action of ICE and the police boxing in the man's car by parking their cars in a manner to prevent the man from driving away. "I don't know, you'd have to ask them [ICE] those questions; I don't have anything to do with that," Madigan says in a seeming disavowal of his participation in the force multiplication process. The advocate then asks, "Is there a problem in Benjaminville with being in your car?" to which Madigan chuckled in exasperation. "They called us, said, 'We have someone barricaded in a vehicle,' and they want us to come help." "So, you are responding to an ICE," says the advocate. "We are not assisting in the ICE raid, the Homeland Security operation, whatever you wanna call it. We are not assisting in that," says Madigan. "You are blocking the street," the advocate says to Madigan while continuing to film the conversation.

"Our job is to keep people from going over there that could potentially be hurt. Some innocent civilian walking by. What if the," says Madigan. "The guy over there's not a civilian?" the advocate says, interrupting Madigan. "What if the person in the car decided to throw it into drive and tried to flee, and it ran a kid over who was walking to the high school right there? We are not going to be here trying to prevent that from happening?!"

While Madigan was focused on the prevention of potential death, this did indicate that he saw part of his role as keeping the driver in place, keeping him from fleeing, as would be indicated by the position in which he and Sunom parked their patrol vehicles, further barricading the man in his car's parked position—in effect, *detaining* him. As such, their positionality, something that is only evidenced by the bodycam footage and not mentioned in the police incident report that Madigan wrote after the incident, was also part of effecting the administrative arrest, itself keeping the driver where he can be easily arrested, not just of keeping people away from the scene who might get hurt.

The advocate then says, "That's your answer?" "To what?" responds Madigan. "That's your answer to why you are here?" says the advocate. "Yes, that's our answer " responds Madigan again, exasperated in his response. The advocate walks back toward the car in which the driver is still locked with his son.

Madigan then says to Sunom, "See. No problem." The advocate can then be seen roughly 10 feet away from the driver's car, standing next to an ICE agent in the street, and the spectator is still watching the entire scene from the side street behind Sunom and Madigan.

Soon after, another neighbor, a white man, walks his dog immediately next to Madigan on the lawn exactly where the advocate had first walked and had been stopped by Madigan, and Madigan makes no attempt to stop the man and his dog from passing there or back into the street in front of the ICE arrest, merely saying to the dog-walker "Mornin.'" The man's whiteness, combined with his lack of "dark matter" and lack of a sousveillant cell phone, affords him no further scrutiny. The man and his dog walk in the street within about 10 feet of the driver's vehicle and down the street. No ICE agents came out to tell him to stay away from the arrest or to give them a "wide berth" as they had said to the advocate. The dog walker merely passes by the scene without incident.

From Madigan's behavior toward the dog walker, we can see that the role of the police in the arrest was no longer to provide scene security to keep pedestrians safe, as was the previously stated pretense. It was as if Madigan and Sunom had given up on maintaining a secure perimeter at all. It became clear that they were solely there to be on hand if any crime *were* to be committed and to add additional law enforcement presence to help ICE effect the arrest with greater symbolic legitimate force—to be a force multiplier for ICE as more boots on the ground, ready to act.

At this point, the advocate moves within three feet of the targeted man's vehicle without any protest from the ICE officers. The advocate then asks ICE, "Do you have a search warrant to search that car?" Madigan looks to Sunom and says, "He just can't help himself, this guy." ICE doesn't answer the advocate. The advocate repeats his question, "Do you have a search warrant to search that car?" and ICE continues to ignore him. The advocate then walks around to the driver's side of the car onto the lawn in front of the driver's home.

Sunom then says to Madigan about the advocate, "Tryin' to beat 'em." "Oh yeah," says Madigan, "That's what he's always tryin' a do. Just, you know, push the limit." "I don't recognize him," says Sunom about the advocate. "Oh, I've never seen him before," says Madigan.

Another neighbor walking her dog passes Madigan and Sunom in the direction of the arrest and asks Madigan, "What's goin' on?" Madigan then says, "Ah, they're just takin' somebody into custody." Unlike with a previous pedestrian who asked a nearly identical question, this time, Madigan makes no ridiculing comment to Sunom. The neighbor then walks with her dog down the street toward the ICE arrest as Madigan removes his gloves. He then walks toward the arrest scene, where the officers are placing something in their vehicle. It is apparent that they have convinced the driver to come out of his vehicle, have made the arrest, and put him in another one of their vehicles. Madigan, roughly 35 minutes after first arriving on the scene, says to the lead ICE agent, "Hey, ya guys all set?" and motions with his hand giving him the thumbs up. "All good?" Madigan repeats. "Hey, just let us clear out," says the ICE officer, to which Madigan says, "OK."

Madigan then walks back to his patrol vehicle, where Sunom is standing. Another ICE agent then walks back to where Madigan and Sunom are standing and says, "We're gonna get out of here." "OK," reply both Madigan and Sunom. "Thank you, guys. I was hopin' ah, you'd get some action," says the ICE agent as he shakes both of their hands, and they all chuckle. "He was smart," said the ICE agent. "Yeah, I'm glad he walked out on his own. It was easier, especially with the kid in the car," says Madigan. "That just makes it so much more difficult than it needs to be."

The ICE agent then gets in his SUV and backs up, preparing to leave the scene with his fellow ICE officers. Madigan gets back into his own parked SUV and waits two minutes for the ICE officers to leave. At this point, Madigan turns off his body-worn camera video. At 11:42 am, after the event in Benjamin Township concluded that day, the "approving officer" for the incident report, Samuel Johnson, modified the dispatch log about the incident to say,

Homeland Security Officers requested scene security as they dealt with a party who was barricaded in a vehicle, in the driver's seat. BPD assisted with perimeter security. Party was taken into custody by Homeland Security. No other assistance was requested. Party was wanted on an administrative warrant.

It is interesting that Johnson refers to the ICE agents as "Homeland Security Officers," a broader term that includes many federal law enforcement officers who have nothing to do with immigration control, such as the US Secret Service. ICE is part of the Department of Homeland Security, though Johnson may refer to them this way to obscure the strictly immigration law enforcement nature of the incident to which the police responded. This, too, should be considered a sanctuary policing practice—not lying, but also not calling attention to how the police may have been indirectly involved in immigration control. Madigan, however, was more forthcoming in the details he included in the incident report for this event. They are worth reviewing in their entirety:

> On 11/14/2019 at 0726 hours, Homeland Security contacted BPD and advised that at the above location they were out with a party who was barricaded in a vehicle and they were requesting police assistance. I responded Priority 1. ARRIVAL TIME: 0729 Hours. Upon arrival I observed four (4) unmarked Homeland Security vehicles with activated emergency lights, blocking in a sedan parked along the edge of the road in front of the above residence. Homeland security approached me and advised that the party in the driver seat of the vehicle had a "Judicial Order" for arrest and was refusing to exit the vehicle. In the front passenger seat was a teenage male, believed to be a family member of the driver. Homeland Security asked for assistance with perimeter security. [Three lines of redacted text blacked out]
>
> INVESTIGATION/ACTION TAKEN: Due to exigent circumstances and being that it was determined to be a civil order without reports of any criminal acts at this time, Ptl. Sunom and I stood by on the perimeter in the capacity of backup assistance and police presence in case of a disturbance or other public safety concern in compliance with G.O. 3.39. At no time did any officer from BPD take an active role in the immigra-

tion enforcement action. Furthermore, no officer from BPD interviewed nor had any contact with the occupants of the vehicle or persons within the residence. [One line of redacted text] . . . our scope and actions were that of protecting the safety of both the Homeland Security officers and bystanders. Furthermore, given that the operator of the vehicle was refusing to comply with orders by Homeland Security to exit the vehicle and surrender for arrest, there was a risk that he may use the vehicle to flee and use same as a potential deadly ramming weapon, thus putting officers and any bystanders who were in the area at risk.

While on site multiple pedestrians and vehicles approached the scene but were directed away for their own safety. While Homeland Security officers negotiated with the operator of the vehicle, three (3) persons, believed to be immigration advocates arrived. One white male arrived and attempted to enter the active scene. For safety reasons I gave an order to the white male to stay away from the scene and out of the roadway. The male was holding a cell phone, presumably video-recording the events, and was confrontational with the Homeland Security Officers and I. A second white male, who arrived with the first male holding the cell phone, remained at a safe distance and did not attempt to interfere nor approach the scene.

The vehicle operator eventually complied and exited the vehicle, at which time he was taken into custody by Homeland Security. The teenage male in the front passenger seat was observed to have exited the vehicle as well and walked over to a female who exited the residence, presumed to be his mother. A third person, a white female walking a dog, also arrived on scene after the operator was taken into custody. Same approached the front yard of the residence in question and appeared to speak with the homeowner.

At this time, I asked if Homeland Security required BPD to remain on location. Same stated they were preparing to transport the party and asked that BPD remain as security until all their units are ready to leave. A few minutes later, upon Homeland Security officers entering their vehicles and leaving, BPD also cleared the scene. The only actions taken by BPD was to provide scene safety on the perimeter for the protection of the Homeland Security officers and any bystanders. [One line of redacted text]

The Homeland Security Office involved in this incident was the Mt. Laurel Office. . . . I contacted Homeland Security via phone in order to document the names of the officers. Same related they would provide individual badge numbers of the officers involved, in lieu of names. The badge numbers involved on scene were . . . .[3]

*　*　*

As we have seen, local police assistance to ICE in the form of preventative perimeter security is a form of sanctuary policing that activates police as force multipliers for immigration control. It is a curious activity, however, as ICE clearly can already manage its own perimeters with its own officers. Dedicating two police officers to stand aside and not really secure the perimeter but rather let pedestrians through the perimeter line, shows that police presence, in the form of *sanctuary policing*, was more about further barricading in an ICE target to effect an arrest. Perimeter security policing as an allowable form of assistance under sanctuary state policy in exigent circumstances should thus be considered primarily as an immigration enforcement activity and part of a force multiplication partnership with ICE. What further capacitated the process was the police body-worn video camera, something that the ICE officer could use to convince the driver to come out of his vehicle. Notably, ICE was able to utilize various moral components of the arrest scene as force multipliers as well, on which it could depend to work toward the goal of immigration enforcement. It is to those moral components that we will now turn.

5

The Morality of Sanctuary Style Force Multiplication

In New Jersey, under the provisions of the Immigrant Trust Directive, the police implement procedures for assessing situations as appropriate or inappropriate for taking action to assist ICE in arresting, detaining, and deporting individuals for immigration law enforcement purposes. These mandates produce a range of shoulds and should nots and standards by which to judge one's action as appropriate or not in the course of navigating through the constantly changing parameters of policing situations in the streets. Implicit in the Immigrant Trust Directive, as in many sanctuary policies throughout the country that I have studied, are value systems that correspond to desired policy outcomes. I say "value systems" in the plural because sanctuary policies are the product of negotiations between immigrant communities, immigrant advocacy groups, law enforcement officials, law enforcement advocacy groups, lawmakers, and executive branch officials such as mayors and governors, including their policy staff, each of whom bring their own value-laden positions to bear upon the final policy texts.

Thus, when immigrant community and immigrant advocacy groups identify forms of local, county, or state government employee cooperation with ICE, they may begin the policy process by drafting policy solutions to completely stop the assistance; such solutions carry certain values that motivate and mobilize the immigrant rights community.[1] This includes the process by which the Immigrant Trust Directive was created—values from which the Immigrant Trust Directive builds are "family togetherness" or "family unity," which is threatened when a family member like a father or mother is deported; and "immigrant trust in the police," which is fostered by the policy. Sanctuary policies may also build from the value of nonviolence—stopping police or ICE from inflicting violence on immigrants during police arrests or immigration enforcement incidents or in the detention and removal process, or staving off violence that may await the immigrant in the country to which they are returned, especially in the case of refugees who had originally fled credible threats of violence in the past. Or, on the other hand, the intention may be to reduce criminal violence against immigrant witnesses who would be afraid to report that violence to the police because of their fear that the local police would report the witness to ICE. Immigrant advocates may argue that the policy promotes the value of immigrant inclusion and recognizes the value of immigrant contributions to the jurisdiction governed by the sanctuary policy; they may also argue that passing the policy is simply the "right thing to do" to recognize a vulnerable population and their inherent human rights, which are being violated by police and ICE.[2]

Advocates then identify sympathetic lawmakers who are willing to sponsor the policy draft and promote it among their lawmaker colleagues, modify its policy language, and negotiate certain provisions to gain enough support to obtain co-sponsorship or legislative votes to pass the policy.[3] If it is not politically feasible to pass such a policy as a law, immigrant advocates may similarly appeal directly to an executive in law enforcement, a police chief, or in the case of the Immigrant Trust Directive, the state Attorney General, to issue the policy as an agency directive. The negotiation process among lawmakers or law enforcement executives is an opportunity for many different power brokers, government staff, constituencies, and lobby organizations to infuse different values into the sanctuary policy, depending on what they would like the policy to achieve in practice. If the values of the immigrant advocates did not win the lawmaker over to supporting the policy, subsequent policy drafts may be written to appeal to that lawmaker's publicly known values based on their past legislative actions and public statements. For instance, sanctuary policy sponsors may include provisions that draw hypothetical connections between the policy's intent to increase public safety as a universal value—something highly regarded across constituent groups of the jurisdiction.

One argument in favor of sanctuary policing policies is that a higher rate of public safety will result, as trusting immigrants who are less fearful of police offering assistance to ICE will come forward with information about incidents that the police are investigating.[4] This value of public safety, however, may overall undermine the value of immigrant inclusion because, in practice, the value of public safety tends to lead to increased support and funding for police and sheriffs, who tend to increase policing activities in immigrant neighborhoods, thus leading to likely increased cooperation with ICE. This can happen, as we saw earlier, if sanctuary policies serve to link police with ICE, such that sanctuary policy serves as a force multiplier for immigration control. This situation also increases immigrant exposure to police violence and therefore runs counter to the value of nonviolence.[5]

In some cases, lawmakers might be in support of immigrant inclusion and the inherent human rights of immigrants, and they might be in support of the values of public safety, but they still don't want to pass a sanctuary policy because they are in favor of voluntarily assisting ICE because it "just makes sense" to help the federal government in deporting people who "shouldn't be here." Sanctuary policy sponsors may court the support of these colleagues in such cases by including language that pertains to fiscal responsibility, which might appeal to the budgetary values of these colleagues. The provisions state, for example, that local resources should be used only for achieving locally determined goals in line with a planned and approved local budget and that immigration enforcement is not a local mandate but a federal one. This value also buttresses sanctuary policies from federal litigation—the federal government is constitutionally limited in its attempts to coerce localities to utilize their local resources to carry out federal projects in which the federal government is the primary responsible authority. Localities can then choose whether to voluntarily participate in federal mandates like immigration control. Thus, the values of state and local autonomy, proper use of local resources, and retaining resources that might otherwise be wasted on voluntary immigration enforcement activities may run through sanctuary policy provisions. Such provisions, however, can contradict values of immigrant inclusion that require the dedication of local resources for projects such as community policing and immigrant-inclusive public services like community health.

Last, sanctuary policy drafts that lawmakers will vote on are inevitably shared with the law enforcement agency policy staff, legal staff, and executive officials who will implement them in law enforcement policy as well.[6] Depending on the values of these agency staff and officials, they may either provide full support for the policy and choose to end all cooperation with ICE, or they may choose to withhold their public support for the draft policy until the lawmaker inserts exceptions or carve-outs to the policy draft that will allow them to voluntarily assist ICE in certain circumstances or to target certain types of individuals. These exceptions can be considered policy provisions that facilitate immigration enforcement assistance inside of sanctuary policies themselves, rendering them tools of force multiplication. These provisions contradict the values of "immigrant protection" in the policy language and insert values about the deservingness of deportation for certain individuals who have, for example, been booked but not convicted of certain criminal violations, who have criminal records that contain certain past criminal convictions, or for one who is a registrant on a state sex offender database. While, as others have noted, psychologically, these provisions, in general terms, set up a "good immigrant" and "bad immigrant" binary value system in sanctuary policies; more specifically, if we consider the ethnographic cases described above, they set up a policing value system that posits a variety of implicit immigrant types, such as those provided in table 5.1.

Table 5.1 Maybe Deportable, Can Assist. . . . . Maybe Deportable, Can't Assist

Immigrants Who May Be Deportable, Can Assist	Immigrants Who May Be Deportable, Cannot Assist
Is a present threat	Is not a present threat
Is a future threat	Is not a future threat
Was a threat in the past	Was not a threat in the past
Is not following the (non-immigration) laws	Is following the (non-immigration) laws / immigrant who may not be following the laws (in the case of a person arrested and booked but not convicted)
Has not followed the laws in the past	Has followed laws in the past
Deserving deportation	Not deserving of deportation
Perpetrator	Victim or witness
Irresponsible (involved in illegitimate black-market work, not responsible for family, is a troublemaker)	Responsible (financially for self and family in legitimate work, hardworking, not troublemaking)
Not doing the right thing	Doing the right thing
Sex offender	Is not a sex offender
Unpredictably noncompliant	Predictably compliant
Armed and dangerous	Unarmed and not dangerous
Difficult, evading ICE arrest	Cooperating with ICE arrest

Police following sanctuary policy, including the Immigrant Trust Directive, make use of variations of these binary valuative assessments of immigrants, rooting those assessments in their witnessed or reported activities, accusations of others against the immigrant, their criminal histories, and in their in-the-moment gut feelings. Such representations of immigrants fit within a broader field of narratives, symbolism, statements, and images that have framed immigrants as criminals and that have existed since at least the eighteenth century. The narrative of immigrants as criminals was intensively reformulated in the 1980s and 1990s and focused on drug-dealing violence-wielding "criminal immigrants," and this specter has also been tailored to the sanctuary city and sanctuary state contexts.[7]

Recently, Cecilia Menjívar, Andrea Gómez Cervantes, and Daniel Alvord have charted the development of the criminal immigrant narrative and point out that the criminal immigrant is the antithesis of notions of the model, law-abiding, hard-working, family-oriented, religious immigrant who contributes to society, in exchange for deserving inclusion.[8] They explain that while many laws in previous eras targeted immigrants for exclusion on the basis of race and perceived criminal threats, they were thought to pose, never before has there been the panoply of federal, state, and local laws that criminalize immigrants as there are today. They contend that this is the result of not only the criminalization of certain behaviors that previously were not criminalized, such as transforming the action of reentering the country after deportation from an administrative offense into a federal felony crime but a more punitive approach to vulnerable populations in general in the United States; advances in technologies of state control and databases designed to combat crime; new forms of surveillance; technologies that allow for the creation of images of immigrants as criminals to be rapidly disseminated and consumed by the public in news media and on social media; and new ways of talking about immigrants as *potential* criminals—a danger to be contained and prevented.[9]

In 1986, the US Congress passed the Immigration Reform and Control Act (IRCA), which not only provided a path to citizenship for many immigrants but also increased border enforcement by allocating significant funds for hiring more immigration officers and technologies, including weapons that they could use. It also authorized a large increase in funding for interior enforcement of immigration laws far from the borders which focused on "criminal aliens," a concept designed to allow local and federal law enforcement agencies to work together to target immigrants who were either undocumented or part of the drug trade. The Immigration and Naturalization Service (INS), the precursor to ICE and CBP prior to 2003, worked with local law enforcement through two programs: the Alien Criminal Apprehension Program (ACAP), and the Institutional Removal Program (IRP). Through these programs, INS conducted "jail status checks," in which INS officers performed on-site interviews with potentially deportable inmates at local jails and state prisons. INS partnered with jail and prison staff, who turned over inmate rosters to INS agents, who would scan the lists for Latin American surnames and then prevent their release from criminal custody.[10] Following the passage of the Anti-Drug Abuse Act of 1988, a new immigration offense was created, the "aggravated felony," for which any noncitizen, including legal migrants convicted of murder, drug trafficking, or firearms trafficking who were housed by local or state law enforcement, must be detained by the INS. Through this period, the federal government could then simultaneously fight the war on drugs and the war on immigration with a combined set of local and federal law enforcement resources, a partnership forged in force multiplication. The narrative of the criminal alien, then, was the hinge on which this force multiplication was justified.

Following the bombing of the World Trade Center in 1993, in 1996, two laws were passed that increasingly criminalized immigrants with the purpose of protecting the country from perceived threats that they posed to national security—the Anti-Terrorism and Effective Death Penalty Act (AEDPA), and the Illegal Immigration Reform and Immigration Responsibility Act (IIRAIRA).[11] AEDPA created special deportation procedures for people who posed a threat to national security, expedited their removals, and limited judicial review of decisions about these individuals made by immigration judges. AEDPA also required mandatory deportation for any lawful permanent residents convicted of an aggravated felony, a category that has come to encompass a wide range of offenses that have been added to the definition over the past thirty years.[12] IIRAIRA streamlined removals by redefining undocumented immigrants who arrived at the country's borders as inadmissible aliens and expanded the grounds for their inadmissibility to the country. IIRAIRA imposed criminal penalties for the creation of fraudulent immigration-related documents and alien-smuggling racketeering; and made the commission of misdemeanors and felony offenses grounds for deportation.[13] Among the significant changes made by IIRAIRA, it made unlawful reentry a felony offense, that is, a *criminal* offense, and called for the expedited removal and criminal prosecution of undocumented immigrants who reenter or attempt to reenter the United States within a certain period after being expeditiously removed.[14] First-time unlawful entry remained a misdemeanor, a civil immigration violation. IIRAIRA also included section 287(g), which, as we have seen, allowed local law enforcement to be deputized to enforce immigration laws in order to target this large new category of criminal immigration law offenders.

Following the implementation of the laws and immigration enforcement programs during the war on drugs and war on immigration in the 1980s and the criminalization of immigrants as national security threats in the 1990s, in the 2000s, a much wider group of immigrants was newly targeted through the Secure Communities program with the dissolution of INS and the creation of ICE and CBP within the Department of Homeland Security following the September 11, 2001, terrorist attacks on the World Trade Center and Pentagon. In particular, with the vast expansion of interoperability of criminal and immigration databases through the Secure Communities program, large numbers of people who had encounters with local and state police for low-level traffic violations and drug possession crimes in particular, and people with no criminal history, were identified for removal after being booked and fingerprinted in a local police station or jail. Essentially anyone processed in a custodial environment, be they individuals booked for misdemeanors, domestic violence victims whose abusers falsely accused them of abuse in turn, gang members, and even any witness who talked to the police was exposed to the risk of being identified and reported to ICE through the Secure Communities program. Through the collection and publicizing of Secure Communities statistics, ICE officials and anti-immigrant public figures could use hard data on immigrants who were arrested to reinforce the representation of the immigrant as a criminal and potential threat and reinforce the perceived need for local police to continue serving as essential force multipliers for ICE.

The impression of immigrants as criminals, however, is not only accomplished through the passage of punitive immigration law and the circulation of images, but also in the course of everyday interactions between police, immigrants, and ICE. Through human interactions, this general discourse on the criminal immigrant becomes inflected with local viewpoints and rationalities, interpretations, opinions, and assessments, and it becomes embodied in police action as they implement sanctuary policies. As we have seen, police rationalize perceptions of immigrants and act spontaneously with these various facts, values, judgments, and feelings at the forefront of their minds. The result is that in a matter of minutes of encountering immigrants and ICE, the police draw upon immigrant narratives, justifications, and rationalities in addition to policies to decide how to implement policing procedures and determine whether or not to assist ICE.

Assisting ICE is then set in motion by police, acting on their practical judgments, empowered by immigration control assistance provisions in sanctuary policies. These policy provisions trigger procedures of law enforcement agencies that might not be explicitly codified in state sanctuary policies like the Immigrant Trust Directive, such as "scene security" procedures. These more specific policing procedures for assisting ICE may be elaborated in agency-specific procedures drafted and issued by the agency's chief and staff, or they may be impromptu and improvisational, influenced by policy guidelines. These procedures, such as obtaining approval from supervisors to go to an ICE arrest of a person at a residential home and to stand in the street to provide scene security, may be inserted into the agency's procedures manuals or General Orders. During the transposition process from a state sanctuary law or policy issued by the Attorney General of New Jersey into an agency-specific procedures policy issued by the Police Chief, the agency's legal staff and sometimes private contractor consultancy firms will import additional layers of values into the agency-specific policy that are implemented and enforced. In many cases in New Jersey, agency-level policies include provisions that are more permissive of immigration enforcement assistance than is permitted by the New Jersey Attorney General's Immigrant Trust Directive.[15]

The police officer, when faced with making a choice about whether to take action to help ICE when they receive a request, inherently considers that question in a field of contending and contradictory value systems, circumstantial facts, and suppositions. Police are supposed to just follow *the* policy, but following their agency policy may itself be confusing and contradictory. Not following an agency policy may subject them to discipline if their management is intent on enforcing the policy, and documented discipline can have consequences, including mandated further training, being removed from duties, being suspended, and ultimately being fired in the case of repeated and serious violations.

In a separate study that I conducted on how police officers are disciplined when they are found to have violated sanctuary policies in San Francisco, California, I found that none of the officers received documented written discipline in their employee files, but rather mere verbal admonishments—a light symbolic slap on the wrist in the form of "don't do it again" statements from their immediate superiors.[16] In some cases, they also were required to undergo training on the sanctuary policies of their department. Effectively, San Francisco, during the period that I studied, did not enforce its own highly public policing policies restricting police officers from assisting ICE in immigration enforcement. New Jersey is an entirely different place, implementing different but very similar policies, and further research is needed to assess if any discipline of violations of the Immigrant Trust Directive has taken place.

In any event, the policy framework into which police in New Jersey situate their actions is a form of textualized and implemented field of competing, professional moral norms. These norms about immigrants and the immigration control situations in which police encounter them are synthesized in their contradiction. This synthesis of norms over time becomes a sort of sedimented, stable, symbolic regime, a reflection of the power assertions of various competing segments of the sociopolitical world. By segments, I ultimately mean people in the field who police look to for guidance on how to appropriately act or who regulate them. These various segments that produce the system of policing norms— the Police Chief and management, the Attorney General and staff, and state and federal lawmakers—establish the policing norms, and police recognize them not only nominally but also as indicators of the line that denotes when the police will be punished if they commit a violation. Police, in their interactions with immigrants, also use norms to achieve their goals—not only to strategize about how to arrest someone but also how to secure their conviction in court. Police use the norms of marking immigrants for deportation assistance in situ as they consider how they might justify their actions later to superiors and the media and how they might explain their value-laden choices made in the face of potentially violent situations. In summary, policies such as the Immigrant Trust Directive serve to provide police with a manner in which to strategically think, justify action, and relate to publics of various kinds.

Law Enforcement Morality as Force Multipliers for Immigration Control

Aside from the policy-produced value systems that police must utilize in responding to ICE, there are also the moral engagements that occur in the field and that can be seen in the BWC of the Benjamin Township incident. As we saw in that instance, Officer Sunom and Officer Madigan responded to the scene to provide scene security for ICE. This action was characterized by the police as protection for the public when Madigan represented it to the immigrant advocates; however, in effect, they were not safeguarding the welfare of any of the pedestrians, the advocates, the neighbors, or the immigrant family. They were providing backup to ICE, in practice focusing less on making the space secure and more on making the act of the immigration arrest secure. By this, I mean that their primary achievement was ensuring that the arrest was carried out without a complicated criminal incident. As such, while they branded their actions as "scene" security, their actions rendered the quality of their assistance "immigration arrest" security, indicating that "public safety" in and of itself was not the motivating value of the police officers, though it was undoubtedly part of their engagement.

ICE thus effectively utilized the local police as force multipliers so that it could make the arrest in the area of the car rather than trying to get the man to come out of his home. This approach also allowed ICE more time to try to work in the middle of the street to convince the man to come out of his car rather than immediately breaking the car window—an act potentially perceived by observers as violence against property and as harm to a child. Policing in this manner, then, served minimally as a provision of sanctuary for the child from greater ICE-inflicted trauma. ICE remained restrained from physically harming an innocent child, someone that the values of sanctuary aim to include in society. In this manner, the local police played the force multiplier role of a de-escalation partner that would allow ICE to save face as a moral agent in the public eye, assisting ICE in branding itself as the good guy. The local police officers expressed that they were rightfully being used as a resource for ICE because they were keeping neighbors safe and kids who might be walking to the nearby school safe from the immigrant father who might ram his car into the ICE vehicles to evade arrest. Local police therefore contributed to the image that ICE's immigration enforcement events are safe in general when police make them safe.

It is also notable that ICE justified police involvement as *reasonable* or *appropriate* in the name of public safety. In the course of the incident, the ICE agents expressly framed the immigrant driver as a potential immigrant threat, spatialized the zone of the arrest as a potential space of danger, and moralized the police and ICE as the heroic protectors of the public. They did not consider the immigrant driver as a member of the public that should be protected. This also rendered the police and ICE as agents who contained the space of threat so that it would not spatially expand or temporally endure.

It is worth noting that when Officer Madigan first arrived at the scene, the loud ICE officer briefed him on the situation, explaining that he wanted the police there "for scene safety, just in case *the family comes out*. We just want you here in case neighbors start comin' out." Given that it is unlikely that the driver would use his car to potentially drive over his own wife, who was nearby, in an attempt to flee, this may indicate that the scene safety was, again, more about protecting the integrity of the arrest than protecting the people from any potential violence. It may be, however, that Madigan and Sunom had both objectives in mind when parking their car to buttress the ICE vehicles to prevent an attempted getaway, as well as when standing in the street and talking to people entering the arrest area. That is, they may have been both concerned about people in the general area getting hurt, including ICE officers, about the welfare of the boy in the vehicle, and about the welfare of the arrest action itself.

What is clear, however, is that the one person whose welfare the police were not concerned about was the immigrant driver, as he had been marked out in their minds as a sort of "past immigrant criminal" who had been previously arrested for murder. No leap in logic is needed to arrive at the conclusion that had ICE decided to break the window of the man's vehicle and forcefully remove him, had he been hurt in the process psychologically, physically, or socially—for instance, through humiliation in the eyes of his neighbors—the police likely would have seen him as the bearer of responsibility for the situation, not only deserving ICE action, but also undeserving of sympathy. I do not mean to construct the officers as "aggressors" and the "immigrants" as "innocent victims" in this framing, but rather to recognize the implications of the various types of behavior, actions, and statements that the police have made, as can be seen in the BWC footage.

It is notable that the moral valuation of an immigrant as a "past criminal" could eclipse the fact that the ICE arrest was only administrative, that it was not enforcing any criminal warrant. While law enforcement officers, under sanctuary policies including the Immigrant Trust Directive, are allowed to assist ICE in immigration enforcement activities when it pertains to people who have been *convicted* of certain crimes, the case in Benjamin Township was not one of these situations. It was clear that Sunom and Madigan were aware that this was not an instance where the criminal provisions of the Immigrant Trust Directive allowed them to participate in the arrest—Madigan told Sunom that the arrest pertained to an "administrative warrant" and was not a "criminal thing," and that's also why Madigan told the ICE officer that he and Sunom would just hang back and let them do their thing. However, the moral personhood of the driver was contested later by ICE when the officer loudly yelled, "You've been arrested for murder before, right?" in the middle of the man's neighborhood, in front of his son, and in front of the local police. While an arrest is not the same thing as a conviction, ICE was publicly shaming the man and attempting to justify their arrest on moral grounds, pressuring the man to exit his vehicle so as to make ICE stop humiliating him and his family and to give any observers a sense of relief that what they were witnessing was appropriate. It signaled that law enforcement considered the driver a *bad guy* and distanced themselves from him as good guys and protectors of them from him.

Such a framing of the driver as a murderer (accused but not convicted) was then placed by Madigan within a valuative framework for assessing who deserves deportation and who does not—a murderer *surely* deserves to be arrested by ICE and deported. Madigan responded to the ICE announcement by saying to Sunom, "Hmmm, hence why he's being deported I guess." Sunom agreed—"That'll do it." It is worth noting that this valuation of immigrants as deserving deportation on the basis of their arrest history is common not only among police but also among pro-sanctuary policymakers and is enshrined in sanctuary policy carve-outs that are premised upon the notion that deporting criminals reduces crime and makes localities and the United States safer—a seemingly logical assumption. Sanctuary policies that call for the deportations of these individuals are then for the purpose of keeping "sanctuary cities safe *from* criminals." In the end, this is the primary ideological foundation of "sanctuary policing" itself.[17] However, statistically speaking, ICE deporting criminals and police helping them to enforce immigration laws does not reduce crime among immigrant populations or the general population of jurisdictions of all sizes and diversity or between rural locations and urban locations.[18] In a comprehensive study of crime data from 3,000 county jurisdictions across the country over a period of nine years from 2004 to 2012, researchers found that when local jails and police assist ICE by detaining and transferring custody of immigrants to ICE for immigration enforcement purposes in response to a Secure Communities–generated immigration detainer, there is no statistically significant effect upon crime rates.[19] It is a point of "common sense" that deporting immigrants arrested for crimes will make places safer, but from a crime-reduction perspective, immigration enforcement and immigration enforcement assistance are ineffective as crime-fighting techniques.

The actions, behaviors, and verbalizations of the ICE officers reflected a similar but different moral valence from Sunom's and Madigan's, emerging from a different organizational culture and policy framework and focused on a different set of organizational goals. ICE's operational objective was focused on effecting the arrest of the man in his car. To do this, they isolated his movement and tried to convince him to exit his car to allow them to arrest him by creating a "nonviolent" spectacle. The lead ICE officer framed ICE's actions of yelling, coaxing, and refraining from breaking the window as just "trying to make it easy" in the course of an inevitable arrest, one that they were *helping* the immigrant to get through in the best way in the context of the possible available routes.

From this perspective, calling the police in to be force multipliers for the operation was working toward this same end—reducing complications posed by the family, neighbors, and pedestrians and further pressuring the immigrant to just "do the right thing" and voluntarily come out of his vehicle to be arrested. Behind the "benevolent usher" image that ICE was projecting, however, was the threat of force, of an impending attack on the car window and physically pulling the man out from his car. Requesting that the local police stand in the street behind ICE multiplied the implicit *threat* of physical force, creating a total threat greater than what would be possible with ICE officers alone. In this manner, sanctuary policing and their restrained "we are not enforcing immigration law" traffic control presence in the street was an internal part of the *force component* of immigration control itself and not just of "scene security" for the protection of the public—not an ancillary or complimentary element exterior to the event.

Familial Force Multipliers

ICE also utilized moral language to get the man to come out of his car, repeatedly framing his acquiescence as *the right* thing for him to do. Appealing to the man to be a good husband, ICE told the driver to "come out so you can let your wife take your child to work. We won't let other people get involved." This framed the man's decision to remain locked in the car as a barrier to his son's ability to work, a choice to place others in the target sights of immigration enforcement, and in this way, attempted to morally place a wedge between father, son, and wife. In a sense, the arrest scenario that penned the man in, combined with the verbal appeal for the man to come out of his car as formulated symbolically, divided the immigrant family into those who were capable (mother) and incapable (father), helpful (mother) and unhelpful (father), responsible for the well-being of the son (mother) and irresponsible (father).

ICE also utilized the moral value of "familial togetherness" as a resource of their arrest, specifically when a second ICE officer attempted to convince the son that he should tell his dad to "get some sense . . . do this the easy way . . . get a bond, he *comes home*." ICE understood the implications of an ICE arrest *for the son* in that he could potentially lose his father. Deportations of parents can leave a family without a parent and spouse for years, if not forever, if the deported immigrant cannot return to be with the family in the United States. Often, the children of deported immigrants may be US citizens and their home country, the United States. Capitalizing on the potential loss of the boy's father, ICE used this as a resource to turn the son into a temporary auxiliary acting on behalf of ICE—a force multiplier of its own kind—toward their objectives.

A professional kinship between ICE officers and police officers also served as a link that made force multiplication possible in Benjamin Township.[20] After first arriving at the ICE arrest scene, Officer Madigan was briefed by the yelling ICE officer and told him collegially, "We'll just hang back and let you do your thing then," to which the ICE officer responded, "Thanks, man," and to which Madigan in turn responded, "No prob, Bro." After the arrest was completed, a second ICE officer then collegially told Madigan and Sunom, "Thank you guys. I was hopin' ah, you'd get some action," after which he shakes both of their hands, and they all chuckle. The three then related to each other in terms of syncing their valuations of how the immigrant driver acted in the incident, showing their affinity in judgment of its appropriateness: "He was smart," said the ICE agent. "Yeah, I'm glad he walked out on his own. It was easier [less "messy"], especially with the kid in the car," said Madigan.

Through this joint agency debrief between law enforcement "bros," ICE and the police in Benjamin Township reaffirmed their shared moral worldviews toward the immigrant to whom they each contributed different moral, material, and strategic resources to arrest. It is also notable that in the hierarchy of authority of the immigration arrest incident, ICE was directing the situation—it was their operation, and it played out through their activities as the lead activities, with the local police taking cues about how to engage the situation not only through reference to their own state and department policies and practices but also from what ICE needed from them. On the other hand, the local officers proactively chose where to stand and determined their own forms of engagement based on the allowances of state sanctuary policy and other agency policies regulating the ways they control public spaces that include third-party observers like pedestrians and immigrant rights advocates. Each agency utilized their respective understandings of what it is to be a good partner in collegial immigration operations, in effect staying in their own respective lanes of responsibility even if they had impacts upon each other's work. It should not be shocking that these agencies, each playing their own role toward reaching each of their respective mutually beneficial objectives, would have an affinity with each other, even in a sanctuary state like New Jersey. But this certainly confounds the view that law enforcement in sanctuary jurisdictions operates with an entirely different moral compass from ICE or that local police could radically disentangle their professional affinities once sanctuary policy is implemented.

The Containment and Co-optation of Immigrant Rights Advocacy

Police in this example also accomplished another force multiplication activity toward rendering the immigration arrest more likely. They delayed and contained various forms of immigrant advocacy from entering fully into the immigration enforcement action. The first form of immigrant advocacy that they affected was that of the driver who advocated for his own freedom by simply sitting in his locked car and refusing to come out. The simple fact that the police responded to such a situation as an exigent circumstance signaled that advocacy for oneself as an immigrant may yield a local police response, which could turn into a police use of force event. This signals not only to the driver but to any immigrant observing the scene that immigrant rights advocacy is therefore something to consider with caution for an immigrant rather than something one should assert to complicate an ICE arrest. In this sense, the police response to the event, at a very basic level, served as a warning to other immigrants of what might happen should they take the same approach as the driver.

This, however, did not stop the driver from remaining in his car, refusing to answer some of ICE's questions, or calling his legal representative. Each of these self-advocacy actions was framed by ICE and the police as "complicating" the situation or making things "more difficult than they needed to be." In attempting to know his legal rights and to have them communicated effectively to ICE, the driver gave ICE the number of the legal representative so that the officer could call them.

ICE ridiculed the legal representative as ineffective and illegitimate and hung up on her. This action was part of ICE's theatrical performance, which sought to undermine the legitimacy of the driver and instead reframe him as a murderer who has no legal ground with which to refuse ICE's demands.

However, when the ICE officer was speaking with Sunom and Madigan shortly afterward, he framed the moral personhood and role of the legal representatives that he called in an entirely different manner:

> "Hopefully, just a couple more minutes, either somebody from the legal team will show up, or he'll come to his senses and . . ." "So, the legal team will hopefully be able to talk him outta the car?" Madigan asked in response. "Yeah . . . or my bosses will gimme the green light, and we'll . . . [break the window]," responded the ICE officer.

Here the ICE officer was planning to turn the legal representative into a force multiplier as well, one that would assist ICE, not the driver, by convincing him to exit the car just as ICE was attempting to turn the driver's son. In this sense, advocacy was perceived not only as a tool of the immigrant to complicate the ICE arrest, but as able to be coopted and repurposed as part of the joint operation. The moral standpoint of the legal representative would, however, need to be shifted from one that secures familial unity and immigrant rights to one that contains immigrant rights and advances the ethics of "cooperation with law enforcement" and "reasonable compliance."

However, when the immigrant advocate arrived on the scene, he filmed the police with his cell phone camera, documented their justifications for participating in the ICE arrest, walked directly into the arrest scene in defiance of the police and ICE, and told the driver that ICE had no judicial grounds to enter his vehicle. Officers Madigan and Sunom at first confronted the man, told him that he was "interrupting" the active scene, and used their local police authority to attempt to disallow the advocate from standing in the area of the street near the driver's car. While purportedly for public safety reasons, this local police action doubled as an attempt to disallow an immigrant advocate to create a sousveillant "watching the state from below" video of the immigration arrest with his cell phone. In this aspect, standing in the street and disallowing the advocate to walk toward the arrest area was done to obscure the arrest from public view and potential scrutiny and to disallow him to confront, delay, or completely frustrate the immigration arrest itself. Madigan did not, however, attempt to strictly enforce a perimeter and acquiesced to the advocate, telling him merely to "stay out of the street."

In a certain sense, Madigan's efforts to contain the immigrant advocate turned back upon him. After informing the immigrant that he did not have to comply with an administrative warrant, the advocate returned to question Madigan about his participation in the event. Madigan denied that what he was doing was participation by defensively asserting, "We are not participating in it; they called us for help because they have someone barricaded in a vehicle. We are just here for scene safety *to keep people away*." In this manner, Madigan selectively chose to appeal to a single set of the moral coordinates in this active moral scene, stripping his justifications of any criminality-based moral assessments of the driver or of keeping members of the public safe and reducing his justification to a bare ethic of "keeping people away"—a more appropriate description of scene safety in terms of keeping the "scene" safe from other people.

As Madigan continued to defend himself, he utilized different moral values to argue his case. When the advocate asked him if he was aware of the Immigrant Trust Directive, a question that itself was laden with the proposition that he *should not* be participating, Madigan responded with a morally emphatic rejoinder about protecting passing children on their way to school from the driver who might hit them with his vehicle. "Participating in the event," then, was morally framed not as keeping people away from the scene or keeping the area safe for the arrest to occur but as preemptively saving children from a potentially dangerous immigrant. Police participation in the form of parking their vehicles in places that would further prevent the driver from driving away and preempting such a getaway from harming a child was a moral act of detention in itself. The same can be said for Madigan's attempt to stop the advocate from entering the near proximity of the driver's car. The police, in attempting to keep people away from the scene and keep it secure from others, along with their values of protecting the public from the harm of the immigrant driver, in fact, also were attempting to maintain the moral personhood of the driver as a potentially dangerous murderer and the rest of the people in his proximity as potential victims needing protection. In short, Madigan was describing himself as a hero, a policing version of a sanctuary provider who might provide members of the public, including "good immigrants" like the driver's wife, with sanctuary from the harm of those who might threaten the sanctuary state's space of safety—that is, from "bad immigrants." His policing was truly a form of *sanctuary policing*.

The advocate, however, asserted that the driver was a civilian with rights, too, that the police were interfering with the advocate informing him of those rights, and that ICE was violating those rights by potentially opening his vehicle and arresting him. This probing and the moral values undergirding it provoked Madigan to later comment that the advocate's consistent advocacy for the driver was tantamount simply to a person "pushing the limit," always testing authority—something annoying, unwarranted, and ineffectual. In any event, Madigan's and Sunom's presence at the event and their engagement with the advocate in these moments in some way served the operation by drawing the advocate away from the arrest itself and keeping him occupied while ICE continued its work. In this sense, the police served as a *detractor* of immigrant rights advocacy.

The entire interaction demonstrates how the anti-deportation sanctuary practices of immigrant rights advocates can clash with the public safety sanctuary practices of police, and therefore the social position and institutional deployment of sanctuary values is a major factor in the outcomes for immigrants themselves. When sanctuary values are taken up in policing policy, they can be mobilized in a manner that perplexes the mind—as in the case in Benjamin Township, and they can be used to target an immigrant father, not wanted for any crimes, for deportation. This is what a sanctuary is when it becomes a policed state.

The Potential Viewer of BWC Footage as Force Multiplier for ICE

One final force multiplier utilized as an instrument of the arrest by ICE during this immigration enforcement scene was the police body-worn camera and what it made available to ICE—*the idea* of a future observer of the BWC footage. While any actual viewer of the BWC video was not present in person at this immigration enforcement event, the idea of an anticipated viewer was used by the ICE agent as part of his strategy to convince the man to come out of the car. In the course of the immigration enforcement event, the ICE officer stopped his cajoling of the driver, turned to Madigan and Sunom, and asked if they were filming the event with their BWCs. When they told him they were, he loudly conveyed his happiness about it to intimidate the driver, something that would be reinforced by comments such as "You are only making it harder on yourself." The potential observer of the BWC that he was invoking was an immigration court judge who might view the video as evidence of the driver's noncompliance with ICE, something that federal prosecutors may use to demonstrate his character as a criminal immigrant more generally and prove his deservingness of deportation. In this manner, the potential viewer of BWC was invoked as a *causal* tool of the immigration arrest.

It was with this in mind that Madigan said to Sunom, "Yeah, they should definitely give those guys body cams." This called attention to the fact, as noted earlier, that while advocates of victims of police force might argue for BWCs to illuminate practices of the police that might have been conducted previously without witnesses, law enforcement themselves, ICE and local police included, see them as assets to use for effecting an arrest or to bolster their court cases against an individual. When the local police utilized their BWCs during the immigration arrest, even when following sanctuary policy provisions, they made possible ICE's use of the BWC indirectly as a direct tool of immigration enforcement coercion. That is, they offered up their cameras symbolically and the hypothetical observers of their videos as force multipliers for ICE.

* * *

As we have seen, when police follow even the most restrictive aspects of sanctuary policies—those that disallow them from directly participating in immigration arrests, making inquiries about immigration status, or enacting immigration-related detentions—while making their services, patrol cars, and body-worn cameras available to ICE at immigration enforcement events, they nonetheless still engage in sanctuary style force multiplication processes that link them with ICE toward effecting immigration arrests. This activity in part relies on officer conceptions of immigrants and their various degrees of deservingness of deportation, their preexisting affinities and notions of professional kinship with ICE officers, their self-image as heroes of the public in a sanctuary state, their tactics and justifications for managing crowds, and their material technologies including their BWCs. Through these means, local police come to conceptualize their actions in moral terms that include sanctuary values, local law enforcement values, and immigration control values operating in mutually reinforcing ways. However, sanctuary policy and sanctuary policing do not always amount to force multipliers for immigration control. In certain circumstances, sanctuary policy does what immigrant advocates want it to do—to serve as what I will call "force dividers" that de-link local police from ICE in particular policing events. The following chapter demonstrates such force division as evidenced in a traffic stop scenario in suburban New Jersey.

6

Sanctuary Policing and Force Division

Immigrants and immigrant rights lawyers have been at the forefront of advocating for "firewall" sanctuary policies that seek to "disentangle" local police from ICE. These advocates commonly portray sanctuary policies as drawing a clear boundary between the roles of local police and federal immigration authorities, relegating the investigation and enforcement of immigration law to ICE alone and "freeing" the police to focus solely on the enforcement of non-immigration-related laws.

When police abide by prohibitions and carry out policing when not at immigration arrest events like the one in Benjamin Township, unless a sanctuary policy's exceptional clauses apply, they must police immigrants in a manner that *avoids* engagement with their immigration status. In these cases, sanctuary policing takes on a more routine policing form similar to the policing of citizens who elicit no suspicions of being undocumented. This does not involve the officer looking away from the individual and their potential law violation, as political pundits have intimated in their critiques of sanctuary cities that "let immigrant criminals off of the hook" for crimes. Rather, the opposite is true—sanctuary policing is a form of *intensively* policing the immigrant, but dealing with their immigration status *as an unknown factor that must remain unknown* while they solve the policing problem—which crime was committed, who witnessed it, and all the other information required to determine guilt or innocence.

When policing according to sanctuary policy, this act of ignoring the unknown but present immigration status involves the officer in a process of force division, whereby the officer is intentionally not engaging immigration status, immigration enforcement agencies, immigration courts, or the detention and deportation system broadly speaking, which includes private detention centers, in order to keep the incident focused on local, state, and federal crimes that are outside of the realm of immigration law and immigration enforcement. Therefore, sanctuary policing does not prioritize local or state autonomy, given that local police still work with and depend upon federal agencies such as the FBI, for instance, to obtain a suspect's criminal history records. Rather, when sanctuary policing is a force divider, it creates a clear distinction within realms of policing at all jurisdictional levels, isolating immigration control and keeping it separate.

From this kind of policing, we can attempt a definition of what a force divider that effects force division might be. The inverse of a force multiplier, a force divider is a capability, capacity, authority, expertise, technique, strategy, policy, or actant that de-links composites of elements that were previously linked through force multiplication, forestalls collaborations between them, denies the flow of certain forms of information between them, narrows the focus of the objectives produced in force multiplication, and assigns narrowed and more specialized objectives to those for which the divided forces were originally created. Force dividers partition and contract the components of force multiplication collaborations into more siloed domains of operation and render those components the sole subjects or directors of the processes that they control. Force dividers end or diminish reciprocal relations and fictive kinship affinities among previous force multiplication partners, redirect forces in divergent directions, deny force multiplication partners the ability to deceive or coerce the participation of others into cooperating in force multiplication processes, and refocus resources in a conservative manner to retain resources among each of the divided forces, which they use toward their narrowed objectives. Force division is simply the process in which such a force divider performs its operations as just described. It should be noted that this is an ideal type wherein such division between elements of force multiplication, between police agencies and ICE, for example, is complete and total. However, in practice, it is more likely that force division occurs to varying degrees, dividing some or many elements of a process of force multiplication but not all—merely producing *near-silos* of more separated law enforcement operations rather than total siloes of operation.

Sanctuary policy provisions that serve as force dividers forestall local police from asking questions about immigration status and the commission of immigration offenses in the course of routine police situations; sharing information with ICE about an individual that may be used to target them for immigration enforcement purposes; detaining them for solely immigration control purposes; participating in immigration enforcement arrest events and other activities; and in the process, narrowing the objectives of local police toward enforcing traffic laws, state and federal criminal laws, and attending to various local disturbances. This, in a certain sense, requires that policing relationships established by local police and ICE are transformed as they can no longer work in certain joint operations, share certain forms of information about immigrants, or pool their resources.

Given the lack of adequate metrics for measuring the number of instances when police operate on the basis of sanctuary policy restrictions and do not investigate immigration law violations or assist ICE or metrics for when they do, it is uncertain how frequently sanctuary policy–initiated force division occurs. The following narrative demonstrates what sanctuary policing looks like when a "firewall"-style sanctuary policy serves as a force divider and has initiated a force division process.

* * *

In mid-January 2019, just two months after New Jersey Attorney General Gurbir Grewal issued the New Jersey Immigrant Trust Directive and one month before the policy was required to come into effect, East Allen Township Police Officer Samuel Arika pulls over a long, white conversion van at around 9 pm. While the Immigrant Trust Directive was not yet in effect, earlier in the day Officer Arika had completed a New Jersey Attorney General online training about the provisions of the Immigrant Trust Directive through the NJLearn training portal for law enforcement officers. When the Attorney General issued the Immigrant Trust Directive back in November 2018, he set the effective date in March 2019 and soon after released a training that could prepare all officers to be ready to implement it in March. This gap also gave agencies time to comply with a provision of the Immigrant Trust Directive that required them to revise their own internal agency policies to render their procedures compliant with the directive. By this point in January 2019, Arika's agency had not yet issued its own department policy—his chief would issue that policy later, on the same day as the Attorney General Immigrant Trust Directive effective date in March.

On this cold evening in mid-January, Arika walks along the sidewalk to the right of his patrol vehicle, which he has parked roughly 10 meters behind the white vehicle. To Arika's right is a one-story commercial building, in front of which is a wide cement patio with a few medium-sized potted trees. While there are no lampposts in the area immediately next to the two vehicles, the sidewalk is lit by the lights on the commercial building, by Arika's patrol vehicle headlights, and by the reflections of light coming from the headlights of cars passing on the residential street to the left of the two parked cars. Cars are passing to Arika's left at about 30 miles per hour and traffic is light.

As Officer Arika approaches the back, passenger-side corner of the van that he has pulled over, he takes out a flashlight and shines it on the passenger side of the van, passing it over the side windows of the vehicle as he reaches the front passenger window and door. On the door, just to the right of the black door handle, is lettering that reads "Carpet Installation," indicating that the vehicle may be a business-use vehicle. Shining the light on the passenger himself, Arika moves his right arm in a motion that looks like he is manually rolling down the window, and the passenger takes a pen out from behind his right ear and manually rolls down his window.

Both the passenger and driver are Latin American men in their mid-thirties with brown skin and short black hair. Greeting the two men in a friendly manner, Arika says, "Hey how you doin' guys? How are you today?" Though they don't respond verbally, the passenger nods his head in acknowledgment, and Arika quickly moves forward with his questions. "Hey, you have yer' driver's license and registration, insurance fer da' car?" The passenger first looks downward into his lap, then points up to a piece of paper poking out of a compartment above the driver's sun visor with his left hand. The driver turns on the overhead light on the ceiling between him and the passenger, takes the piece of paper out of the compartment, and passes it over to the passenger as Arika rests his white-skinned left hand on the passenger door's windowsill. In Arika's left hand is his flashlight which he has turned to shine on the lap of the passenger, who is holding the documents that Arika has requested. The light further illuminates the inside of the entire front cab of the vehicle, and the driver's face can finally be seen.

The driver then softly and deferentially asks Arika, "Wha'd I do, Sir?" Not fully hearing him, Arika asks, "I'm sorry," inviting the driver to repeat his question. "What'd I do?" "Two things," says Arika. "Number one, you didn't maintain your lane, you went over ah . . . the yellow lane markings . . . OK? . . . And then secondly, the license plate, the light, is like danglin,' from thah, from thah car, obstructing the New Jersey portion of it. It makes it difficult ta' see. On the car? Alright? . . . Ahm, everything alright? Were you . . . usin' yer phone or somethin'?"

At this point, Arika has positioned himself closer to the door of the van, which itself is set slightly higher off the ground, and his BWC is pointed into the door panel rather than the window, so the faces of the passenger and driver are not visible to his BWC. All that the viewer can see are reflections on the car door of small rectangular red and green lights and small square white lights from the commercial building to the right of and in front of the van, along with the sidewalk. These lights are bordered by Arika's body's shadow on the door and the black inside of the zipper of his police jacket to the right of the video's view. The entire door is also reflecting a faint purple flashing light coming from the top lights of Arika's patrol vehicle, further signaling that this situation is, in fact, a "law enforcement incident."

It is likely that in response to Arika's inquiry into why the driver might have gone over the street lane markings when driving, he nodded his head as Arika continued to say, "Alright . . . cuz you clearly went over the lane marking." Realizing that the driver might not understand what Arika is saying, Arika politely repeats, "You know . . . the yellow lane marking? The double lines . . . Ya went over it . . . just near Townhouse Motel. Da motel ova'der [over there]? Ya even heard the ripple in the road from your tires hitting the, the ripple marks. So, what . . . you 'er on yer phone or sumpthin'? . . . . . . No? Ow-kay. . . . Maybe you wah-just navigatin' da bend but . . ." "No, no," says the driver.

Arika's BWC's view then shifts upward to where we can see slightly into the van. Arika moves the beam of the flashlight in his left hand from the men in the van to the van registration card that he is holding in his right hand, which is still resting on the passenger window sill, and says to the men, "So where you guys comin' from?" "I coming from, from, Hamilton," the driver then says in English with a native Spanish speaker's inflection. "Ow-kay, were you workin'?" asks Arika. "Yeah," responds the driver. "Ah-aight, so it's safe to say you weren't drinkin' or anything like that?" asks Arika with a tone of sympathy for the driver, signaling that he wasn't assuming that the driver was drunk, demonstrating a degree of good faith and that he was on the driver's team in any case. "Noooo, no, no," responds the driver, moving the pitch of his "no's" from high to low through his response in a way that signaled slight surprise at the idea of such a possibility. "Ahr-uht," Arika responds in a rather terminating way as if his search for answers about why the driver might have failed to maintain the lane had come to a dead end. Then, renewing his friendly tone, Arika continues, "Okuh, you have your driver's license?" "No, driver's license, no, I don't have no driver's license, my driver's license expired [inaudible] so we need to write to come get so . . ." responds the driver before Arika interrupts with, "Do you *have* a valid driver's license?" "No, no, no, I don't have one," says the driver. "Alright, do you have yer ID on you?" asks Arika. "No sir, no," responds the driver. "You don't have any ID.?" responds Arika. "OK, can you jus' step outta da car?"

Arika then steps away from the passenger side door and walks in front of the van, shining the flashlight on the hood of the vehicle as he passes into the street next to the driver's door, which, like the passenger door, also has "Carpet Installation" painted on the side. Cars can be seen passing under the black night sky and widely spaced-out street lamps in front of a row of two-story houses on the other side of the road. Traffic seems to have picked up a bit and Arika is standing about halfway into the lane of the two-lane street. Cars take turns on each side passing on the street to avoid him. The driver gets out of the vehicle and we can see that he has a short haircut buzzed on the sides. He is wearing a dark winter jacket that covers a winter vest over a grey t-shirt, light blue jeans, and black casual boots. As he is getting out of his vehicle, Arika asks him, "Yer saying you don't have any ID on you at all?" "No, no," says the driver. "You don't have yer wallet?" asks Arika. "No, no, I don't have it." Says the driver. "Alright, let's just walk right to the front of your car," instructs Arika. The two walk toward the front of the van and stand in front of the vehicle's beaming headlights. Arika continues, "You don't have a wallet on you at all?" "No sir, you can check it, all my stuffs or no," says the driver, and he zips down his jacket, holds each side of the front of the jacket, and opens them up to show him that there is no wallet in any of his inner pockets while saying, "No, no."

Arika shines his flashlight on the driver's winter vest and into the visible areas of the inside of his jacket and says, "Alright, were you ever issued any tickets or anything?" Arika asks the driver. "Tickets before?" asks the driver. "Yes," says Arika. "No, no, no sir, no," responds the driver. "You've never driven before?" asks Arika, but before the driver responds, Arika moves to the side of the driver, now standing on the white line marking the outer side of the lane of the street, and asks the driver, "Can you jus' turn around and put yer hands on yer head?" The driver does this, and Arika uses his left hand to do a minor check for weapons on the driver's back, outside of the view of the BWC. The driver turns back around unprompted and Arika continues his questions, "Where do ya live?" "I live in a Rauntsburg," says the driver as he puts his left arm down. "You live in Rauntsburg? Yer whole life?" Facing a momentary blank stare from the driver at the question Arika quickly continued, "Er a like a long time?" "Yeah, yeah, a long time, long time."

The driver then says, "I'm sorry sir, please forgive me," while Arika takes out a pen and looks in his pockets for a small notebook he can give to the driver to write down his details. "Where ya goin', yer goin' . . . ta *Hamilton?*" asks Arika. "No, no . . . [points down the road in front of him in the same direction his van is facing] . . . yeah [nods], I go to Hamilton. I got to . . . pack a tha car and go to tha other house," says the driver. "How come ya didn't tell yer boss that ya didn't have a license?" asks Arika. "I told my boss, butta he don't care," responded Arika. "You told yer boss, and yer boss didn't care?" said Arika with mild surprise and a tinge of judgment. "Seriously, no, no, I told my boss, I explained to him, but he told me . . . [with his hands in his jacket pockets, he opens his arms as if to shrug and chuckles] . . . he said . . ." "Figure it out?" Arika added, finishing the driver's sentence. "He said, 'It's the first time, so don't worry, nothing gohn be happen.' I say yes, I know, but I not lying, because you know, I have to pay taxes . . . I explain that I, " says the driver.

"Alright, can you write down . . . I'm gonna have you write down yer name and yer birthday, and yer address," says Arika. "OK," says the driver. "Exactly as it appears," continues Arika. "OK," affirms the driver as he takes the pen and small notepad from Arika's right hand. Arika briefly turns to look down the street behind him as cars continue to pass the two men, and as the red lights from his patrol vehicle flash on the front faces of the residential homes across the street. Arika turns back to the driver and shines his light on the notepad so the driver can see the area where he is writing down his information, while the passenger remains in the cab of the van. Looking at what the driver was writing, Arika stops him and says, "That's fine; you can stop there." "It's OK?" asks the driver. "Yeah. Lemme see . . . yeah, yer good," says Arika and then motions with his fingers for the driver to return the pen and notepad. After the driver does this, Arika asks, "Ahm, you have yer boss's business card?" "Uh, no, no, that's all the papers," as he motions to the registration and insurance papers that Arika is holding for the van.

"Ah k, you can just have a seat, you can have a seat back in the car, just gimme . . ." says Arika before the driver begins softly pleading with him, "Gimme a break." Arika says, "Sorry?" "Gimme a break if I have to pay a ticket, " the driver continues. "I gotta, I gotta check it, I gotta see what's goin' on," says Arika as he begins to walk back to his patrol vehicle and motions toward it with his right arm holding the registration and insurance information. "Why don't you just give yer boss a call, ah-ight? And just let'im know you got stopped," says Arika politely. "OK," says the driver. "Just gimme a moment, I'll be right back up to the car; you can just have a seat," says Arika and then turns to walk back to his patrol vehicle. It is worth noting that during this traffic stop, unlike the traffic stop narrated in this book's prologue, Arika did not ask the passenger, who is also an immigrant, his name, about his identity documents, or whether he has a driver's license or about anything related to his immigration status.

Arika then opens the door to his patrol vehicle and gets in. He turns on the left overhead lamp to give him some light and clicks the end of his pen. Arika types in some information on the computer keyboard, which is more like a black desktop computer keyboard with tall protruding keys. Two white boxes come up on the screen and Arika moves the arrow onto one of them and clicks on the mousepad. On the screen is a list of data with five columns, none of which are legible by the BWC. With his right hand, he touches the mousepad to move the pointer over various parts of the screen while looking at the notepad with the driver's personal information on it in his left hand. He stops on one of the lines of data and double-clicks. It was not what he was looking for and he returns to the previous list, likely a list of individuals with similar names to the driver. After setting down his notepad, he moves the pointer to another line in the list, and with his left hand, he double clicks on the mousepad button. He then moves on to complete a different search task and brings up a different list of information following a robotic chirping sound that comes from his computer.

At this point, a woman's voice comes on over his patrol car radio as he continues typing, "5-1-0-6, There's gonna be a correction. The Ford, not payment of insurance [not understandable]." Another voice comes on over the radio, "Pam, thank you." Arika continues his computer search, clicking through various screens and typing with both of his hands. More talking over the patrol vehicle radio can be heard along with the clicking from each keystroke that Arika takes, and each of the dings, bells, and electronic noises that indicate he has executed a search request and it has returned something to him.

After returning to another list on his computer screen, Arika takes the notepad back into his hands and begins flipping the pages from back to front, looking perhaps for a blank page. He puts the notepad into a pocket in his police uniform and opens the door to get out. It appears that he has finally found the details of the man he was looking for—the driver. He closes his door and begins walking back up to the van on the driver's side. He turns his flashlight on again and shines it back on the vehicle just a few feet in front of where he is walking and the circle-lit area moves with him. With his right hand, he holds the notepad and knocks on the closed driver's side window, where on the other side, the driver, now wearing a backward-facing navy blue and red baseball hat, had been facing toward the passenger. As Arika knocks, the passenger turns his head around to see Arika and manually rolls down his window.

"Sir, what's yer birthday?" Arika asks the driver. "0-2-25," he responds. "I'm sorry?" says Arika. "0-2-25," repeats the driver. "2-24 . . ." says Arika. "0-2-20 . . . 0 . . . 2 . . . 22" says the driver. "0-2 . . . 22?" asks Arika. "Nah, no," says the driver. "0-2 . . . 0-2 . . ." says the driver, and then with a finger on his left hand, he motions as if he were writing the numbers in the air, "0-2 . . . 24 . . . 80." Arika then tests the driver by asking, "How old are you?" The driver pauses. Seeing that he is not immediately responding and may be lying, Arika repeats his question, "How old are you? Cuántos años?" (How old are you?). The driver begins to stroke his chin while looking forward. He says, "I close to . . . ahm . . ." as if he were thinking about his answer. "What are you thinkin' about? How old are you? What is your age? Cuántos años?" asks Arika, verbally pressing him. With each question, Arika gets more emphatic and gestures with his right hand, holding a pen up and down in a punctuated way. "I have ah, 30, 30, 36 . . ." says the driver. "Well, what are ya thinkin' about?" says Arika, potentially catching the driver in a lie. The driver chuckles and starts to smile.

Arika continues, though still in a friendly but authoritative tone, "It's a simple question, what's yer age, right?" "Yeah," says the driver. "Right? I mean, you ask me, I'd tell ya 'Hey, [opens his right hand towards his chest] I'm 29'. Right, it's a simple question [moves his right hand, dropping it forward, punctuating the word 'question']. OK? You're not bein' truthful with me, and I don't appreciate that," Arika says while moving his pointing hand in a short zigzag motion in front of his waist as if dotting each end of an invisible banana as he says each word. "This is yer time to correct that. OK?" he then says, while using his right hand in a punctuated manner to point down to the ground, as if he were pointing to each of the words he was saying, as if they were the firm truth, as firm as the concrete he is pointing to beneath his feet. The driver stares at him blankly. "This is yer time to correct it, OK?" Arika repeats. "OK," responds the driver and nods his head. "D'you understand?" he says while changing his gesturing right hand into a horizontal position and patting it downward as if hitting it lightly on a tabletop. "Yes, sir," responds the driver. Then, while pausing briefly, Arika takes his notepad into his right hand, and over the radio on his uniform, a voice can be heard saying, "70, what's yer status?" followed by another officer's voice responding with the same audio quality as a call box at a restaurant drive-through.

Arika flips a page in his book and says, "You have yer phone with ya?" "Yes," says the driver and turns his head to look at the middle area of the cab of the van. "Here?" says Arika as he points into the van. "That's yer phone?" "Yeah," says the driver. "OK, pull up yer, pull up yer Facebook," Arika says. "Nah, I don't have Facebook," says the driver. "I'm sorry?" says Arika, thinking the driver is lying. "I don't have Facebook," reaffirms the driver. "Pull it up," insists Arika, "Lemme see." After 12 seconds of silence, Arika says, "I see it! I see the Facebook app. Why don't you press on it? Right, why don't we go to your profile? Why don't we see what yer real name is, right? You wanna cut the, the B.S. [bull shit]? You wanna start bein' truthful?" The driver mumbles something not understandable with the BWC audio. "You're lying to me, OK? By giving me a fake name. What you wrote down–it's fake. Right?" says Arika. The driver stares at him with a blank expression, motionless, caught in a lie. "Right? Pull up your profile," says Arika. "I'm not lying to you," the driver says with a slight emphasis, though not aggressively and without any anger, but rather just in his own mild defense. "Pull up yer profile on your Facebook. What are we going away from your Facebook for?" says Arika. "My WhatsApp, I have a different name, and my Facebook, I have a different name," says the driver. "OK, lemme see," says Arika. "I'm not lying to you," repeats the driver. "OK, lemme see," says Arika with a slightly raised tone of his voice, though without anger which indicates that he knows he's catching the driver in a lie. "Alright, it's a simple, " says Arika. "Like in my Facebook, I have a different name, so . . . I'm not lying to you," says the driver.

"George David," says Arika viewing the driver's Facebook profile on the driver's cell phone. "Yeah," says the driver, "I'm not lying to you." "OK, go to yer info. Go to 'About', right? It's gonna have yer birthday, right?" [10 seconds pass] "Ju . . ." says Arika. "So that my info," says the driver, "I'm not lying to you." "You are, though," Arika says, "Yer name is not . . . [flips the notebook page back] Valenciano Thomson . . . it's George David. What's yer last name? I need you to give me your actual information before this goes down a *very bad* path for you." The driver, looking at him blankly, then briefly turns to look back down into his lap, potentially at his phone. "'Cause you're lying to me, I'm not stupid. Alright?" says Arika. "No, sir, I'm not, I'm not, " says the driver. Arika then moves to give the driver his notepad and a pen and says, "I want you to write down your information exactly how it appears on your passport. This is your last chance." The driver takes the notepad and looks at it. He then looks back up at Arika and says, "On my *passport*?" "Noo, I want you to flip this around. I want you to write your name exactly how it appears on your passport," says Arika.

While he is writing, Arika walks toward the front of the vehicle and uses his uniform-worn radio to call his agency dispatch. "5 at 9, 5-1-0-6 when yer clear would you stop by there? 10-4." A faint voice can be heard responding back over the radio, saying, "10-4." Arika walks back to the driver's window, where he is still writing down his information. After roughly 25 seconds, he hands the notebook and the pen back to Arika. Realizing that all the information that the driver gave him previously might have been untruthful, Arika repeats his earlier question, "Where do you live? Dónde vive?" The rustling of Arika's jacket on the BWC mic makes the location inaudible in the recording.

"Diego Jorge . . . Sanchez?" says Arika after looking at the notepad, now again pointing down with each name that he says. Jorge is the Spanish version of George, the name he used in his Facebook profile. Diego, however, is not the Spanish equivalent of David, the other name on his profile. Diego responds, pointing out the open van window at the notepad, in a soft way, "Diego, Sanchez," and then continues to look at Arika blankly. "What, Valenciano [the name he'd previously written down] . . . is yer . . . ," says Arika. "No, no, that is just like I told you. I have on my Facebook, a different name," says the driver. "OK, well, why did you give me this information before, this fake information? You gave me a fake birthday, right? And a fake name. How come?" says Arika. "Who told you to do that?" Arika says, indicating that he might be seeing culpability for the situation to extend beyond merely the foreign driver who is on the job. "'Cause my boss; told me, something happen," says Diego. "'Cause this is what you wrote," says Arika. "Yes, sir," says Diego and nods his head, accepting responsibility, "I apologize. It's my fault." "Who's yer boss?" asks Arika. "My boss?" "Yeah." "He's Marcus Porter," says Diego. "Marcus Porter, P-O-R-T-E-R?" asks Arika. "Yeah," responds Diego.

"Do you have warrants or anything?" asks Arika, "Do you have like warrants for your arrest?" "No. No, no, no, I have, " says Diego. "You just didn't wanna get tickets?" asks Arika. "No, no, no. Like I tell you, if I have to go to court, I have to," says Diego. "If your boss told you to jump off of a bridge? No, you made that decision, a'aight?" interrupts Arika, trying to teach Diego a moral lesson about responsibility and individual obligation. "No, no, now I say sorry, Sir. If I have to go to court, if I have to pay tickets, I understand. I did a something bad so, " says Diego. "I don't appreciate your dishonesty this whole time throughout this stop. We coulda been gone. You coulda been on yer way, right? Instead, now we're prolonging everything. Alright, just give me a few minutes," says

Arika, and then he flips back a page in his notebook and begins walking back to his patrol vehicle as a black pickup truck passes him on his right side in the street.

On his body radio is heard, "0-6 Dispatch, ... to 40." Arika opens his patrol driver's door and sits in the driver's seat. He places both hands on the keyboard of his patrol car's mounted laptop, pauses for a few seconds, and then pulls out his notebook. He flips five pages from the front to the back of the notebook, sets it in his lap, and then places his hands back on the keyboard and begins to type in a combination of hunt and peck style typing and touch typing. He keeps his hands above the keys but places his hands in standard positions and uses multiple fingers to type. As he types, he makes mildly loud clacking noises with each keystroke, which are followed by various robotic-sounding cascading beeps from the laptop as it shows search results. "Lo-cal, a-lert re-cord with war-ning," is said by an automated search assistant. With Arika's right hand, he pauses his fingers on the mousepad and with his left, he takes up his notepad again. He double-clicks on the mousepad button and says something under his breath to himself that is not understandable to the viewer.

On his patrol laptop, he reads a few lines of text and then clicks again on the mouse button, which pulls up a mugshot of Diego that clearly had been taken at another time by police. Arika again whispers something to himself, clicks out of the screen with the mugshot, and then hits the down arrow button many times, which allows him to scroll down through many lines of tabulated text. He navigates to one place in the list and clicks once on it, bringing up a pop-up box with text. He begins to turn the paper pages of his small notebook, re-reading some of the things that he and the driver had written down. He then picks up his patrol car radio, brings it up to his mouth, and pauses, pulling it away briefly as if stopping to think about something before he radios into his dispatcher. He pauses for ten seconds. As he thinks, he softly swings the radio away from his face and back again, away, and back, and then sighs. Then he pauses again, still and silent. He then brings the radio up to his face again, activates it, and says, "5 at 9th Dispatch, you can start me the next 45." He puts the radio back in its holster, and we hear "[Beep] Received, starting the next 45," come back over the radio from the dispatcher.

Arika then takes up the notepad to look at something briefly and returns his hands to the keyboard, navigates the mouse to a part of the screen, and clicks the mouse button. He navigates through three tabulated lists of information, each with the background of the screen black and the text in a very small white font. On the third screen, he moves the mouse to various parts of the screen and clicks in different places roughly ten times to select different items rather than navigating to other screens. After doing this, he returns to the home search screen and clicks, eliciting a laptop sound that resembles a mouth harp being struck in a classic country song. After clicking one more time, the beeping cascade sound is repeated, and the laptop again says, "Lo-cal, a-lert re-cord with war-ning." He picks up the notebook and examines the information written in it, comparing it to the laptop screen. His laptop then says, "Ah-lert, wanted person, Ah-lert, wanted per-son. Male, white Thir-tee-fiiive. [Diiiing, Diiiing] Ah-lert, suh-spen-dehd dry-verse-lie-scence. [Diiiing, Diiiing] Ah-lert A-T-S ac-tive war-rant." Arika begins to type some more, takes his notebook off of the dash just above his steering wheel, and flips through pages as the radio dispatcher says over the radio, "5-90, Collins is your ah, co-company." This may refer to the surname of the officer who will be providing Arika with backup assistance for the stop.

After finding a page in his notebook, Arika rips it out and keeps it and the notebook in his left hand. With his right hand, he picks up the patrol car radio speaker microphone and brings it to his face. [4 seconds go by as he pauses] The laptop sounds a cascading beep, and with his right hand holding the radio speaker microphone, he presses a button on the computer and brings the radio back to his mouth, pausing in contemplation for three seconds. Dispassionately, as if with an attitude of "No big deal," Arika responds, "10-4, I'm 10-4, just standin' by. He's got active warrants." It's clear that there are no ICE administrative warrants issued for Diego in the National Crime Information Center database since no alerts popped up on Arika's laptop when he ran Diego's name. Diego has a state driver's license, which would indicate he has some form of legal immigration status or even naturalized citizenship, but even legal immigrants may become deportable if they commit certain crimes.

In New Jersey, beginning in May 2021, undocumented immigrants could by state law obtain a state driver's license using an Individual Taxpayer Identification Number or ITIN number. At the time of Arika's traffic stop of Diego in January 2019, however, he would not have been able to get a New Jersey license without citizenship or one of the acceptable forms of legal noncitizenship such as permanent residency. It would still be unclear to Arika whether Diego was a citizen or if he has any one of the many noncitizen legal immigration statuses that would make him eligible for a license that could be suspended. Despite Diego obviously being a foreigner with warrants, someone whom ICE might prioritize for immigration enforcement, Arika does not further investigate Diego's immigration status by, for instance, calling ICE's Law Enforcement Support Center to see if they know anything about Diego. Instead, Arika keeps the stop focused on the traffic warrant. His simple act of restraint makes him and his sanctuary policing a force divider from ICE rather than a force multiplier for ICE.

Arika then places the radio speaker microphone back into its holster, and the dispatcher asks over the radio, "Where on 6 are you on 2's location?" Arika flips his notepad closed and takes the radio back up into his hands as another officer's voice comes over the patrol radio, "5106, about to clear up." Without speaking, Arika then returns his radio speaker microphone back to its holster. He tears another sheet out of the notepad and places the sheet and the notepad in a compartment in between his seat and the front passenger seat. He then takes a plastic paper-letter sized 9- × 12-inch brown case, opens it, and shuffles through various pieces of paper, closes it without removing anything, and places it back in the passenger seat. He takes into his lap a plastic brown accordion folder and opens the top flap in time to hear, "588, what's yer 20?" and with his right hand, picks up his radio to respond, "33, just past . . . townhouse." He then takes out a light-colored piece of paper from the accordion folder, puts it on a wood clipboard, and takes the two sheets he had ripped out of his notepad and places them in the visor above his seat. He clicks his pen and starts writing a ticket for Diego. He takes the notepad back out and begins to write in it for about twenty seconds before putting it into a pocket in his uniform.

As he returns to writing up the ticket for Diego with his right hand, his arm pushes the right flap of his jacket over the body cam, covering it. In the dark interior of his jacket, the viewer is packed away, still close to the officer's chest, and still listening to the writing activity taking place on the other side of the officer's clothing. While we can't see it, we hear Arika tapping on the space bar and mouse buttons of his laptop after about ten seconds. After about a minute, Arika, still keeping us in the temperature-less dark, goes back to intently scribbling on the ticket for another minute and a half. By this point, nearly twenty-five minutes have elapsed since he first pulled over the driver. After nearly two more minutes, we are finally able to peek out of the inside of Arika's jacket to see him finishing his writing and tearing off a page of the ticket to give to Diego. He places that ticket in the visor above his seat and separates the two back sheets of the ticket from each other, placing them back on the clipboard under the clip and placing the clipboard back on the passenger seat.

Arika then refocuses his attention on the vehicle's registration card and insurance card, holding the registration card, which is light-colored with a red-colored banner, closer, and the white insurance card just above it in his hands in front of his chest. As Arika puts the two cards down and uses his right hand to select something on his laptop, for the first time, in the reflection of the laptop screen, we can see a blurred mirror image of his face, tinted with rose, the color of the screen's glass. His square white face with a sharply geometrical jaw evokes the kind of strength of someone who stays in good physical condition. Arika types in the license plate of the vehicle in the laptop search, which leads to two cascading beep sounds and a pop-up box of search results in white text.

He then places the car's insurance and registration cards on top of the yellow ticket in his left hand, switches them to his right hand, hits the three against his leg as if smoothing out playing cards that he just shuffled, looks at the time on his phone, pauses in silent stillness as if resetting, and opens his patrol car door. Rather than walking back to the driver in the street as he had walked from the van to his patrol car, instead, he walks back around the rear of his own vehicle, back onto the sidewalk, in front of the commercial building and its potted plants. This time, without his flashlight on, he walks up along the passenger side of the van toward the passenger door and window, up and around the front of the van, and back around to Diego's window, which is still open.

"A'aight," says Arika as he raises his right hand, holding the ticket, insurance card, registration card, and now lit flashlight and points at the passenger of the van. "Sir, *you* have a valid license? No . . . a'aight.

Ahhhm," says Arika in a calm and neutral tone. The passenger can be heard faintly saying something unintelligible on the BWC. Arika continues, "Ah, just one second, OK . . . Ah, Diego, step outta the car." Diego opens his car door and steps out in front of his open door. "You have anything on you?" asks Arika to which Diego responds by again opening his unzipped outer jacket, revealing his inner winter vest. "Why don't you drop that, drop yer belt, leave it with the car," instructs Arika. Diego begins to take off his belt, pulling it out of the loops of his pants and placing it back on his driver's seat. "Alright, let's walk back here," says Arika. As they get to the back of the van, the two stand in the ten meters between the van and the patrol vehicle. "Alright, Diego, you've been dishonest with me this entire time. OK?" Arika says, still in what sounds simultaneously dispassionate and slightly annoyed but not angry. "With your . . . the fake names, date of birth, and stuff like that." "You said you give me my, a second, my second, a second chance, " says Diego. "Yeah, and you still gave me the wrong birthday," responds Arika. "No sir," pleads Diego with a tone of righteous indignation. "If you give me a chance, I can bring my passport. That's my real name, sir," says Diego while motioning with his full right arm toward Arika's patrol vehicle. "That's your real name? Yeah, that's your real name. It's the wrong birthday. OK," says Arika. "No, sir," says Diego, this time shaking his head and continuing to raise his arm toward the patrol vehicle. Emphatically, he continues, "I'm honest with you, I can give you my passport." "OK, what's yer birthday?" asks Arika. "0-2-29-84," says Diego, now pointing and lowering his hand with each number said. "0-2-29-84, OK," says Arika. "I appreciate it 'cause you say you give me the second chance," says Diego. "And you say your passport's gonna be at your house?" asks Arika. "Yeah, ihsss in my house," responds Diego with a nod.

"Alright, well, we'll square that all away, but at this point, you have several active warrants for your arrest, OK?" says Arika. "I have what?" asks Diego. "Active warrants, traffic warrants and stuff, so . . . we gotta go back to the station and deal with it," clarifies Arika. "Tram-fic warrants?" Diego says with a facial expression showing he is confused. "Yeah, traffic warrants . . . and yer license is suspended," says Arika. Diego stares at Arika still with a confused facial expression. Arika continues, in a manner to inform and lecture Diego, "Yer not supposed to be drivin' . . . even though you don't have a license, it's still suspended. Yer revoked, sawh . . . unfortunately it is what it is. We'll go back to the station, and we'll deal with it, but . . . you coulda been honest with me to begin with, and we didn't have to go through all this. You coulda been pretty much on yer way home. We coulda dealt with it, whatever warrants we have to deal with, and right now, instead, we prolonged everything. . . . It's at a point where you, ya jus', yer actin' silly, to be polite about it. So."

As Diego continues to stare blankly at Arika as he finishes chastising Diego for his dishonest behavior, Arika's dispatcher can be heard over his uniform-worn radio, "[Keeegh] 20-2-2." Arika instructs Diego, "I'm gonna need you to just turn around and put yer hands behind yer back. Turn around," and Arika points his finger behind Diego and spins his hand to demonstrate a turning motion. Diego, first looking slightly down as he realizes that he is being arrested, says, "OK," and points to the van with his left thumb. "Can I, can I let you know him," Diego says trying to indicate that he wants to alert the passenger of the van that he is being arrested. "I'll talk to him," says Arika, in a polite tone. "Can I take a my phone, cause," says Diego. "I'll get it. At this point, you just gotta put yer hands behind yer," says Arika, reassuring him. With his right hand, Arika takes hold of Diego's right arm, which Diego has already placed behind his back as he turned around.

Arika's dispatcher calls over the radio, "509 [bleep], 509, you got the I-M on the second person, correct?" Arika takes out his metal handcuffs, clicks them on Diego's hands, and says, "I'll make these nice and loose for ya'. I just wished you'd been a little bit more honest with me to begin with." [Click, click, click, click, as the handcuffs close in] As Arika finishes putting the handcuffs on Diego, the BWC viewer again is placed in the dark behind the black of the lightless inner part of Arika's jacket. "I'm gonna put you in my car," Arika tells Diego. "OK, OK," he responds. After some sounds of Arika's jacket rubbing against his BWC, Arika says to someone talking to him in the distance, "Just one second, sir." In the distance can be heard a person at the front of the van talking to Arika and Diego. Diego then again asks Arika, "Can I let, you know, go talk to him?" "Just one second, I'm gonna go talk to him. I'll talk to him," Arika repeats to reassure Diego. As Arika's jacket moves to the side of his BWC to the point where we can see Diego near the opened patrol vehicle's rear passenger side door, Arika tells him, "Can you have a seat in the car." Diego begins to duck his head down and slightly bend over to get into the patrol vehicle when Arika says, "Just watch yer head gettin' in. I know it's dark."

Arika closes the patrol car door and, roughly thirty minutes after the beginning of the traffic stop, turns to walk back over to the van. Standing in front of the passenger's window are two people, a man and a woman, who had not been at the scene previously and who seem to be talking to the passenger through his open window. Also at the scene is another, just arriving East Allen Police officer whom Arika begins to talk to as he approaches the couple. "Ahm, he gave me a fake name, he's suspended, he's got warrants and stuff," Arika says as if it's all rather trivial to him. We don't, however, get a chance to see the backup officer himself as he is out of Arika's BWC's view.

As Arika walks up to the two people talking to the passenger, he says, "How we doin' guys?" to greet them. Seeing that the van's driver's side door is still open in the middle of the street, he walks back around the back of the van, over to the door, and closes it. He then returns to the sidewalk and walks back up to the two people talking to the passenger. To the woman, who is Latinx in her thirties, wearing black-rimmed glasses and plain civilian clothes, Arika says softly, "Ahm, can you just help, can you assist with being an interpreter?" She says, "Yeah," to which Arika responds, "Thank you. So obviously, you know, he was lying about his name, right? [The woman speaks to the passenger in Spanish but it is not fully captured by the BWC.] OK, so he still didn't give me all his correct information. Eventually, I figured it out. He has multiple warrants and stuff, so he's arrested. They're minor warrants, so he'll probably be released. Ahm, [woman continues to speak to the passenger in Spanish] . . . OK, the van's gonna get towed."

The woman then asks Arika, "Can we take it?" referring to the van. Arika asks her in response, "Do you have a license?" She then says, "Well, I don't, but he does," referring to the man who was standing next to her. While many citizens do not have a driver's license, this was a moment when again, Arika may have suspected that the woman might not be a citizen, though Arika did not inquire into her immigration status. Arika then says, "I'm sorry?" asking for the woman to repeat what she said. The passenger, however, breaks into the conversation from the van, saying to Arika, "He's my family." The woman says, "I have a license, but I don't have it on me, but he has a license on him." Arika then asks her,

"And it's valid?" "Yeah," she responds. "No issues with it or anything?" Arika asks, and she chuckles.

Arika then asks her, "Who is the ah? Who is the owner of the company?" She turns to the passenger and says, "¿Quién es el dueño de la compañia?" (Who is the owner of the company?) The passenger then says to her, "Yo soy el dueño de la compañia." (I am the owner of the company.) "He says he's the owner of the company," she tells Arika. "*You're* the owner of the company?" Arika says in a sort of comedic surprise, given Diego's previous account in English, which the passenger wasn't part of, telling Arika that "his boss" had told him not to worry about driving unlicensed and to lie about his personal information. "So you know, he doesn't have a license," says Arika. "But the insurance is from another lady," continues the woman. "OK," says Arika trying to wrap his head around what is and isn't the truth. "So, *you're* the owner of the company, so he was lyin' about that too?" says Arika, beginning to laugh before he says, "Not good, not good." The passenger then says to the woman, "El no entiende nadie." (He [Diego] doesn't understand anyone), says the passenger. The woman then says to Arika while chuckling, "He didn't understand you."

Arika then responds to the passenger's comment in a matter-of-fact manner, "That's not true, but." The woman translates what Arika said back into Spanish. "A'aight. You have a valid license? And you want to take the responsibility of drivin' a van?" The woman grins and chuckles. The man hands Arika his driver's license for him to inspect. Arika then activates his uniform-worn radio and says, "5 at 9th. Dispatch, I was able to get a licensed driver. Ahm, you can just put return request back at the top of the list." He then says to the other officer on the scene, "I just gotta go check on this real quick." Dispatch then responds, "509, did you make contact with him on the scene or asking to call him to cancel?" "No, can you call and cancel, please?" says Arika back into his uniform radio. "Affirmative," says the dispatcher.

Arika, then pointing at the passenger, says, "Ah, so you have your ID? Identificación por favor." (Identification please.) Arika's jacket covers the BWC, so we cannot see what the passenger is doing. As he opens his jacket again, we can see that the other officer who is with Arika is a tall white man with a crew cut who is standing to his right and roughly a meter and a half from both the van and the passenger's family member who will drive the van away. Arika takes out his notebook again and begins writing with the passenger's ID in hand and his jacket re-covering most of his BWC, allowing us to only peek out of his jacket once in a while. He then says to the passenger, "Still 1 Spruce?" referring to the address he sees on the passenger's ID. The passenger can be heard correcting him. "OK," says Arika. "And what's a good telephone number for you?" asks Arika. "Telephone?" "Yeah." "5-2-9-9-4-2-2-4-8-5" says the passenger. Arika then repeats back, "5-89." "5-29," corrects the passenger. "5-29 . . . 9-4-2-2-4" repeats back Arika. "A'aight. Ahm, yer gonna get a ticket too for letting him drive without a driver's license, OK." The woman then translates this into Spanish for the passenger. The passenger then speaks back to the woman in Spanish. "Because he told me, unless he's lyin', he said he told you that he didn't have a license, so yer gonna get a ticket and yer gonna come to court," Arika tells the passenger. "A'aight, on the plus side, I'm not gonna tow the van anymore, so save you money that way and let yer family take it, OK?" The woman repeats this to the passenger in Spanish. Arika opens his jacket back up to show the passenger's family member seriously looking at the passenger through the window.

Arika, returning to the dishonesty as a central factor in the stop, takes the opportunity to moralize the passenger, saying again, "A'aight, no more lyin'. Alright, if he'd just had been truthful, he woulda still 'ave had the warrants, but he wouldn't of [have] had the criminal charges on top of it." The criminal charges that Arika was referring to here were charges incurred due to his dishonesty. While his traffic charges consisted of failure to maintain his lane and that one of his vehicle lights was improperly mounted, he also had eight failures to appear in traffic court, and his dishonesty led to one additional criminal charge for obstructing justice and one criminal charge for contempt of court.

"Alright, you guys are free to go," says Arika, though all three—the passenger, his family member, and the woman, seem to stare at each other in a tense silence. "He's just getting one, OK?" clarifies Arika, explaining that the passenger wasn't facing criminal charges. "Thank you," says the woman.

Arika then turns to walk back to his patrol vehicle. The other officer then says, "Thanks, man." "It's all good!" Arika responds, perhaps indicating that he covered for the newly arrived officer while he continued to be at another policing incident. As he walks behind his patrol car, Arika continues, "It's all good, I was out here forever, so I just wanted to speed 'er up." "You leavin' now or are you just gonna leave 'em out there?" says the other officer to Arika. "What's up?" says Arika, to which the officer repeats his question. "Yeah," says Arika.

Arika opens the back driver's side door in his patrol car, and Diego says, "I don't know, one number, maybe to call the family." Arika walks over to the passenger side where Diego is sitting and says, "You have anything in the van you need, man?" "Yes, please!" responds Diego. "Whadda ya need?" asks Arika. "I need my phone because I need to call him," Diego says, perhaps referring to the passenger. "Yer phone? Ahh, I'll grab it." Arika walks back up to the rear of the vehicle, through the steam of the now running van's exhaust, and calls out to the passenger who is standing on the sidewalk in front of his opened passenger door, "Sir, can you just grab his phone?" The second officer then reaches over toward the passenger as he hands him the driver's phone. "That's his phone?" Arika asks the passenger, who nods and says "Yeah." "OK, so he [Diego] has yer number?"

The passenger moves out onto the sidewalk, closing his van door behind him. Arika tells him, "He's not goin' tah county [jail] or anything, to my knowledge. He's got a coupla traffic warrants, alright, ahm. An hu'll be able tah make a phone call 'imself," says Arika to the passenger, who looks at Arika with a quiet inquisitive expression. "We're gonna-llow him ta make phone calls himself when we get back. OK?" Without saying anything, the passenger then glances back over to Arika's patrol vehicle, bites his lower lip, and looks back at Arika as he continues to listen to what he says. "Sao, he has his phone. He has anything else in the car that you think you might need?" asks Arika. The second officer chimes in, "A wallet, 'er ?" Throwing both hands in the air, the passenger looks at the second officer and says, "I'dunno." "Alright, he asked for his phone, so I'm gunna take that, and I'll have 'im, I'll have 'im give you a call when we're done, are-aight?" says Arika. The passenger looks back at Arika's patrol vehicle with a solemn stare and nods his head. "We gotta process him and stuff, so we just gotta take some information from him and whatnot, are-aight?" continues Arika. "Alright," says the passenger. "Thank you," says Arika, who then turns to walk back to his patrol car.

Arika walks back to his vehicle, opens the door, sits in his seat, and says to Diego, "Are-aight, I got yer phone, sir." Arika then takes the yellow citation slip of paper from off of the dash above his steering wheel where he had previously placed it, makes a long sigh, and picks up his patrol car radio speaker microphone.

"5-at-9, Dispatch. All units'll be clear. One adult male under. Here em'mout [I'm out] . . . [he turns off his overhead light inside the car] . . . at this location," says Arika into his radio. He sets the radio speaker microphone back in its holster to the right of his seat, and it makes a plastic clicking sound. He sits in the dark of the car, and the only lights shining into the vehicle are a faint white light from a streetlight ahead of and across the street from his car and a flashing pale blue light from the top of his patrol vehicle. He turns the flashing lights off, puts the transmission into drive, and rotates the steering wheel as he begins to drive away. Diego remains silent in the back seat in handcuffs. As Arika drives, he quickly takes a white piece of paper from the left of his lap with both hands, and with his right hand places it in the visor above his head in one smooth motion while his left hand re-takes the steering wheel slightly before his right hand does too. In the dark of the night, Arika continues driving while we listen to the rumbling and knocking of various pieces of equipment on the console of his vehicle. We see roughly fifty small round lights illuminated on his otherwise totally dark patrol vehicle laptop screen and his black dispatch radio and lamppost-illuminated trees pass through the view of his windshield.

Arika comes to a stop and, in the dark, takes out something unseen to the BWC which he rapidly clicks in his hands just before rubbing his hands back and forth as if to warm them. He immediately turns to his vehicle-mounted laptop to type something in. The cascading beeping noise indicates that the system has yielded a result and he continues to type while slowly bringing the vehicle back into motion and soon after moving his hands from the keyboard back to the steering wheel. Once the car is back at full street speed, he brings *both hands back to the keyboard* while he holds the steering wheel in place with his leg and continues typing while driving straight for roughly ten seconds. The laptop yields another cascading beeping sound, and he turns on his right blinker before putting his left hand back on the steering wheel to make the turn. Once driving straight again, he returns both hands to the keyboard to type, and again, a search return beep. This continues two more times over the next twenty seconds. He pauses, sighs, makes three sounds with his mouth, "Chuh, chuh, chuh," and says to Diego, "Sorry, do you still live at 548 Chestnut Street?" "Yes, sir," Diego responds from the back of the vehicle. Arika briefly goes back to typing, indicating that what he may have been working on while driving was his police report of the incident.

Diego then says, "Can I ask a question, sir?" "Yes," responds Arika. "Probably today, I go back my home?" asks Diego. "Ahm, so say you just gave me the fake name, right? Ahm, and I arrested you for the fake name. You would be processed, and then I'd give ya, ah'd, you'd get a court date, almost just like a ticket, right? Even though yer under arrest, you know, you'd get released. Ahm. In this, though, you do have some traffic warrants, so we have to clear those warrants up; ahm, I don't know what they are 'cause they're not in front of me. I think one is out of East Allen for $500; ahm, one might be outta Robbinsville. . . . So [Arika holds his hand open and flat to the ceiling and waves it side to side where Diego can see it] I don't think that. . . . Most likely, you'll be able to get out today and just have tah go back to court. But ya can't keep forgettin' about these things; you have ta go ta court 'cause it's not going to disappear," says Arika. "No sir, it's my fault, this. My boss, my boss, he said, " says Diego.

"Well, let's be clear, your boss was the person sitting in the passenger seat," says Arika. "Yeah, I know, today, today only, today. I'm honest with you, he, stopped drinking in New Brunswick," says Diego, perhaps meaning that his normal boss, who had hired him, stopped working that day to go drinking in another city, New Brunswick, New Jersey. "Yeah, the *driver*," says Arika referring to the man who showed up and drove the van away. "Yeah, he's my boss, and he's the driver. I work for him, and I need to come to my home, and he said, "No, take a the car to . . ." says Diego. "Who owns the company? Who *owns* the carpet company?" asks Arika. "Da' um, Da' um, I think he's da guy's, da cousin, da cousin to my boss," Diego responds, not really sure. "His name is a Thomas." Arika then says to Diego, "The person who owns the, the company, was the guy sitting next to you." "Yeah, Thomas, his cousin, I'm not sure. I'm not workin' for him; I work for the guy who was staying in New Brunswick." This may have meant that the person who usually drove the van and

Diego's boss is the man who showed up to drive the van away, but that previously in the night, he told Diego to do the driving despite having a suspended license, so that *that* driver, the owner, could stop in New Brunswick to drink rather than drive, and that the passenger is Thomas and was only serving as Diego's temporary boss today. Or it all might have just been a poorly delivered lie. "He hiring me, so . . . I don't know much about Thomas," finishes Diego.

Arika sits in silence saying nothing back to Diego for roughly a minute while he waits for the red traffic light to change green and then begins to drive, still in silence. After about a minute, Arika calls over the radio, "5 at 9, dispatch, I'm out at 30 . . . Is the port still occupied?" "[Bleep] That's affirmative." "10-4, out 30," responds Arika. "Received 20-59," says the dispatch. Arika puts the car transmission in park, the two sit in silence, and Arika turns off his BWC.

* * *

As we have seen, provisions in sanctuary policies that disallow police from investigating immigration status information so that they may investigate other infractions and crimes should properly be understood as something unique, as sanctuary policing. Though this approach may appear to be very close to forms of policing citizens, the presence of a known unknown–immigration status–makes it slightly different. As with policing that aims to be race-blind and that is regulated by policies prohibiting race-based policing, but that does not erase the race and racism of officers, the race of those they police, or the factors that define what race means in their particular society, sanctuary policing is designed to be immigration status–blind, but must still manage situations that involve the citizenship status of the officer and the immigration status of an immigrant *as an unknown*. Immigration status is still a factor of the policing scenario in a sanctuary state—not only the immigration status or citizenship status of the immigrant but also the citizenship status of the police officer and the power dynamic that imbalance presents. Sanctuary policing is one way of dealing with this factor—it is a mode of ignoring immigration status as a present but to-be-unknown factor, and this approach allows police not to ignore traffic infractions, warrants for an immigrant's arrest, crimes, or criminals, but rather to all the more intensively focus on them. Sanctuary policing is a way to keep immigrants "on the hook." Given that many immigrants live in mixed immigration status communities and may have undocumented family members, coworkers, neighbors, or bosses, this type of policing pertains to all immigrants, not just those who are individually exposed to immigration enforcement or targets for deportation.

This approach to policing should be considered a "force divider" in that, in the words of immigrant advocates, it, to some extent, "disentangles" policing incidents from immigration control. Since sanctuary policies typically include exceptional language that allows local police to cooperate with ICE in other circumstances, the force divider provisions do not completely silo police from ICE. That is, they do not end the cooperative professional relationship. Rather, they merely separate or silo the particular policing incident when local police do not link with ICE to enforce immigration. The force division processes operationalized by restrictive sanctuary provisions reduce the focus of the activity to non-immigration law enforcement such as payment of traffic fines, as was the case with Diego. Thus, police may participate in these two modes of sanctuary policing when interacting with immigrants and with ICE—force multiplication and force division. The activation of each mode is determined by the circumstances that meet policy requirements, officer norms, and discretion, and, as we will examine in the following two chapters, the manner in which they engage, utilize, adhere to, take up, embody, and are driven by the inherent authority of sanctuary policy, and the law more generally, at their disposal.

7

The Authority of Sanctuary Policy

The power and authority of sanctuary policy begin well before and extend well beyond the period of implementation or when it is "effective" as an enforceable law. At the time of Officer Arika's traffic stop and arrest of Diego in January 2019, the Immigrant Trust Directive had only been issued but had not yet become effective, that is, active. What *was* effective at that time was the previous Attorney General Directive 2007-3, issued by the previous Attorney General Anne Milgram. That policy supported officers in proactively cooperating with ICE to enforce immigration law in a more permissive manner. However, the mere fact that Attorney General Gurbir Grewal issued the Immigrant Trust Directive in November 2018, announced it to the public, and created a training module for police officers to watch prior to the effective date was sufficient to influence Arika's policing behavior and implement it immediately in a traffic stop. While by law he could have taken every opportunity to assist ICE prior to the effective date of the new Directive, which "repeals and supersedes the provisions of AG Directive 2007-3," Arika nonetheless conducted it without recourse to immigration enforcement.[1] The reason could be that officers throughout the state understood the "intent" of the policies of the present Attorney General, the highest law enforcement officer in the state, who wanted this new regime to come into being.

Policy intent is a sort of intuitable, personalized element of policy texts, expressed in some ways explicitly, and in other ways, implicitly. It refers to that which the policy author intends the text to mean, and how they intend for it to have an effect on government operations or their jurisdiction, and generally provides an interpretive frame for understanding the literal words used in the policy. A policy's intent can be adopted and adapted to inform further policies; it can allow for a flexible expansion of the policy's scope through the implementation and enforcement process; it can connect policy texts past and present through interpretation as new situations pertinent to the policy domain come into existence and challenge the original policy text; and it may be modified through the interpretive process.

Such interpretive modifications to a policy's intent are used to create policy amendments or wholly new policies and render old ones inactive. It is often the case that policy intent is invoked by policymakers who want to render a policy ineffective as well. When sanctuary policy texts are read to disallow immigration enforcement entirely, a policymaker who wants government workers to provide a new form of assistance to ICE may, for instance, make arguments against literal readings of an existing sanctuary policy that "prohibits the use of city and county resources for immigration enforcement purposes" by saying, "Well, but the policy authors didn't intend to provide sanctuary to *criminals*. Sanctuary is only for *law-abiding* immigrants."

The intent is therefore something that runs through policy but that also exceeds it. Intent is based on the contextual factors of a policy author's actions, behaviors, and private and public statements when participating in proposing, voting on, adopting, signing, and implementing a given policy. Past policy intents may be referred to in policy battles in which policymakers seek to bring policy texts into alignment with hypothesized, conceptualized, perceived, or interpreted governmental circumstances. Policy intent may be evoked by policymakers who want to move beyond a literal reading of sanctuary policy but who are faced with new situations that pose a challenge or problem for government systems that had not been anticipated by the authors of the original policy text.

The New Jersey Attorney General's Immigrant Trust Directive was written to be implemented in all law enforcement environments and has very specific language about the kinds of immigration enforcement assistance law enforcement officers may and may not provide to ICE and under which circumstances. However, if ICE implements a new nationwide program that solicits a new form of assistance from local agencies, a new state Attorney General may invoke Attorney General Grewal's policy intent in the Immigrant Trust Directive to justify issuing a new directive to law enforcement. The purpose would be to create additional sanctuary provisions to prohibit the new form of immigration enforcement assistance. In this way, sanctuary policy intent may remain relatively consistent while policy texts may differ. Policy intent may "travel" from one policy, policy era, policy jurisdiction, or "policy world" to another.[2]

Policy intent is imputed in this way to policy texts by various policy authors over time and cannot be said to be the product of just one sole author. In every case of policy creation within a given policy domain, an author jumps into a moving river of policy, so to speak, picking up the current where the last authors left off. Even if their authored texts differ in specificity, there may be some kind of textual torch or baton that has been taken up and passed along many, many times. There are also cases when policy intent is completely abandoned and new policy intent is created seemingly out of whole cloth. However, it is never the case that policy intent is born from no past precedent. Policy intent is merely gathered and assembled from other sources, other policy streams, policy fields, and policy worlds, and reconstructed in a new way, giving rise to policy from something.[3] In this manner, policy intent has a power and authority of its own that is exercised through and beyond individual policies such as the Immigrant Trust Directive.

The Commander in New Jersey's Sanctuary Policy

In order to unify "bodies" of policy and to wrangle together the diversity of voices and author intents running through them, a certain individual "subject" in policy or "commander in policy" is textually produced. The commander in policy is not that individual policy's author, for instance, the New Jersey Attorney General Gurbir Grewal. Rather, the commander in policy is the artificial "person" voiced by policy readers when they read a policy silently to themselves or aloud. It is an abstract, absent "speaker" and commander with a neutral, generic voice. The commander in policy is a textual someone who is meant to be no historical anyone and who can be read and understood by everyone regardless of the reader's or interpreter's background, immigration status, race, religion, or political affiliation.

A particular author may have written down the specific words included in a policy text, but that author's individual identity is effaced when such words are adopted as policy and placed in a policy system—a body of policies—that is timelessly tensed in the present through authoritative commanding language such as those in a county administrative code or a police code of general orders. Police officers may be able to associate particular policing policies such as "Chief's Bulletins" issued by a still-acting Police Chief as *his or hers* and hear that particular voice when they read the text to themselves or out loud. However, the particular words are still not the chief's alone. Policing policy language includes the inputs of various other people—legal staff, consultants, community experts, and advocates who reviewed and modified the personalized policing policy prior to its issuance. The chief, in these cases, serves as the textual figurehead of the policy and is proffering their identity at the service of personalizing what the policy would otherwise submit into the general, universal voice of the commander in policy. As soon as that particular Police Chief leaves their post, or if the policy text is adopted into a general policy and procedures manual, the words are absorbed into the trans-era, collectively produced voice of the commander in policy, as are policies that are passed by city, county, state, and federal legislators into the various legal codes of government.

Examining the power and authority in policy and law is not a new project. Building from the philosophical works of Thomas Hobbes and Jeremy Bentham, legal philosopher John Austin, for instance, developed the "command theory in law," which largely determined that the commander I have been describing is "the sovereign" itself issuing commands "from above" to subjects "below" that have the obligation to obey—that is specifically to do something that follows the command or else be punished.[4] The sovereign, for Austin, could be a specific person or body of persons—that is, *their office or institution*, not the specific individuals—who receive habitual obedience from the bulk of the population and who do not themselves obey any other person or institution. H.L.A. Hart responded in 1961 to Austin's theory of law, retorting that not all laws are commands made by a sovereign but that some are rules made by the people—in particular, customary laws as Aristotle and Plato had contended long before him—and that laws may facilitate behavior rather than coerce it.[5] Most importantly, Hart found the foundation of law to reside in the practice of law-applying officials.[6] In connection to these theories of law, Ronald Dworkin later argued that law emanated from a single will rather than a sovereign.[7]

I will not attempt an additional theoretical critique or development of the command theory of law and the responses to it; or of accepting that the power and authority in policy and law, the commander in policy, including sanctuary policy, is merely the sovereign, the voice of the customs of a people, singular will of the people, or the collective voice of law-applying officials. I'd rather like to take as a starting point the ethnographic data to understand how the commander in *sanctuary policy* functions, how it is stylized, and how it is formulated in law enforcement discourse in New Jersey. The distinction between the personalized voicing of the policy author and that of the commander in sanctuary policy is most clearly perceived when two forms of policy statements are made—a statement explaining a policy that is made at a policy issuing press event, and the text of the policy itself.

On November 29, 2018, the day that New Jersey Attorney General Gurbir Grewal issued the Immigrant Trust Directive, flanked by uniformed police officers and management, he spoke to members of the media:

> We are announcing new rules to strengthen trust between New Jersey law enforcement and our state's diverse immigrant communities. We are issuing new rules that draw a bright line between Federal Civil Immigration Authorities on the one hand and state and local law enforcement officers on the other. And we're telling our friends and our neighbors who have been living in fear, you can trust state law enforcement. You can trust state prosecutors here in New Jersey. Earlier this morning, I signed Attorney General Directive 2018-6 known as the Immigrant Trust Directive. This directive will apply to all law enforcement officers in this state. We are limiting the types of voluntary assistance that we will provide to federal civil immigration authorities. And in doing so, we are telling our state law enforcement agencies to focus their resources on their core priorities such as solving crimes and protecting the public rather than advancing Washington's immigration agenda. Now while there are many aspects to this directive, the most important take-aways are as follows: under the Immigrant Trust Directive, New Jersey police officers cannot participate in federal immigration raids; cannot stop, question, arrest, search, or detain an individual, solely because they believe the person might be undocumented. They cannot provide ICE access to state and local law enforcement resources including equipment and databases, unless those resources are already available to the public. And they [quickly shakes his head] cannot ask individuals about their immigration status except in the rare instances when it is relevant to a specific criminal in-

vestigation. With this directive, we hope to draw immigrants out of the shadows and into our communities. Nothing in this directive restricts officers from complying with federal law. Nothing in this directive prevents officers from enforcing valid court orders, including warrants signed by state and federal judges. And nothing in this directive provides sanctuary for those who commit crimes in New Jersey. If you break the law in New Jersey, if you assault someone, if you rob someone, if you defraud someone, we will hold you accountable no matter your immigration status.[8]

In the Attorney General's comments, he called attention to the power and authority from which the Immigrant Trust Directive was issued. That authority was personalized as a "we"—a group of specific law enforcement officials that included himself and the state law enforcement management standing with him at the press event. His speech was directed at a personalized public at that moment, and his message was given directly to press people in attendance who were documented on video. No doubt, his speech was, if not written solely by his staff, reviewed by people other than himself and was likely the product of a collective effort. Nonetheless, it was written in a voicing that signaled to the audience that the words were coming directly from him. The speech itself would not be included in a depersonalized state law code or law enforcement code but would live in that one moment and in the news reports posted online. It addressed fears of the public that his sanctuary policy would give people who commit crimes a free pass, allowing them to prey on others. It sent a message to those very people who might consider committing crimes, a message directly from the person of the Attorney General to those individuals via the media. In short, it was his voice being read from a piece of paper by him. In real-time, it was perceived as coming from him and was therefore a representational form that extended not just his office but him personally, in time and space.

By contrast, the New Jersey Immigrant Trust Directive that he had issued that morning functioned differently. In its textual style, Grewal and his policymaking staff invoked the commander in policy as an auxiliary authority, as a textual, aesthetic force multiplier to ensure its efficacy among police officers around the state to whom sanctuary values and rhetoric were foreign and potentially unwelcomed. The commander in policy served as an emissary of sanctuary, sanctuary values, sanctuary movements, sanctuary state advocates, and the Attorney General's Office to local officers in a discursive register that would communicate the policy's mandates in a type of language that would more effectively ensure officer compliance. Its words were not a humanitarian appeal to their sense of right and wrong or an impassioned argument that they should love immigrants. It was constructed in the artistic form of the cold, unforgiving, universalistic command that carries hidden with it an implied message—"do it or be disciplined."

The initial section of the Immigrant Trust Directive explains the historical context and reasons for issuing the policy and addresses what the Office of the Attorney General anticipated from the public to be misunderstandings about the policy. It addressed fears about immigrant criminals and included information about past policies that this directive would repeal and supersede. However, the meat of the policy, that is, the part that all law enforcement agencies throughout the state would be required to integrate into their department policy and procedure codes and manuals, was written in the depersonalized, interest-neutral, generic authoritarian voice of the commander in policy:

I. Racially-Influenced Policing—No law enforcement officer shall at any time engage in conduct constituting racially-influenced policing as defined in Attorney General Law Enforcement Directive No. 2005-1.

II. Enforcement of Federal Civil Immigration Law

   A. Use of immigration status in law enforcement activities. Except pursuant to Sections II.C and III. below, no state, county, or local law enforcement agency or official shall:

   1. Stop, question, arrest, search, or detain any individual based solely on:
      a) Actual or suspected citizenship or immigration status; or
      b) Actual or suspected violations of federal civil immigration law.
   2. Inquire about the immigration status of any individual, unless doing so is:
      a) Necessary to the ongoing investigation of an indictable offense by that individual; and
      b) Relevant to the offense under investigation.

B. Limitations on assisting federal immigration authorities in enforcing federal civil immigration law. Except pursuant to Sections II.C and III below, no state, county, or local law enforcement agency or official shall provide the following types of assistance to federal immigration authorities when the sole purpose of that assistance is to enforce federal civil immigration law;
   1. Participating in civil immigration enforcement operations.
   2. Providing any non-public personally identifying information regarding any individual.
   3. Providing access to any state, county, or local law enforcement equipment, office space, database, or property not available to the general public.
   4. Providing access to a detained individual for an interview, unless the detainee signs a written consent form that explains;
      a) The purpose of the interview;
      b) That the interview is voluntary;
      c) That the individual may decline to be interviewed; and
      d) That the individual may choose to be interviewed only with his or her legal counsel present.
   5. Providing notice of a detained individual's upcoming release from custody, unless the detainee:
      a) Is currently charged with, has ever been convicted of, or has ever been adjudicated delinquent for a violent or serious offense, as that term is defined in Appendix A;
      b) In the past five years, has been convicted of an indictable crime other than a violent or serious offense; or
      c) Is subject to a Final Order of Removal that has been signed by a federal judge and lodged with the county jail or state prison where the detainee is being held.
   6. Continuing the detention of an individual past the time he or she would otherwise be eligible for release from custody based solely on a civil immigration detainer request, unless the detainee:
      a) Is currently charged with, has ever been convicted of, or has ever been adjudicated delinquent for a violent or serious offense, as that term is defined in Appendix A;

b) In the past five years, has been convicted of an indictable crime other than a violent or serious offense; or
  c) Is subject to a Final Order of Removal that has been signed by a federal judge and lodged with the county jail or state prison where the detainee is being held.

  Any such detention may last only until 11:59pm on the calendar day on which the person would otherwise have been eligible for release.

C. Exceptions and exclusions. Nothing in Sections II.A or II.B shall be construed to restrict, prohibit, or in any way prevent a state, county, or local law enforcement agency or official from:
  1. Enforcing the criminal laws of this state.
  2. Complying with all applicable federal, state, and local laws.
  3. Complying with a valid judicial warrant or other court order, or responding to any request authorized by a valid judicial warrant or other court order.
  4. Participating with federal authorities in a joint law enforcement taskforce the primary purpose of which is unrelated to federal civil immigration enforcement.
  5. Requesting proof of identity from an individual during the course of an arrest or when legally justified during an investigative stop or detention.
  6. Asking an arrested individual for information necessary to complete the required fields of the LIVESCAN database (or other law enforcement fingerprinting database), including information about the arrestee's place of birth and country of citizenship.
  7. Inquiring about a person's place of birth on a correctional facility intake form and making risk-based classification assignments in such facilities.
  8. Providing federal immigration authorities with information that is publicly available or readily available to the public in the method the public can obtain it.
  9. When required by exigent circumstances, providing federal immigration authorities with aid or assistance, including access to non-public information, equipment, and resources.

10. Sending to, maintaining, or receiving from federal immigration authorities information regarding the citizenship or immigration status, lawful or unlawful, of any individual.[9]

While the legal authority to issue the New Jersey Immigrant Trust Directive text was granted by the state legislature to the Attorney General, and in issuing this policy, Gurbir Grewal exercised this power, the aesthetic quality that he lent to the wording of the policy text itself voiced the generic universalist tone of the commander in policy as a force multiplier. The policy was not "said" with all of the colloquialisms of the voice of Gurbir Grewal, as in the press event—he adopted the voice of the commander in policy as if putting a powerful puppet on the hand of the policy and then making it speak like a state.

French sociologist Pierre Bourdieu, in his essay "The Force of Law," called this the "neutralization effect" or the "universalization effect," a voicing created through passive and impersonal constructions designed to mark "the impersonality of normative utterances and to establish the speaker as universal subject, at once impartial and objective."[10] Bourdieu argued that it was not merely a textual fabrication but a product of the entire "juridical field." Within this field, certain forms of rationality formulate such a universal "juridical sense" or "juridical faculty," which in turn determines, or in his terms, "subordinates," the system of juridical norms. For Bourdieu, those who could participate in the creation of this universal legal subject were themselves those who had been trained and certified in the manners in which to master the world of legal resources "amassed by successive generations"—the "canon of texts and modes of thinking, of expression, and of action in which such a canon is reproduced and which reproduce it."[11] Rather than building from popular notions of justice, customary law, or a sovereign will of the people, for Bourdieu, the universal juridical attitude emanated from rules internal to the exclusive, juridical field itself, something that Gurbir Grewal is part of, as a trained, professional lawyer, president of the South Asian Bar Association of New York, and member of the Asian Pacific American Lawyers Association, in addition to serving as Attorney General of New Jersey. Within this context, Bourdieu proposed that improvisational legal expression was possible as long as it was in harmony with the internal schemas elaborated in the juridical field, and to the extent that it is, it could form part of the universal attitude, or in my terminology, the rationality and voice of the commander in policy.[12]

Bourdieu argued that formalizing legal doctrines and procedures and treating them as "universal"—that is, disinterested, unbiased, and applicable to all people, required the complicity of those who are dominated by that law. The only way that such law becomes truly legitimate is if the people recognize it as legitimate and applicable to them. Thus, Bourdieu held that this required the formalization and systemization of a jurist professional ideology, which is a rather arbitrary set of legal principles, ethics, and practices as if they are neutral and autonomous of the law and of specific jurists themselves.[13] The universal voice of law then occurs when one group's principles are universalized in law and recognized by all sectors of society and subsequently when the text of law itself becomes autonomous from the specific people who elaborated it, wrote it, passed it, and ruled on it.

The universal subject of law produced through the processes Bourdieu describes, which I have been calling the creation and voicing of the commander in policy, is not merely a regime that lives in policy and legal norms, in formalized legal documents, or in discourse. At an existential and psychological level, it lives in us. Law, autonomous from its authors, uses each of us and works with us as collaborators and as force multipliers. Most of us live and operate outside of the juridical field—most of us are not lawyers, lawmakers, or judges—but we nonetheless still proactively assist policy and law by carrying it into new legal domains and new territories wherever we go. We interpret law and modify our behaviors, imagine how we should act according to law or in defiance of it in new scenarios we face.

The commander in policy, whose voice we hear with our own ears when we speak aloud the words in laws and policies, including the Immigrant Trust Directive policy text, is modern government's replacement for the voice of God, the voice of some kind of "mortal god" if not Hobbes's Leviathan.[14] This commander in policy is not a god that is to be understood at a personal level, a god or specific sovereign king that one can have a relationship with, that responds to prayers and requests, one with interest. Living according to policies and laws and interacting with them is like interacting with a subject that cannot interact with us.

All we do is project our own intentions and interpretations onto that atemporal and nonpresent subject of policy through policy advocacy campaigns and amendments to bodies of policy. We tend to believe that we understand the intentions of the original policymakers, but in fact, we don't really know entirely. We amend policy not only in our own image but also in the image of the commander in policy, and we make the commander in policy speak back not to us as individuals or to particular subject groups but to everyone simultaneously.

The commander in policy is a subject that is to be understood outside of the reader's self and outside of the reader's world in an empty space, yet somehow here—an authority whose tenseless commands are applicable everywhere in specific jurisdictions of the corporeal world. The tangible space of the commander in policy is the ideational world of our minds, on the material space of paper, the PDF, the digital space of document databases, and in the field when its commands are uttered by potentially anyone with any degree of "juridical capital"—theoretical and practical knowledge of the law, to use Bourdieu's term. That is, this commander can be invoked, conjured, mobilized, and used by anyone, powerful and powerless alike, police and policed.

The commander in policy is produced collectively by historical people who have each voiced singular, particular interests and opinions about what a policy text should say. These particular interests and opinions emerge in the context of broader social and class struggles and become focused on how policies and laws should be written. Contending political forces and power blocs each attempt to assert their own voices in policy texts and to silence their competitors—they each vie for "narrative dominance" or for their text contribution, vision, solution, or narrative about the policy issue to dominate and be reflected in policy and law. However, when writing up the formal policy language and having it "legalized" by government attorneys, the particular voices of interested policy authors are neutralized and harmonized with other bodies of legal doctrine. The resulting text is written in the voice of the commander in policy, one that reduces this cacophony of competing voices to a singular legalistic, neutral, and commanding dialect. Yet the commander in policy's neutrality is not without its contradictions. Competing policy provisions within a single policy text reflect different, competing strategies for addressing social and administrative issues, for instance, those devised by immigrant rights advocates on the one hand and those by sheriffs on the other.

The commander in policy is then what we have taken as a modern replacement for the Word of God, and we have made policy our replacement for commandments. The commander in policy is the secular god that governments and the publics they represent impel their subject populations to obey. It is a discursive epiphenomenon seemingly separate from but lassoed by law-applying officials and autonomous from any identifiable sovereign. The author of specific sanctuary policies like the Immigrant Trust Directive and the subject of policy that I have called the commander in policy therefore as has been noted, is not the same person. The author of a policy can be named—for example, Gurbir Grewal. The person voiced in the policy once passed—the force multiplier in the policy—is unnamed. It is not the particular state regime that we can map throughout all of the agencies and institutions of the state and its particular representatives in time. The subject or person of policy, the commander in policy, is a type of ghost—one that has a hand in how people are governed, managed, and controlled, how we are cajoled and incentivized.

That is why it is so hard to revolt and rebel against *policy*, against *law* as such—because the target of such rebellion is not present and yet is still expressing, and moving the state, albeit through other people's bodies and mouths. Policy is something to be interpreted by government priests—bureaucrats, the department heads who give guidance and training on these aesthetically impartial policies, the courts and legal scholars, and social scientists like me. Policy needs its own priests, deacons, and police to breathe its words in the streets, invoke its language, and apply it. Without them, individual policies become stale, useless, ignored, and forgotten, while the commander in policy in general lives on. Policy is the expression of a secularized church of believers in the state who use the state to manage their lives and arbitrate their problems on the basis of this atemporal policy and its interpretations.

The only way to change the expression and the resource management system that the commander in policy directs is to make further policy, to contribute to feeding the commander in policy new policy texts so that it will say something else. But it is not certain that the commander in policy will say exactly what policy authors want it to say—there are too many people feeding it bits of policy text and policy intent on any given issue, such as sanctuary and immigrant assistance. Aspirational amendments may not be amendable to the precedent and intent-latticed policy field. When sanctuary advocates are successful at passing new sanctuary policies and at making the commander in policy speak anew, they anticipate to a certain degree that the world will take form in its image, but it doesn't. While the commander in policy produces systematic behavioral change when voiced—and when people, like the police, try to follow its commands—a wide variety of behavioral aberrations that are unexpected are produced as well. Reflecting a more general principle of force multiplication, force multipliers, including the commander in policy, are not bare instruments, objects to be used toward affecting only the goals of the user. Force multipliers are subjects themselves with their own unique capacities and partners, which influence the outcomes of the process in which they play a part. When sanctuary movements partner with the state and with its commander in policy to construct sanctuary policies, each as force multipliers for the other, unexpected outcomes are produced, as we have seen in the policing events narrated in this book.

The commander in policy alone does not determine the outcome of how its words are interpreted or applied in the world. Nor does our invocation of the commander in policy ensure our influence upon or control of the processes we are part of. To a certain extent, we impute ourselves into policy and inflect its application, and to another extent, it inhabits us and takes hold of the manner in which we engage the world experientially. In reading or referring to a policy text in the course of daily life, the imagined voice of the commander in policy is our own voice in our head. We project ourselves into the voice of authority, welding ourselves to the commander in policy and its mandates of authority as if it were us giving the rules to the world or at least reviving them in the world from their stale, placeless policy repositories. Some may utilize perhaps an imagined other voice that is not their own but that is akin to another government voice that they may have heard utter a governmental rule in their past. When reading the Immigrant Trust Directive text in our heads, we are unlikely to "hear" Gurbir Grewal's voice. Through our voice speaking the commander in policy's words, we tell ourselves what to do according to policy and law. We listen to our own personal internal "legal compass," a form of policy-awareness conscience, what Bourdieu called a "juridical sense" or "juridical faculty"—a superego formed in the relation between our personal judgment and the commander in policy's rationality. As we breathe life into the words of policies and laws, we serve as force multipliers for them, commanding ourselves and sinking ourselves deeper into their knowledge and power. We accept it or reject it as if we were accepting or rejecting our own words uttered in our own voice.

The commander in policy gets its power from institutions that enforce its dictates through force, punitive mechanisms, and rewards. It also gets its power from everyday uses of it that reaffirm its utility. No one is in full control of the commander in policy—it is perhaps the most powerful epiphenomenon of our time. At the same time, it is at the instant fingertips of all who have access to the internet, easily conjured with cell phones through keyword searches on government legislative databases, infinitely reproducible in the form of PDF files that can be emailed to an infinite number of recipients, posted and shared endlessly by those with the technological access and infrastructure to do so. The commander in policy is absent and yet seemingly so present that it can be endlessly quoted in specificity, interpreted, adapted, and applied in our everyday lives. We can paraphrase and misquote it, misunderstand it, and imperfectly project ourselves and our own prerogatives into it when advocating for or passing new policies and laws or taking action in events.

We trust in this commander in policy to transform our world for us and tell others what to do. Social movements, including sanctuary movements advocating for sanctuary policies, look to this commander in policy to be the bearer of the terms of our lives, including immigrant lives and police lives, despite this commander being no one with no human body and no resources. People with human bodies and governmental resources then attempt at every turn to claim that they are the true representatives of this commander. On behalf of this commander in policy, real people lock immigrants away, keep them in jail, detain them, and deport them. And yet, this same commander in policy is who we trust to hold those people who do the locking up accountable. Our projections into and demands of this commander in policy make it an unforgiving authority that provides no leeway in some instances, a reasonable caretaker in others, a protector in others, a provider of sanctuary and safety, and the decider of who deserves deportation.

The commander in policy is simply an expression of our will to control the world through a godlike authoritative agent that transcends religion and the particular historical configurations of any state or ideology. It is our collective disavowal of our actual inability to control the world. It is that in which we seek sanctuary to solve our collective problems, to bring order to disorder, and to invoke inside of us so that we have the authority to face powerful institutions and disenfranchised outsiders alike and harm and chaos of all kinds. This is the silent partner of sanctuary movements and immigrant-friendly officials that empowers police in New Jersey to serve both as a force multiplier for ICE and force divider from ICE.

Police, the Emissaries of Policy and Law

A primary function of local police is to serve as emissaries and surrogates, that is force multipliers, of policy and law itself, and therefore of the commander in policy. Police voice the dictates of policy and law in the field, making them understandable to people without much knowledge of the law as well as to each other; and they invoke the law instrumentally, come into relation with it, and allow its authority to inhabit them and work through them. As many scholars have explained, police do not uniformly apply policy and law like passive machines but rather selectively and improvisationally interpret law and policy, including sanctuary policy, working with it in the course of using their discretion and attempting to achieve their objectives among a variety of possible courses of action. The following narrative demonstrates how police serve as force multipliers, that is, partners working on behalf of and in coordination with the commander in policy, as well as force multipliers for ICE.

* * *

It is just after midnight on March 1, 2018, eight months before the Immigrant Trust Directive will be issued. Two patrol officers—Officer Grant Kowalsky and Officer Brian Flanagan—are driving their patrol vehicles in suburban Benjamin Township, New Jersey. They see a Mexican man in his early forties who is driving an SUV late at night on the way home from a casino. Kowalsky and Flanagan, each in their own vehicles, drive up behind and to the side of the man's SUV. The driver, alarmed at this police car formation, immediately pulls over before either patrol car has flashed its overhead lights. At this point, Kowalsky turns on his BWC and says out loud for the recording that he is conducting a traffic stop because the man's rear license plate is unclear—a traffic infraction—and for "failure to maintain the lane."

As the man pulls over, Kowalsky sees him quickly swallow the blue contents of a small travel bottle of mouthwash and thinks it is suspicious, perhaps indicating he had been drinking alcohol and is attempting to mask the smell on his breath. Once he is stopped, the officers question the man, who is named Mario, through his passenger-side front window and interpret him to be very nervous. He tells them that he is scared of them and upset for having lost $2,500 at the casino. After looking at his driver's license and an honorary police society membership badge that his boss had given him, they ask that he step out of his vehicle and search his body but find no illegal substances or weapons. Mario can more clearly be seen to have light brown skin, be slightly overweight, nearly bald, and wearing a thin, black, fleece, zip-up, collared jacket and blue jeans. On Kowalsky's written report for this event, he describes Mario as having an "orderly" appearance. They detain him by having him sit down on the curb behind and to the side of the vehicle and ask him about what he had been doing that evening. To the right of the curb is a long stretch of lawn, and in the distance are street lamps and the lights of one-story, tan commercial buildings. The officers do not conduct an intoxication test but it seems clear that Mario is not drunk. Mario does not understand why he has been pulled over and thinks that the police are being discriminatory toward him. Though he speaks English fairly well, he asks them to provide him with a Spanish interpreter to help him understand their questions. They deny his request and do not provide one for him, saying it's too late at night and that there is no one available.

While questioning him as he sits on the curb, the police officers want to search his car and ask for his permission. At first, Mario is open to it, telling them there is nothing illegal in the SUV, and Flanagan goes to get a consent form from his patrol vehicle. Flanagan returns, holding a white piece of paper and shining his flashlight on it to show Mario, and says, "Ah'aight, man. Listen, this is the voluntary consent to search form. What's yer name?" "Mario Cabrera Figueroa," Mario responds promptly. "OK, yer gonna say yer name for me when I read you, ah, this form," says Flanagan. "Right," responds Mario affirmatively. Then looking down at the paper. Flanagan says, "OK, it says, 'I', yer name. " "Mario Cabrera Figueroa," Mario interjects. Then, reading quickly in a monotone, hurried-while-reading- through-the-specific-legalistic-required-words-of-the-text-of-the-form-to-get-to-the-end manner, Flanagan says, "OK, 'hereby-authorize-Patrolman-Kowalsky and-Patrolman-Flanagan [he looks up from the paper, pauses momentarily, and looks into the eyes of Mario before continuing], police-officers, Benjamin-Tonshi'Police-Depar-ment-to-conduct-a complete-search-of-my-Ford-Explorer-located . . .'" "Can I, can I talk to my lawyer before I do that because I don't know if you guys have a da right to do it," says Mario, interrupting Flanagan's "generic" legalistic vocalization of the form's text.

Flanagan, as if woken from a trance or possession by the commander in policy, jerks his head up to look at Mario as himself, as Flanagan, back in his personally annoyed stance and means of expressing *himself* rather than the commander in policy. He positions his head tilted slightly forward toward Mario as if pulled by his intensely staring eyes and the disruption of the formal documentary process of asking for and providing consent for a search. "Can I jus' make a phone call? Can I speak a my lawyer really quick?" says Mario while staccato pointing with his right index finger toward his Ford Explorer. "I'm asking for your *consent*!" says Flanagan with an annoyed, emphatic, tone. "I'm not gonna, I'm not gonna say anything. Can I speak to my lawyer?!" Mario says again, staccato pointing forward with each word he says. "Can I speak to my lawyer really quick?" Mario asks. "No!" says Flanagan firmly. "The one ihsss taking my case?" Mario continues. "No," repeats Flanagan. "So, I'm not gonna let you sorsh [search] my, my. . . ." says Mario. "OK," says Flanagan. "Because I don't know what is your righsss [rights] and what is my righsss," says Mario while shrugging.

The two officers deactivate their BWCs to have a private strategy session, and when they reactivate, they mention that there is a small white "pill" in view on the floor below the driver's seat. This may be a narcotic—something that would give them "probable cause" to search the vehicle—to conduct a "PC Search" or "Probable Cause Search"—without Mario's permission. They begin the search as four more officers and superiors arrive on the scene, and the "pill" turns out to be a white mint or antacid, but the officers continue their search of the vehicle's contents.

As they search the vehicle, Mario, in response to one of the officers questioning him, unprompted, tells him, "I have four kids," while holding up four fingers on his left hand. "They *need* me here. I don't need to get myself in trouble. And I'm *legal* too; I'm not illegal," referring to his immigration status. "I totally respect ya," says a recently arrived sergeant named Bill Conti. "And I feel really offended for all this to be honest with you," Mario says, pointing to the four patrol cars that are now parked at the event, rendering it a public spectacle.

Soon after, Officer Kowalsky finds an "airsoft" gun—a pellet gun that is used for sports and firearms training and which was illegally modified to look identical to a real handgun. By law, airsoft guns are required to have a plastic orange tip at the end of the muzzle to distinguish them from real guns, and the state had recently passed a law prohibiting the removal of this tip because people were using them, once modified, to conduct robberies. Mario's illegally modified airsoft gun, which looked like a real SIG Sauer handgun, is found lodged between his driver's seat and the center armrest. Mario claims that his four-year-old son had dropped it there after they were playing with it but the police officers do not believe him. In the pouch behind the front passenger seat, the officers also find a slingshot, a knife, and a baseball bat which Mario seems to be unaware of.

Finally, in the trunk of the vehicle, the police officers find a few bags, and they think Mario may be involved in some kind of fraudulent enterprise. One bag has file folders with bank statements, W-2 "Wage and Tax statements," and other financial documents of many people. The other bag contains new Central American and Mexican passports, Mexican ID cards, US driver's licenses, and new credit cards in these individuals' names. Mario claims that they were the property of his colleague who owns and loaned him the vehicle, not his, and that his colleague owns a tax accountancy office. While the police can't arrest him for having all of these personal documents and financial statements, they find it very strange that he has them and believe that they can arrest him for having an illegally modified airsoft gun. As airsoft gun infractions—"imitation firearm" statutes—are new in New Jersey state law at this time, the police officers are not yet confident in their knowledge about the exact provisions of the law that might apply to this context.

After finding the airsoft gun, Officer Flanagan steps away from Mario's vehicle and walks back toward the rear of his own patrol car, and up on the grass to use his cell phone to pull up and read various New Jersey statutes to figure out which statute they should use to charge Mario and how they should proceed in making the arrest. Leaving other officers in charge of standing with Mario to continue questioning him on the curb, Kowalsky walks back to Flanagan as well to join him in finding the appropriate statutes. When he gets within two yards of Flanagan, Kowalsky stops and turns to his left, where their superior, Sergeant Conti, gets out his cell phone to look up the statute on imitation firearm tips. Another sergeant, John Supiso, is seen illuminated by the light from his flashlight reflecting back up from his hand, which is holding the airsoft gun. "I'm pretty sure there's a statute that he's not supposed to have that within reach to him, one, and he's not supposed to have it without an orange tip. I feel like we've charged people with it before," says Kowalsky to Conti. "A BB gun?" says Conti with mild surprise, "I would look, you very well could be right." Flanagan has not moved from his position, standing with his eyes glued to his cell phone. "Well, Brian's [Flanagan] tryin' ta see. I thought we'd charged someone before," says Kowalsky. Conti and Kowalsky step over next to Flanagan. "That's why he [Mario] didn't want us ta search," says Flanagan, still holding his cell phone with both hands and intently looking at it. "Yeah, a hundred percent," adds Kowalsky. Conti steps immediately to the right side of Flanagan and leans to look at what is on his cell phone screen. "He's got all . . . he's got like a bat in there, a slingshot. I don't know what he's doin' that he needs a," says Kowalsky. "I mean . . . bat and slingshot, you can't charge 'im with that," says Conti, "I mean, whattaya, whattaya gonna charge a bat and slingshot? Unlawful possession ah weapons?" "I believe a slingshot may be a prohibited weapon," says Kowalsky, who is standing to the immediate left of Flanagan, "I could be wrong." "Any, any kid tha's in the possession of a slingshot would be arrestable?" says Conti who continues to chew his gum.

Then, with his head down, still staring at his cell phone screen and slipping back into the monotone that he had used when reading the text of a consent form to Mario, Flanagan begins to quickly read the text of New Jersey statute 2C:39-4(2)e on imitation firearms aloud to Conti and Kowalsky: "Imitation firearm: Any-resident-in-possession-of-imitation-firearms-under-circumstances-that-would-lead-an-observer-to-reasonably-believe-it-was-possessed-for-an-unlawful-purpose-is-guilty-of-a-crime-of-the-fourth-degree."[15]

Switching back into his otherwise normal speaking tonation, speed, and liveliness and out of the "generic policy-reading" voice reserved for quoting the commander in policy, Flanagan says, "I'd say that fits. 39-4e." Finally looking up from his cell phone, Flanagan turns his head to his right to hear Conti saying, "Do you think it's unreasonable? Do you think . . ." says Conti. "I mean, I think, it has the orange tip smashed off. That's definitely not something that somebody who's carrying it for target shooting or practicing in his basement," Flanagan says to him before looking back down into his phone. "Read that one more time," says Conti. "Especially in reach to the driver?" poses Kowalsky.

Then returning to the identical monotone policy-reading style and speed as before, he repeats: "Any-resident-in-possession-of-imitation-firearms-under-circumstances-that-would-lead-an-observer-to-reasonably-believe-it-was-possessed-for-an-unlawful-purpose-is-guilty-of-a-crime-of-the-fourth-degree." After moving away from his position looking over at Flanagan's phone while he had been reading, Conti says, "As, as long as you can articulate that you believe it's gonna be, it's for an unlawful purpose." Kowalsky plays with the handcuffs attached to his belt as he listens and steps to the side.

At this point, Kowalsky breaks away from the conversation to walk over to his patrol vehicle. Conti also tells Flanagan, "I'll be right back," then walks back to his patrol vehicle and turns off his BWC while calling another officer. Kowalsky opens the front passenger door of his own patrol car, gets his cell phone, closes the door, walks back to Flanagan, and says, "I'm pretty sure slingshots are prohibited." Flanagan is again intently looking at his phone and reading. Kowalsky joins him, putting his phone in his right hand, just at the top of the view of his BWC.

The two officers continue to stand nearly motionless, aside from small movements of their fingers typing occasionally on their phones as they look up and read statutes. Finally finding the statute he has been looking for, Flanagan says, "Slingshots! Bing!" "Which is illegal," says Kowalsky referring to the slingshot being an illegal weapon to possess in New Jersey. "Yeah, 39-9, Can't manufacture 'em or transport 'em," Flanagan continues, citing New Jersey Code 2C:39-9.[16] Under 2C:39-3e, possession of a slingshot in New Jersey is also made a crime of the fourth degree. "That's under 39-9, look under 39-4 and 5," continues Flanagan. "No, what I'm under, I'm on 39-1 . . . this is jus' definitions," says Kowalsky. "39-4, 5 it'll be, uh, where it should list the slingshot," says Flanagan, trailing off.

Flanagan steps a few feet into the grass and begins to make a call on his cell phone. "You callin' Tye? Ask him about the gun; the slingshot's *definitely,* " says Kowalsky. "It's definitely under 39-4e is the gun," interrupts Flanagan emphasizing the "E." "The imitation firearm, the 4e," finishes Flanagan. "Eh, but I don't know if . . . ah'aight," concedes Kowalsky, "The slingshot definitely." "The, the *gun* definitely," clarifies Flanagan, "39-4e, imitation firearm. A hundred percent. If the hunter's tip is broken." Kowalsky, who is not fully convinced, says, "Ask what Tye thinks," referring to another one of their superiors. After letting the phone ring for a while, Flanagan says, "I dunnknow, maybe John's [Sergeant Supiso] on the phone with 'im" [with Tye]. "He might be," says Kowalsky. "Yeah, he didn't answer," says Flanagan. "He might be on the phone with 'im," says Kowalsky as Flanagan ends the call and returns to examining the statutes.

"He's [Mario] up to no good. I don't know what he's doin'; he's carryin' that thing," says Kowalsky, referring to the airsoft gun. "Right," affirms Flanagan. "Like where it is [where it was found in the car]," continues Kowalsky. "That stuff in the back, he's takin' to an accountant, I'm wonderin' if he's like a bookie or somethin.'" "Ahddon'know," says Flanagan.[17]

After focusing on his phone, perhaps texting with someone, Kowalsky touches his body-worn radio, which makes a beeping noise. "Gah-head," says Kowalsky. The voice of a dispatcher says something unclear to the BWC, and Kowalsky responds, "I'll give you a call." Flanagan is back looking at his cell phone, and Kowalsky, too, returns to reading on his phone. A fourth, recently arrived officer named Sean Hayes then walks briefly toward Kowalsky and says, "Eh, is Tye comin' down?" "Yeah," responds Kowalsky.

After entering numbers on his cell phone, Kowalsky turns away from where Mario is sitting on the curb and says, "Hey, what's this guy's CCH look like?" "CCH" refers to a search on the New Jersey Computerized Criminal History database, an additional criminal background check that officers can request from dispatch on Mario. After twenty seconds, he says to Flanagan, "He's got *multiple* unlawful possession charges." "Of guns?" asks Flanagan, looking up from his phone. "Of just weapons, but," says Kowalsky. Then, returning to talk to the person on the phone, he says, "How recent are we lookin' at? . . . Ah'aight . . . He's probably gonna get taken into custody. He's got some weapons on 'im now. We'll let you know . . . ah'aight, thanks." "I would think 39-4e, yeah 4e. That's the charge fer this," says Flanagan to Kowalsky as he ends his call.

Kowalsky takes his phone and begins dialing another number. "I'd say we take him for 39-4e and check 39-4d; it's slingshot, so let's," says Flanagan. "Yeah, " says Kowalsky.

Officer Hayes, who had been continuing to question Mario, then calls over to Kowalsky and Flanagan, "Yo!" Kowalsky and Flanagan walk back toward Mario and Hayes, who asks, "Somebody wanna stand with him real quick?" Hayes then looks to Kowalsky and says, "I wanna talk to you real quick about this," and they return to the area where Kowalsky and Flanagan had been standing looking at the statutes on their phones. "Turn off to discuss," says Hayes prior to turning off his own BWC. "Turning off body camera to discuss investigative strategy," says Kowalsky.

After their unrecorded discussion, the officers proceeded to arrest Mario for having the imitation firearm without reading him his *Miranda* rights, place him in Kowalsky's patrol vehicle, examine the airsoft gun as a group, and commiserate about everything that Mario said to them that they thought was bullshit. Kowalsky, with his BWC turned back on, gets in his vehicle with Mario in the back, closes the door, and puts on his seatbelt. He puts the car into drive and radios his dispatch to let them know he's made the arrest and is headed back to the station. After driving for roughly six minutes, Kowalsky arrives at the station, parks and turns off his vehicle, asks Mario for his phone number, puts his own gun in a lock box in the garage, and turns off his BWC.

According to the Benjamin Township Police Arrest Report, the officers booked Mario for "Unlawful possession of imitation firearm," statute 2C:39.4E for the airsoft gun, "Prohibited weapons/devices," statute 2C:39.3E for the slingshot, and "Trafficking Personal Identity Information," statute 2C:21 for the passports, IDs, tax documents, and bank cards. Mario's car was impounded, and the vehicle identification number for the SUV was registered under Mario's name as the owner, not under the name of any other individual as he had claimed. Kowalsky's arrest report narrative explained that he fingerprinted and photographed Mario as part of the booking process and filed a warrant that listed Mario's charges before transporting him to the county jail and turning him over to their custody. The police maintained possession of the airsoft gun, slingshot, financial records, ID documents, and credit cards as evidence.

That same day, also on March 1, the Benjamin Township Police Department received an ICE detainer asking them to hold Mario for an ICE interview, transfer of custody, or for information on when and where he'd be released by the agency. Given that Mario was transferred that same day to the county jail, ICE additionally sent a detainer to the jail. It stated that ICE had determined that probable cause existed that Mario was removeable from the United States due to

> the pendency of ongoing removal proceedings against the alien; Biometric confirmation of the alien's identity and a records check of federal databases that affirmatively indicate, by themselves or in addition to other reliable information, that the alien either lacks immigration status or notwithstanding such status is removable under US immigration law; and/or statements made by the alien to an immigration officer and or other reliable evidence that affirmatively indicate the alien either lacks immigration status or notwithstanding such status is removable under US immigration law.

This is standard language on all detainers that the ICE officer checks off prior to actually obtaining a judge's opinion that probable cause exists. The arrest report then notes that the following morning, one of the agency's detectives, Adam Kelly, contacted an officer of ICE's Homeland Security Investigations, Special Agent César Martínez, to share the information about Mario and the evidence they had found from his SUV that he was involved in some kind of immigrant benefits fraud scheme. César Martínez was the ICE agent who had issued the ICE detainer for Mario the day before. After being briefed on the investigation by a Benjamin Township Police Department lieutenant, Detective Kelly inspected Mario's impounded vehicle in the police department's secure impound lot, and the various bags, including IRS notifications and financial documents, many of which were unopened envelopes. He conducted an impound inventory of the vehicle and noted in his report that he saw the following:

A black and white backpack suitcase containing similar bank mail and IRS notifications, along with ledgers and file folders containing personal identifiers, bank accounts, and Temporary Tax Identification number information in the cargo portion of the [SUV]; A black folio folder containing ledger notes, fingerprints, an ink blotter, and card stock in the cargo portion of the [SUV]. I immediately recognized those aforementioned items as consistent with identity theft. Based on my training and experience, I recognize multiple foreign nationals and/or immigrants receiving bank and government mail to a common address to be an indicator of that location and those persons' possible involvement in government benefits fraud.

Special Agent César Martínez, Homeland Security Investigations, assisted me in reviewing the previously described documents. During our review we located and inspected four separate Mexican Driver's Licenses. . . . Based on our training and experience we observed inconsistencies in the appearance quality and physical construction of the documents. We additionally observed inconsistent fingerprint and anti-counterfeiting measures built into the individual identification cards. During our inspection we located multiple homemade advertisements that translated from Spanish to English stated "we process driver's licenses" and provided the telephone number [redacted]. We additionally discovered multiple ledger entries in various notebooks that referenced "$2800 for Driver's License." We additionally discovered multiple various forms of paperwork providing Temporary Taxpayer Identification Numbers (TTIN) from the Internal Revenue Service. Many of those TTIN correspond to various names on the IRS Notices and Bank mail seized from the various locations. At that time, based on our training and experience, we suspected that Figueroa was accepting money to create fraudulent Mexican driver's licenses in the name(s) of individuals associated with the "back-stopped" TTIN. The Driver's License, mail to the Annapolis residence, bank information, and a printout from the Maryland Comptroller stating the associated person has two or more years of income tax returns filed can then be utilized to fraudulently obtain a Maryland Driver's License from the Maryland Department of Motor Vehicles. We additionally located a lease agreement signed by Figueroa for a storage unit I at the "Public Storage" located at 4239 Yorkshire Avenue in Benjamin Township.

Special Agent Martínez [ICE-HSI], Special Agent Ryan Wagner, United States Postal Inspectors Service and I met with Figueroa in the

Detention Area Interview room. At that time, I read Figueroa an Arrest Warrant Notification advising him of his criminal charge. Figueroa acknowledged that he was aware of his criminal charge but refused to sign the document. SA Martinez and I then read, and translated, a Chasen County Rights Form to Figueroa. Figueroa immediately asked for his lawyer. A CD-R recorded copy of our meeting with Figueroa was logged into property under this CFS#.

Special Agent Martínez and I then went to the "Public Storage" facility and met with Talia Simmons, the manager on duty. I inquired as to the validity of the lease document and if it was current. At that time, she told us that she knows Figueroa as a customer, and that he rents storage unit D23. She further related that Figueroa had missed "several months of rent payments" and as a result the unit had a manager's lock installed on that date to bar entry to the storage unit until payment is received. I subsequently prepared an affidavit of probable cause in support of a search warrant for the storage unit D23, located at 4239 Yorkshire Avenue in Benjamin Township. The affidavit was submitted to Assistant Prosecutor Julie Operns, Chasen County Prosecutor's Office, for review.

The complaint warrant that Kelly submitted to the New Jersey Superior Court accused Mario of

> facilitating a fraud or injury to be perpetrated by anyone, specifically possessing more than approximately 60 pieces of mail, IRS notices, Mexican Driver's Licenses, Passports, Fingerprints, Passport Photos, and Tax Return Documents pertaining to more than 10 separate individuals; along with ledgers, notes, and instructions documenting how to create fraudulent Mexican Driver's Licenses in the name of individuals backstopped with IRS Individual Taxpayer Identification Numbers, for the purpose of obtaining government issued Identifications, all in violation of N.J.S. 2C:21-17.3B(2) (2nd Degree Crimes).

On March 2, a judge reviewed and approved the affidavit and search warrant for Mario's storage unit. That same day, Detective Kelly, his Lieutenant, and ICE-HSI Special Agent César Martínez executed the search warrant of the storage unit and according to Kelly:

A systematic search of the premises was then conducted. I acted as evidence officer, collecting all items located and placing them on a Benjamin Township Inventory List. Nothing was seized during the search of the storage unit. . . . Digital images taken during the execution of the search warrant were logged into property under CFS#18-5982-AR.

On March 2, Mario also appeared before a judge of the Superior Court of New Jersey who issued a pretrial release order which would have allowed him to be released immediately from jail to go home subject to certain conditions, such as telephonically reporting once every other week and in person once every other week; refraining from possessing a firearm or other destructive weapon; refraining from excessive alcohol use or the use of narcotic drugs or other controlled substances; and to appear for all court hearings in person. However, rather than releasing Mario that day, the county jail, according to Mario's release form, "released" him into the custody of ICE.

Four days later, on March 6, 2018, Kelly met with IRS Special Agents Karen Forester and Bernard Clark, ICE-HSI Special Agent Martínez, and Special Agent Ryan Wagner of the Postal Inspectors Service. The three briefed the IRS agents on the investigation and reviewed the seized tax documents. Kelly noted in his report, "At that time, we did not uncover any evidence of loss on the part of the IRS, or that the documents were being used in an attempt to defraud the IRS." IRS's Special Agent Clark told Kelly that he'd contact him if the IRS would investigate the matter further. In response to this author's public records request for such communications, Benjamin Township provided no further records of communication from the IRS, and therefore, it is likely that the IRS's investigation of Mario's activities didn't advance further.

On March 17, after a "thorough review" of Mario's case, the Superior Court of New Jersey admitted Mario into the Pre-Trial Intervention Program, a court program where first-time offenders are supervised by probation officers and are provided various supports to avoid future criminal behavior. Individuals are selected for the program prior to their court case moving forward and being decided upon by a judge. It is unclear why Mario was released from ICE custody and allowed to enter this program. The probation department was placed in charge of closely monitoring Mario for thirty-six months. According to the Chaser

County Prosecutor, "If the conditions of the supervision are fulfilled, the charges against the defendant will be dismissed. If the defendant fails to fulfill those conditions, the defendant will be terminated from the [Pre-Trial Intervention] Program, and the case will be prosecuted by this Office." On November 19, 2020, according to a letter from the Chasen County Prosecutor to Officer Kowalsky, Mario completed the terms and conditions of the Pre-Trial Intervention Program, and the court dismissed the charges against him. It is unclear if he faced any immigration enforcement consequences aside from being transferred initially to ICE custody from Chasen County jail.

* * *

The arrest and subsequent investigation of Mario demonstrates how within the context of a single case, local police can serve as force multipliers of multiple types. First, police serve as force multipliers *for law itself* by instantiating law and the authority of the commander in policy in specific events—police make law present, enunciate it, strategize with it, and involve it in their decisions and actions. Without this embodiment and enunciation, policy and law otherwise would merely remain "on the books" in networked, digital databases. Through accessing it via police officer cell phones in the course of an arrest, police bring the law into their minds and bodies in live situations, and the law utilizes police as its emissaries who lend it credibility among other officers and those whom they police. Second, within the same arrest event, police may operate as force multipliers for transnational policing agencies like ICE HSI, as local police investigate potential violations of state laws regarding the trafficking of fraudulent documents. These investigations, when linked with ICE and its capacities, double as investigations into transnational criminal networks in which people like Mario might merely serve as a local point person. Police seamlessly and without issue pivot between these force multiplier roles, activities, and foci and offer up their locally contingent visions, prerogatives, authorities, and networks to the process of force multiplication that also makes use of the resources of ICE toward shared objectives. This case thus demonstrates how local law enforcement may use ICE to achieve its goals just as much as ICE can use local law enforcement to achieve its goals—police act as force multipliers for ICE and ICE acts as force multipliers for the police.

Conclusion

Sanctuary is an elusive concept that has driven social movements, politicians, and, as I have argued in this book, *policing* judgments, decisions, and behaviors. Not only does it refer to a set of values of protecting immigrants from the harm of their many pursuers, but also to a type of policy that links local police to ICE, such as in New Jersey in some cases, while in others, it separates the spheres that the police are called on to police into distinctive crime control and immigration control spheres. In law enforcement, the implementation of sanctuary policies creates a new form of policing that I have called sanctuary policing, one that takes immigration status into account only to avoid it, and takes into account immigration enforcement only to relate officers to it differently.

When serving as a force multiplier for ICE, police who implement sanctuary policies provide various forms of ancillary collaboration, support, and cooperation for ICE that looks like the local policing of traffic violations and crime, the investigation of state law, the protection of the public, and the controlling of scenes for public safety purposes. Upon closer scrutiny—through the view of the police officer's body-worn camera—we can see that what passes for merely local law enforcement and public safety can double as immigration enforcement assistance with an immigrant-friendly face. Police, when they follow sanctuary policies, serve as force multipliers for ICE if they respond to ICE phone calls for backup in exigent circumstances of ICE's own making and design; when they park their vehicles in a manner to detain immigrants for ICE; when they stand in the street at a distance to direct traffic, engage pedestrians, prevent immigrant advocates from disrupting ICE arrests, and otherwise stand ready to act *if* a crime is committed at an immigration enforcement event; when they respond to civil administrative ICE warrants in the NCIC; and when they serve as videographers for ICE and provide them with the ability to verbally coerce immigrant targets. When enacting sanctuary policies, police act as partners to de-escalate immigration enforcement situations; to make immigration arrests simpler, safer, and faster; to reduce harm to "good immigrants" and other members of the public while allowing ICE to potentially harm and humiliate "bad immigrants"; and to keep immigrant advocates occupied and away from spaces where they might intervene in the immigration arrest. Through sanctuary policy carve-outs, exceptions to policy prohibitions of immigration enforcement assistance that allow police to assist ICE, the police relationship with ICE and their status as force multipliers is normalized as legitimate, reasonable, and necessary—it is the relationship through which sanctuary states purge themselves of those perceived to threaten its peace and safety.

Therefore, collaborations and joint operations with ICE are still valuable to sanctuary states and to local police that implement sanctuary policies. When local police, sheriffs, prosecutors, and state police participate in joint operations with ICE that is focused on criminal activity such as human trafficking and worker exploitation, these relationships are revived, as is the role of local and state law enforcement as force multipliers for immigration control. It is in these joint operations allowed by sanctuary policies that police may provide even the most minute forms of assistance, such as passing a detained and handcuffed immigrant's wallet to an ICE agent or frisking an immigrant's leg while ICE questions them about their immigration status, that police turn what in other contexts would be solely criminal law enforcement into immigration enforcement. When they mix and offer up these local law enforcement capacities and tasks as force multipliers for ICE, they assist in the immigration enforcement process as well. It is these small acts of assistance, cooperation, and collaboration that form the basis of mutual projects, professional kinship, and the achievement of joint goals that are only possible when force multipliers link their agencies together.

It is also through these joint operations and instances when local law enforcement comes to the aid of ICE that shared viewpoints about immigrants and the morality of immigration enforcement as something inevitable, good for the sanctuary state, and good for public safety are revisited. It is in these events that policy terms such as "exigent circumstances" are defined and instantiated in real-time officer responses. In these moments when ICE and local police share space, old formulations of the "criminal immigrant" are mobilized in a new sanctuary policy tone. Through a sanctuary state–specific framework, not only are criminal immigrants judged as deserving deportation, but so are immigrants who have no weapons and are not being charged with any criminal charges but who once may have been arrested—but not prosecuted or convicted—for an alleged murder. These judgments form the basis for justifying sanctuary policing that assists ICE in targeting them, using their family members as immigration control auxiliaries, safeguarding the immigration arrest area, amplifying the violence threat component of immigration control, and acting as emissaries of public safety and immigration control to members of the public.

It is through the logic of sanctuary policy that police are afforded the ability to further argue to members of the public that when they provide such forms of immigration control assistance, they are not "actively participating" in immigration enforcement. Due to the prohibitions in sanctuary policy that bar them from directly laying hands on immigrants or conducting investigations based solely on immigration status or violations of immigration law, police defensively assert that what they are doing is merely scene safety work or crime-fighting—keeping people safe, and keeping them away, or keeping criminals from exploiting good immigrants and others—and it is *not immigration control*. In this sense, the sanctuary policy allows police to maintain an image of themselves as heroes of those who deserve protection in the sanctuary state, that is, as sanctuary providers, not those who merely target fathers who are taking their sons to work and who separate families. Such are the rationalizations of individual police officers who themselves are conduits of systems of authority much larger than themselves and from which they receive universalistic legal commands that they, in turn, must represent as emissaries in arrest events. Through this command structure, sanctuary values and the values of the state to maintain order are united, and police become the face of sanctuary when a state becomes a type of sanctuary that needs to be policed. This is not a sanctuary that exists in an unconditional safe space but one that operates according to rules that determine how the sanctuary is to be governed, who may remain protected, and who must be turned over to face harm, as was the case in the ancient Hebraic Cities of Refuge.

By contrast, police serve as force dividers when they implement policing procedures to account for and ignore immigration status and immigration law violations so as to intently investigate, arrest, and prosecute non-immigration laws that immigrants may have broken and enforce warrants for their arrest. In these limited and likely rare cases, police refrain from engaging ICE and withhold their local resources from immigration enforcement, de-linking them momentarily from the long-established force multiplication culture nourished by informal practices of providing collegial notification to fellow law enforcement officers and more formal, routine, and automatic forms of interoperability such as the Secure Communities program. Sanctuary policy provisions that serve as force dividers forestall local police from asking questions about immigration status and the commission of immigration offenses in the course of routine police situations; sharing information with ICE about an individual that may be used to target them for immigration enforcement purposes; detaining them; participating in immigration enforcement arrest events and other activities; and in the process, narrowing the objectives of local police toward enforcing traffic laws and state and federal criminal laws and attending to various local disturbances. This, in a certain sense, requires that policing relationships established by local police and ICE are transformed, as they can no longer work in certain joint operations, share certain personal information, and use their own resources effectively for their own operations rather than pooling their resources. However, local police in New Jersey never fully cut ties with ICE. Rather, they continue in other policing incidents when allowed by sanctuary policy to return to the relationship and serve as force multipliers in immigration arrest events, joint operations, and joint investigations all over again. In fact, in some cases, police do not consider sanctuary policies to be binding law, but rather to be mere guidelines to be generally followed but not strictly adhered to.

This is because force multiplication is not about merely allowing one's law enforcement agency to be used by ICE, but rather force multiplication empowers police as subjects of immigration control, even in sanctuary jurisdictions. Local police may also use ICE for their own local ends of investigating crimes and targeting the people that they don't want in their communities. This linking of local contingent, *nonscalable* policing resources to broader policing networks through ICE allows local police to broaden their impact and policing visions so that they do not need to try to "arrest their way out of the problems" they face but to overcome the churn of daily policing that seems to have no effect on crime. Sanctuary policing in its force multiplier mode is therefore an aspirational form of policing carried out with restraint, holding back their desire to directly arrest immigrants or detain them in their local jails, but also with purpose. That purpose seems to never be one guided by an ethic of anti-deportation values of protecting immigrants. Rather, it is carried out with an eye toward getting criminal immigrants out of the sanctuary state for good, and they are utilizing allowable immigration control mechanisms to do it. In the spirit of sanctuary, then, police don't directly carry out stereotypical immigration enforcement actions, but they go to work on the environments immediately surrounding such actions; they don't call ICE to tell them when they will be releasing an immigrant from their jail, but they will covertly collect an immigrant's home address or work address information and provide it to ICE so ICE can go on their own to arrest them somewhere else at a later date.

While I estimate that sanctuary policing is currently rare even in states with sanctuary policies, it is still nonetheless a unique and significant form of policing that may increase with time as unauthorized immigration increases. This is the case not only in the United States, but anywhere that people cross borders to seek refuge from the many forms of life-threatening harm and where governments do not provide formal legal status to the sanctuary seekers. With shrinking governmental budgets available to grant services and benefits to immigrants and refugees and an increase in war, environmental disasters, climate change, and inequality, governments that decide they cannot afford the expense of incorporating immigrants will spend the money they have on the more expensive task of internally policing them instead. Sanctuary policing will be carried out anywhere that governments seek to utilize immigrants as force multipliers who can serve as police informants in immigrant communities—witnesses of crimes who will come forward with information about criminal immigrants that the police can target, arrest, and prosecute with the purpose of making the sanctuary safer.

In New Jersey, the future of sanctuary policing is uncertain. Since the time of the Immigrant Trust Directive's implementation in 2019, Attorney General Gurbir Grewal left his position in July 2021 to become the

Director of the US Securities and Exchange Commission's Division of Enforcement. Andrew Bruck became the Acting Attorney General, followed by Matthew Platkin in February 2022. Matthew Platkin has continued Grewal's public support for undocumented immigrants in many ways. He supported Dreamers—immigrant youth who were brought to the United States as minors and who remain undocumented—by calling upon the federal government to reduce barriers that Dreamers face to obtaining health care. He and his predecessor Andrew Bruck also stood up for the continuance of Deferred Action for Childhood Arrivals (DACA). Platkin also supported the New Jersey Domestic Workers Bill of Rights, a state labor law that regulates the working conditions of this class of workers, many whom are immigrants.[1]

The status of the continued implementation of the New Jersey Immigrant Trust Directive, however, is not clear. It is uncertain to what extent it is still *living* policy in the practices of local police agencies that had modified their internal policies or created new policies compliant with the directive in 2019, or if its provisions are being enforced by the Office of the Attorney General. Given that only half of the state's law enforcement abided by the Immigrant Trust Directive's mandate to create or modify their own internal policies to render procedures compliant, it is also a question whether sanctuary policing has ever existed in the agencies that never created their own internal policies.

The Immigrant Trust Directive's section titled "Annual reporting by law enforcement agencies" requires local law enforcement on an annual basis to report "any instances in which the agency provided assistance to federal civil immigration authorities for the purpose of enforcing federal civil immigration law."[2] They must report these instances to the county prosecutor's office and those offices must compile reports submitted to them and submit a consolidated report to the Attorney General's Office. The Attorney General in turn "shall post online a consolidated report detailing all instances of assistance . . . during the prior calendar year."[3] However, the Office of the Attorney General only issued such a consolidated report in November 2020 for data collected pertaining to 2019, the first nine months of the directive's implementation. It is thus unlikely that law enforcement agencies are reporting instances of providing immigration enforcement assistance to their county prosecutors or that the Office of the Attorney General is reminding them to do so. It is also unclear if any officers who have been hired by local law enforcement agencies are receiving training in procedures to implement the Immigrant Trust Directive after the initial wave of training occurred in late 2018 and early 2019.

In December 2021, to further codify sanctuary style policing provisions and render them independent of the will of a particular state Attorney General, immigrant advocacy organizations worked with state assembly member Raj Mukherji and state senator Joseph Cryan to introduce a bill to the Assembly and Senate called the New Jersey Values Act (originally A6222 and S4289). Much like the California Values Act, also known as SB 54, the New Jersey Values Act prohibited state, county, and municipal law enforcement agencies from the various forms of immigration enforcement assistance activities also outlined in the Immigrant Trust Directive and prohibited 287(g) agreements. What was remarkably absent from the bill was any language that might allow local law enforcement to cooperate with ICE in exceptional circumstances—it does not provide allowances for joint operations, responding in exigent circumstances, or for targeting individuals on the basis of criminal charges or criminal histories. The only such language allowing for law enforcement to participate in immigration enforcement under the bill pertains to instances when ICE provides a judicial warrant that legally mandates local law enforcement to cooperate.

Under the bill, healthcare agencies, education institutions, libraries, and state youth shelters were permitted to ask information from service seekers relating to their citizenship, immigration status, place of birth, social security number, or individual taxpayer identification number to determine eligibility for services, benefits, or programs provided by the institution, but not for any other purposes, such as for immigration enforcement. The bill also extended beyond law enforcement in another way—prohibiting local and state staff from permitting ICE on the premises of these institutions in restricted areas, or otherwise assisting in immigration enforcement. Finally, the bill additionally revised various parts of state law so that various government service provisions were modified to disallow the use of immigration status as a factor that may bar the provision of those services to undocumented immigrants.

Upon re-introduction of the bill in the new 2022–2023 session in January 2022, it was referred in both sides of the house to their respective

Law and Public Safety Committees. While it did not move further than that in the Assembly, in the Senate, it was subsequently transferred to the Senate Judiciary Committee, where it has languished ever since. In order for it to move any further toward becoming a law, it will need to be reintroduced by Democratic party leadership, and immigrant advocacy groups such as the ACLU continue to call on state lawmakers to do so. As this book has shown, however, the language of this bill, as with the Attorney General Immigrant Trust Directive, will not ensure that local police stop assisting ICE as force multipliers. Should this bill become law, it is very likely that police will comply with the law and continue to provide ancillary public safety policing for immigration enforcement events, claiming that they are not directly "participating in immigration enforcement operations." The bill also does not address whether local law enforcement may participate in joint operations that are primarily about crime and not merely immigration law, such as those convened by ICE's Homeland Security Investigations and in which local law enforcement provides complimentary policing services that are supportive to the immigration enforcement aspects of those joint operations.

Sanctuary policing as a form of force division from ICE and force multiplication for ICE will continue throughout the country as well. More than 700 counties have created policies that limit when their local police and jails will hold people for immigration enforcement purposes; 196 counties have policies to limit when police and jails may notify ICE each time they release a potentially deportable person; 240 counties have policies limiting local law enforcement from allowing ICE agents to interrogate individuals who are detained in local custody; more than 160 counties prohibit their local officers from asking people about their immigration status; and more than 175 counties have created policies that prohibit local government staff from using local resources to assist ICE or participate in joint operations with ICE.[4] Both Republican and Democratic US presidents have utilized local law enforcement as force multipliers for immigration control through the previous administrations back to that of Ronald Reagan. The adoption of sanctuary policies under the vocally anti-immigrant President Trump was however rapid and extensive. The adoption of sanctuary policies and the implementation of new federal programs that incorporate the resources of local police as force multipliers go hand and hand. We can expect therefore that sanctuary policies and the policing mentalities they make possible are not going away any time soon.

The cases presented in this book should call attention to the fact that all spaces, including sanctuary spaces, are policed. They operate according to some set of rules that establishes barriers and boundaries that include some and exclude others. The safety provided to those who are included is the product of the intensive sanctuary policing of those for whom sanctuary is denied. Therefore, sanctuary as policy, sanctuary as social order, and sanctuary as policing remind us that no zones, even safe zones, are outside of governance and regulation. Rather, they are themselves the product of regulation and some form of policing, be it informal community oversight and accountability measures or codified and institutionally backed with force and state-legitimated police violence. Sanctuary spaces, whether entirely safe spaces for everyone or not, will always depend upon some regime of regulation backed by mechanisms of enforcement that reinforce that regime. Sanctuary, as I've written elsewhere, therefore *is* a style of governance, and along with religious activists and immigrant rights lawmakers, police of various kinds are also its unwitting and reluctant protagonists.

ACKNOWLEDGMENTS

This book would not have come to fruition without the financial support of the Rutgers University Pratt Bequest Fund and the institutional support of the Rutgers Law School Center for Immigrant Justice. In particular, Center Founding Director and Professor Rose Cuison-Villazor, who first invited me to join her in a project on the implementation of the New Jersey Immigrant Trust Directive that lasted from 2020 to 2022, who supported this body-worn camera project in 2022–2023, has been a continual base of enthusiasm for the work, an advocate for sanctuary-focused research, and an inspiration as a pathbreaking scholarly contributor to the field of sanctuary studies.

Much of this book builds from previous research that I directed on the New Jersey Immigrant Trust Directive that was conducted by Rutgers Center for Immigration Justice Fellows Patrick Johnson, Joseph F. Lin, Samantha S. Hing, Diana Woody, Tiffany Fahmy, and Alexandra Tran. The research findings of our final project report provided the structural framework for understanding the extent to which law enforcement agencies in New Jersey were implementing the New Jersey Immigrant Trust Directive throughout the state. This framing considerably rooted my understandings of what was happening in the ethnographic descriptions presented in this book. At the Center for Immigrant Justice, Program Coordinator Habibah Johnson also helped immensely by fielding calls and emails from law enforcement records custodians and collecting hard copy files of body-worn camera videos from certain agencies.

As the book builds also from and discusses previously unpublished research that I conducted on the implementation of sanctuary policies in San Francisco, thanks are due to the funders of those projects, including the Wenner-Gren Foundation and the US National Science Foundation.

The book gained from the seemingly unending encouragement and support of Edward F. Fischer, who read preliminary drafts of the book's chapters and provided critical feedback as well as suggestions for the publication process. As the idea for this book started as merely an article, it owes a great debt to David Westbrook and Douglas Holmes, who read the first draft of the article version and provided feedback that lit a fire under the project and inspired me to develop the nascent ideas into full chapters. Also, thanks to Mark McGuire and Ayşe Çağlar for reading an initial draft of chapter 3, "Capturing Migrants with Police Body-Worn Cameras." Thanks are also due to Jeffrey Kahn, who, in the process of exchanges about his book *Islands of Sovereignty,* inspired me to write on the topic of police body-worn camera footage of immigration enforcement assistance in the first place.

At NYU Press, Senior Editor Jennifer Hammer has been a ray of light, bringing the book through the publication process from start to finish with enthusiasm and support. Thanks also to NYU Press Editorial Assistant Brianna Jean for her logistical support, Senior Production Editor Alexia Traganas and staff copyeditors, the senior editorial staff and Director Ellen Chodosh for their careful consideration of the book, and to two anonymous reviewers for their critical feedback. Also, I want to thank César Cuahtémoc García Hernández, who encouraged me to publish the book with NYU Press.

I'd like to thank the many law enforcement records custodians, patrol officers, and supervisors who searched for the body-worn camera videos that I requested, took the time to redact them and make them available to me, and fielded my many follow-up emails and calls. This work often comes on top of many other day-to-day policing activities and while done behind the scenes is incredibly important for the continued engagement of the public in the institutions that govern them.

Last, I'd like to thank my parents, Mike and Maureen; Marjorie, my stepmother; my children, Bea and Evla; my brother, Joel, and sister, Kate, for the unending support and joy they all bring me; and most of all, God for being the basis of everything good in my life, including this book.

METHODOLOGY

Surveillant Anthropology

To better understand how force multiplication links federal immigration control with local police in the United States, and in particular when local police interact with undocumented immigrants in jurisdictions governed by sanctuary policies, in October 2023, I submitted thirty public records requests—digital letters—by email under New Jersey's Open Public Records Act to local police agencies. I sought police officer-recorded body-worn camera (BWC) footage of arrests of people who the police agency or the jails where they had been transferred had received ICE detainers for them over the past two years.[1] I also requested BWC footage for instances when police gave other forms of assistance to ICE or US Customs and Border Protection (CBP).

These thirty requests sought 118 BWC videos, which recorded the arrests of roughly ninety individuals over the period from March 2018 prior to implementation of the state's sanctuary policy, the Attorney General Immigrant Trust Directive, until November 2020, nearly two years after its implementation. These thirty requests amounted to every incident identified in the arrest records, ICE detainers, incident reports, and warrants of 416 New Jersey agencies provided through similar public records disclosure to a team of law school researchers that I co-managed in the two previous years. In response to my request, the agencies sent me fifty BWC videos. The videos that I obtained have proven to be the most illustrative documented data of police cooperation with ICE in a sanctuary jurisdiction that I have seen.

The scope of the requests made the project "multi-sited"[2] in its focus on videos that not only display content of policing in many sites throughout New Jersey but also that illuminate a multi-sited object of study—an heterogeneously emplaced, singular state policing system structure spread across multiple localities; in part, "non-local"[3] in that it remotely studies aspects of policing that transcend localities and that relates them abstractly together by means of policy and transnational information-sharing databases, infrastructures, and policing norms that policing agents appropriate; "multi-scalar,"[4] in that it analyzes immigration enforcement assistance as a nested policing capacity that simultaneously enacts local, state, national, and transnational state resources, infrastructures, roles, and authorities in carrying out police activities locally; remote in that I set foot in none of the sites studied nor interviewed none of the police officers involved;[5] and a form of "studying up" in that the police and ICE, which are the primary subjects, hold state authority over society including academia, however provisional that may be.[6]

I had previously studied the police in the San Francisco Police Department, who operate under department sanctuary policies, by attending a course at the San Francisco Police Academy, conducting ride-alongs over a series of a few months, and interviewing key staff and management, including the Chief of Police. I observed patrol officer interactions with immigrants, thinking that it would finally let me see the truth with my own eyes beyond the facile journalistic caricatures of law enforcement in sanctuary cities. At that time, in situ participant observation, which, after all, was mostly observation and just a little participation in policing, provided some insights into officer perceptions of their general interactions with people who spoke English as a second language or who spoke no English at all. However, it was ineffective as a method for providing data on interactions specifically with undocumented people largely because the officers involved in the arrests that I witnessed did not ask about immigration status and therefore they did not know who was undocumented when conducting their work. Their agency had a sanctuary policy in effect, and their choice to not ask about immigration status or participate in other forms of immigration enforcement assistance may have been reinforced by an awareness of me watching their work with an interest in the implementation of their agency's sanctuary policy after all.[7] From participant observation, I got the impression that their sanctuary policies were working just fine. But I always wondered how they acted toward people who spoke English as a second language or no English at all and who had black or brown skin when I wasn't doing ride-alongs with them. Immigrant advocates at the time had continued to report that local police, in certain cases, did cooperate with

ICE when the public was not watching. BWC would prove a way to find out how the police in sanctuary jurisdictions acted when anthropologists or the media weren't present.

From 2020 to 2022, I co-managed a team of Rutgers University law student researchers to obtain internal documents from more than 400 of the 600 law enforcement agencies throughout the state about the manner in which they were implementing the New Jersey Immigrant Trust Directive. Documents from various police agencies showed that they were continuing to cooperate with ICE in ways that were both allowable by their sanctuary policies and, in certain cases, arguably in violation of those policies. Rather than just rely on the summaries of the incidents created by the officers, I submitted four rounds of requests to the agencies for BWC videos of the incidents in 2022—in mid-October, in late October, in mid-November, and in early December. The agencies sent me the videos relatively quickly. The statutory duration for public agencies to respond to a records request in New Jersey is seven business days. But the agencies that I requested records from were allowed to and did request under the open records law more time to respond so that they could identify the BWC videos in their file systems and in some cases redact certain elements. The redactions included dedicating staff time to making auditory redactions of personal information provided by arrested individuals, such as their phone numbers, social security numbers, home addresses, and other personal information. In other cases, agencies visually redacted elements of the video, such as applying blurred areas to parts of the scene such as police patrol car laptop computer screens and identification cards such as driver's licenses. In total, the fifty BWC videos I received from nine agencies represented a positive response from 30 percent of the agencies requested and 42 percent of the total BWC videos requested.

BWC arrived in my email inbox in October and November 2022. As I watched the videos for the first time, I felt "the field" via the range of emotions similar to when doing in situ fieldwork—interest, boredom, annoyance, skepticism, anger, surprise, and shock. The videos allowed me to control the research analysis and the digitalized field in other ways, of course, by pausing, rewinding, and relistening, adjusting the audio and changing headphones, and minimizing or maximizing the image to see or hear more or less intensely. I wouldn't say it was a *hyper-*

real form of field observation, but it was augmented: enhanced in one way yet limited in another. I couldn't participate in the physics of the event, for instance, or smell or touch anything, or directly engage the people in the video.

Soon after watching the BWC videos, it became clear to me that they had the potential to better illuminate my anthropological object—sanctuary policing—than participant observation, allowing the anthropologist to virtually observe police activity in a manner that is potentially much richer in detail than what is captured in police arrest reports, jail documents, court warrants, and even by the anthropologist's own perception when in the field. While being there in person long enough to see the object of our studies with our own perceptive organs and minds for long enough and working collaboratively with other researchers and research participants has been a highly effective methodology for better seeing what sociologist Erving Goffman calls the "backstage" of sociocultural life, this did not serve the study of sanctuary policing in my case.

To be more specific, ethnographers who study the police, be they sociologists, anthropologists, or criminologists, have long been inspired by Goffman's conceptualization of "frontstage" and "backstage." The frontstage, as it has been applied in studies of the police, refers to the public-facing, reputation-maintaining, public relations–managed "official image" of police work, whether that includes news articles, police arrest reports, or official department policies. The backstage refers to how police officers *really* think and behave in the street and behind closed doors when journalists are not present, or how informal policing rules operate in practice,[8] all of which is guarded by a police officer tight-lipped "blue code of silence." In ethnographic studies of the police, long-term participant observation has been the primary method to illuminate the backstage and what is kept out of public view. Scholars may also examine the frontstage as what the officer says they do or thinks that they do and the backstage as what they *actually do*. As such, frontstage and backstage may not only be about concealment of police secrets from the public but also from their own self-awareness of what they are actually doing in practice.

In some cases, however, participant observation is not capable of illuminating the backstage for a variety of reasons. It is often the case that when the researcher is studying up, participant observation is impossible. In 1969, anthropologist Laura Nader called upon researchers to study up by researching "the colonizers rather than the colonized, the culture of power rather than the culture of the powerless, the culture of affluence rather than the culture of poverty."[9] Nader, reflecting upon anthropology in her time which had focused in manifold ways on rural peasantries and indigenous populations throughout the world, was assessing the importance of studying those increasingly few in our world who "by their actions and inactions, had the power of life and death over so many members of the species"[10]—on the middle and upper classes. Utilizing anthropology, anthropologists could interrogate the reasons not just why people might be poor but why some people become so affluent and powerful. The subjects of these studies she proposed might be powerful institutions and bureaucratic organizations, industry titans, universities, the Pentagon, law firms, the banks, the landlord class—the "most powerful strata of urban society," and the networks of power, relationships, policies, legal practices, white-collar crimes, and payoffs that they maintain in order to subordinate the poor.[11] To make this shift in focus, Nader foresaw, would also present new ways of seeing those who anthropologists study when they "study down" and the process in which they are entrapped. In this sense, her call was not to *only* study up but to study up and, with renewed vision, study down, and "sideways"—to study the same social classes or segments as the anthropologist's, including knowledge workers, the managerial class, culture workers, or those who might otherwise share a similar sociocultural disposition as well.[12] The purpose of this approach was to educate citizens about the major institutions that governed their lives so they could better "cope with, the people, institutions, organizations which most affect their lives" and to "plug in . . . to exercise rights other than voting as a way to make the 'system' work for them."[13] As such, the ethnographer's task was to describe the cultures of bureaucracy.

However, even then, Nader recognized that in certain settings, such as a law office that does not want to be studied and that prevents a researcher from conducting participant observation, the methods of participant observation should not stop the anthropologist from studying up. Rather, anthropologists should explore other more useful methods, such as the analysis of personal documents, public relations documents, internal documents, and memoirs, and also conduct interviews to investigate certain problems and situations in which participant observation is not suited or fails.

While the police are popularly seen as the quintessential state representatives who use sanctioned violence to enforce order, bring laws to life, and punish those who confront state authority and its distribution of resources in society, including property, studying the police can, in many ways be a project of studying up. Beatrice Jauregui, however, has pointed out that police, especially line officers or constables in her field site—Uttar Pradesh, India—are routinely exploited by their police administrations, politicians, and members of the public who can call upon people more powerful than the police to get them to do things against their will.[14] In this sense, studying the police may consist of, at times, studying up, studying sideways, and, in other cases, studying down, and this can be contingent upon the constantly shifting status of the police. It should not be surprising therefore that participant observation has been an effective method to directly study the police, who are not as closed off to general research as one might expect of such an institution that, in many ways, operates through secrecy.

Since police, to varying degrees, are transparent about their work in some cases and, in other cases, very secret, scholars of policing since the 1950s have used mixed methods approaches to understanding who police are, how they think and behave, how they interact with rules governing their work, how they wield authority and play a role in governing society. Participant observation has undoubtedly illuminated some of the most significant understandings of the police and provided an on-the-ground, narrative, and analytical richness to academic renderings of policing.[15] Police ethnographies based on in-person participant observation have countered official narratives about the police through a humanization and historicization of particular agents, officers, police management, police auxiliaries, security officials, private security sector guards, and community member policing volunteers in policing systems throughout the world in a manner that complements statistical renderings of policing effectiveness, policing strategies, police policies, and criminological metrics.[16]

To gain further insights on policing unobtainable through participant observation *with* the police, scholars have also used mixed methods to conduct ethnographies of a uniquely placed anthropological force multiplier—the *policed*.[17] In these cases, the ethnographer conducts participant observation research among populations that are subject to police action not only to learn about policing from their perspective but to put themselves in the target sights of the police and experience their tactics, strategies, and interpretations of law as the police enforce it through action taken also upon the body of the ethnographer. This includes studies of protestors, football fans, hooligans, racialized and working-class neighborhoods, and undocumented immigrant border crossers.[18]

Of particular mention here is Jason De Leon's work, which uses methods from archaeology, forensic anthropology, and linguistic anthropology, as well as participant observation and ethnographic interviews. De Leon sought to understand not only how undocumented immigrants are policed by border control officers and their surveillance technologies, but how immigrants are deterred, killed, and disappeared by the many actants that make up the desert through which immigrants attempt to clandestinely cross the US-Mexico border. De Leon studied deterrence of border crossers by conducting an archaeology of sites where migrants left belongings, deceased bodies, body parts, and shelters; conducting participant observation with and interviewing migrants who had successfully or unsuccessfully migrated through the desert and been hunted by border agents, neo-Nazis, and animals; participant observation and interviews with border agents who patrol the same areas where his immigrant participants have attempted to pass through the desert; photos of migrant sites, migrants, migrant families, institutions helping migrants, and photos taken by migrants on cameras that De Leon gave them in the course of crossing the dessert; and, most heart-wrenchingly, an account built from participant observation and interviews about an Ecuadorian family that attempted to find one of their family members who went missing in the desert and was never found, and separately to obtain the body of and grieve the death of another one of their family members that De Leon and his students found deceased in the Arizona desert when conducting their archaeological fieldwork. To understand how the CBP and the desert together inflict violence upon the deceased bodies of immigrants, DeLeon and his students also studied the process of decomposition and scavenging of immigrant bodies using surrogate animals, five pigs that he purchased and had killed in the desert. Placing a video camera near the bodies, he documented in video and audio the two- to three-week process of decomposition, scavenging, and scattering of the carrion by various predators, mostly various birds and dogs, and treated this as a form of disappearing that was anticipated and utilized by CBP as a manner in which to amplify deterrence and therefore part of policing the border.

Laurence Ralph, in his book *The Torture Letters: Reckoning with Police Violence*, examined the culture of silence about torture that Chicago Police Department officers inflicted on Black witnesses, suspects, and other members of the Black community in the 1970s and 1980s. Ralph could not directly observe this police practice, which occurred decades before his fieldwork in the 2010s, because it was intentionally occluded from public view, and city government leadership had given the police torturers political cover so that they could continue their violence behind closed doors in a black site.[19] Ralph creatively examined the present social consequences of past police torture, the persistent inattention to reckoning with police torture, as well as its ongoing disciplinary operation upon people—torture has instilled a general fear of police and this allows police to continue to terrorize Black people with impunity today.

Ralph publicly solicited interviewees from a wide variety of public spaces in Chicago to participate in group interviews in which he facilitated discussions about police torture that were sparked by various materials he shared with participants—for instance, court transcripts and open letters that he wrote to various people related to the issue of police torture. Through these conversations, he sought their input on the formation of the open letters and published them as chapters of his book. This process allowed him to unearth the culture of fear that the police had produced in Chicago and the complicity of various police actors, politicians, and, more generally, the public in maintaining the open secret of police torture.

Building from an anthropology of the policed approach, Yarimar Bonilla and Jonathan Rosa have conducted what they call "hashtag ethnography"—online and offline fieldwork into the unfolding event of the police shooting of Michael Brown in Ferguson, Missouri, and the transnational response in tweets on the social media platform Twitter (now X), in the streets of Ferguson, and at many offline locations throughout the world where protests occurred.[20] Their semiotic approach allowed for a reexamination of the multi-sited ethnographic study of police and policing, including the nonpolice institution sites, social movements, and forms of expression in analog and digital formats. Through this work, they reconceptualized the field as a dialogical space gathered together by a single hashtag #Ferguson and studied how new mediatized publics were forged, images and videos circulated, and meaning was made and contested on- and offline. They questioned whether such research constituted an ethnography of a "non-place," a "virtual world," and whether the research was a new form of "armchair anthropology," a derogatory framing of early anthropologists who did not conduct fieldwork in the geographic locations in which they wrote about but rather relied upon secondary literature to inform their accounts of foreign peoples, all from the comfort of their library armchairs. Ultimately, they found hashtags to be "entry points into larger and more complex worlds . . . a window to peep through" that allowed them to "follow" individual users and place their tweets in broader on- and offline contexts.[21] In sum, theirs was a study of the multitude of views of what police practice is, what the meaning and effects of police violence were, and how police violence is represented. With a mixed online and offline approach, Beatrice Jauregui also utilized social media sites of police union activists who were vocal in public news stories about police rights. This work, following years of participant observation in Upper Pradesh, India, included observation, interviews, content analysis of court writs and judgments, executive orders, internal police memos, posts on social media sites, news stories, and various other archival documents.[22]

Utilizing methods other than participant observation to study the police hasn't just been developed when researchers encountered roadblocks to gaining access to powerful policing groups or policing processes that are purposefully concealed from the public—for instance, the activities of secret police, undercover police, police management, or to see aspects of police work like unlawful interrogations and police torture. Rather, researchers have used methods other than participant observation to see the same phenomena that they could see with participant observation in *additional* ways, to see new aspects or sides of policing that were not afforded through participant observation. These additional methods may be used to study up, down, and sideways.

Katherine Verdery examined how the secret police in communist Romania in the 1970s and 1980s operated by analyzing her own Secret Police file after the files had been decommissioned.[23] She interviewed the retired Secret Service agents who had been surveilling her during a previous era when she had been conducting participant observation fieldwork on an unrelated topic.[24] In her decommissioned secret security files, she studied how the Secret Police inserted informants into her network to influence her and, by changing her network, attempting to reformulate her personality. She also interviewed the informants in her close intimate friend network and professional network, who she read in her police file had informed on her. In effect, she turned the Secret Police's force multipliers—their informants—into anthropological force multipliers—research informants about the Secret Police. In this way, in the late 2010s, she was able to look back and analyze how the Secret Police operated in the 1970s and 1980s, how the networks they created operated in her life and, more generally, in the country. She studied how truth and knowledge were instrumentally formed by the Secret Police and used for political and security purposes. Finally, she compared the work of secret police, who not only seek to extract information but produce effects on the population, to the work of anthropologists who have their own "informants" and who may seek to influence the public sphere with their writing. This, of course, follows implicitly on her earlier participant observation experience, which didn't directly focus on policing, but as she conducted the fieldwork on peasant life in Romania, she experienced surveillance as part of her fieldwork, always knowing that her work was being watched, followed, listened to, and documented.

Anthropologist David Price has also used archival documents—correspondence, oral histories, published sources, and more than thirty thousand pages of FBI, US State Department, and other government documents released under the Freedom of Information Act. His formal requests document how the repressive postwar McCarthy era in the United States shaped postwar anthropology by conducting surveillance on anthropologists, policing anthropological scholarship and anthropologists' participation in public discourse, and using anthropologists as informants against their colleagues.[25] This, of course, took the form of an inquiry not just about secret policing agencies like the FBI but also examined the actions of congress members and senators who "badgered witnesses at loyalty hearings and the college and university administrators who scrutinized their faculty for signs of thought crimes or activist inclinations."[26] While Price's work is not "police ethnography" per se, he renders a portrayal of the FBI through the stories agents tell of their suspicions of subversive anthropologists in government documents and communications, those who they thought threatened the social order, and the statements and writings of anthropologists themselves. This historical approach, which relies on substantial public disclosure of previously classified records, has an ethnographic sensibility and has contributed greatly to the anthropological understanding of secret policing. Price effectively transformed the FBI archive into anthropology's force multiplier.

Anthropologists have also used video footage to study policing and immigration control primarily through the view of two types of video cameras—the anthropologist's video camera and cameras used by members of the public to film policing incidents unfolding in front of them. When anthropologists and other social scientists use their own cameras to collect social science data and analyze it according to a specific methodology, pairing it with in situ observation, participation, and other ethnographic methods, this is part of what Hubert Knoblauch and René Tuma call the "videographic" tradition in empirical social science research.[27] Videography is the conjoining of video analysis and ethnography wherein video recordings of sociocultural processes are created by the social scientist to study the field. The ethnographies produced from videography are "video-based ethnographies" in their terminology.[28] Videography entails conducting research prior to setting up a camera to determine research questions, determining the manner in which the camera will be involved in the field site, obtaining the video data through the on-site presence of the ethnographer with the camera, followed by processes of reviewing, coding, and analyzing the data to better understand forms, patterns, and structures of actions that occur in the field. This also includes working directly with research participants, holding discussions with them, conducting interviews, as well as collecting documents and artifacts ancillary to the theme of the ethnographer's video recordings.

The focus of video-based ethnographies has been on social situations, events, interactions, practices, and communicative action, and involves single or multiple cameras that may be fixed in place or mobile, mounted on moving actors.[29] Videos are treated as ethnographic data that relate to the fieldworker's experience in the field and are used to elicit ethnographic knowledge of the field. One example of the use of this kind of anthropological camera is Jason De Leon's recording of the decomposition and scavenging of the bodies of pigs in the Sonoran desert to understand how the desert as a type of force multiplier for border control officers disappears migrant bodies as a form of immigration deterrence.[30] In this case, De Leon uses the camera as an anthropological force multiplier that allows him to maintain a continual, month-long presence in the desert with virtual open, recording eyes and ears without himself being exposed to the desert's dangers. This is not to say he does not expose himself to the desert in the course of all of his other archeological and sociocultural research in the desert. Further, the recording allows De Leon to observe a form of auxiliary border policing that he could never observe through participant observation due to the need for uninterrupted access to this site for the duration necessary to observe the full decomposition process.

The second type of camera used to study the police is that used by members of the public for non-research purposes to document police activity. In police studies conducted as early as the mid-1990s, Charles Goodwin, in his article "Professional Vision," analyzed the way that the court case of the Los Angeles Police Officer group beating of Rodney King, which was filmed by an amateur videographer from his home, was a process whereby police experts and defense lawyers used the video to explain the professional, embodied ways of interacting with King in the course of their beating of him.[31] Goodwin's own work examined hundreds of hours of courtroom video not only of the Rodney King beating case, which ended up exonerating the officers but also of other courtroom cases. In this particular article, he demonstrates how the interpretation of video of police violence is marked through discourse, broken down into pieces that can be highlighted, coded, and framed so as to illuminate a shared, that is, collective, way of viewing suspects in the course of a police violence incident. His work also showed how, from the court stand, the police may train a jury about how to watch a video of policing with the vision of a police officer. Once the jury is properly trained, police could convince the jury that the person in control of the situation in Los Angeles was not the police, who were supposedly responding to King's agentive actions, but King himself who they argued was resisting arrest and being aggressive even while being unarmed, outnumbered, and brutally beaten.

Among a variety of approaches to surmounting the barriers to accessing the institutional spaces and processes of powerful actors like the police, some anthropologists have engaged in remote ethnography, which transforms a variety of people, technologies, networks, and information sources physically located remotely from the anthropologist in off-limits-to-the-anthropologist field sites into anthropological force multipliers, allowing anthropology to go where anthropologists cannot. Hugh Gusterson's book *Drone* is a fascinating example of how remote ethnography can bring the reader into a multitude of physical off-limits sites without the author having accessed them personally to conduct in situ research.[32] Gusterson's remote ethnography takes the reader through the vast, dispersed "network of sites, expertise, and experiences" where drone warfare has taken place, including Creech Air Force Base in Nevada, from where drones are flown, to

> bases in the United States where drone operators sat in trailers operating drones thousands of miles away; the bases in the Middle East and North Africa where the drones were maintained and from which they flew; the CIA and military command centers where video data and other kinds of intelligence from drones was monitored and analyzed; the White House, CIA, and the Pentagon where lawyers labored to torture national and international law so it would legitimate extrajudicial killings; the think tanks that produced reports about the ways in which drones would finally make victory possible; the Congressional offices where members of Congress and their staffers did their best to pay no attention to drone warfare; and the remote landscapes in Iraq, Afghanistan, Somalia, Pakistan and Yemen where children heard the incessant buzzing of drones through the night and lived in terror.[33]

Gusterson's "panoramic" approach that sought to show drone warfare as a global phenomenon would be impossible with participant observation, a method requiring access to all of these places, many of which also would require security clearances. To study the apparatuses of drone warfare, rather than conduct multi-sited ethnography, he dispensed with participant observation and interviews of drone operators and elected an approach of no-sited ethnography. The materials Gusterson used to understand drone warfare and drone operator burnout were newspaper articles, first-person accounts by drone operators, gray literature on drones produced by think tanks and nongovernmental organizations, transcripts of other people's interviews, and watching drone operators and their critics talk on videos. From the "immersion in these sources" as he describes it, he inductively saw patterns.[34]

Most paralleled to the production of ethnographic descriptions from BWC videos that I have created in the current book, Gusterson, in an opening vignette to *Drone* included a *New Yorker* account—journalism in the vein of "thin description"—that covers the content of a Predator drone as it approached a target, a Taliban leader in Pakistan, the release of two Hellfire missiles that executed the man, and the aftermath of the scene in Pakistan and at the Langley Central Intelligence Agency (CIA) headquarters where the journalist watched.[35] Gusterson uses this to analyze the vision of drone-empowered executioners, the CIA, the operations crew supporting drone flight, drone operators, and how drones transform modern warfare into what US President Barack Obama framed as a form of "aerial policing."[36] Gusterson examines how the video is framed by these actants, how it is an asymmetric gaze (the state sees the target, the target does not see the state), silent and absent of smell, touch, and taste. Aside from his reflection on his methods for immersing himself in the materials to write his book, Gusterson also demonstrates how, despite the distanced ability of drone operators to kill their targets, drone technology, in particular, the video capabilities,

> gives drone operators a sense of experiential immersion in their victims' deaths. The emotional force of this mediated experiential proximity is amplified by the requirement that drones linger after a strike to assess the damage and count the dead. Thus, the impersonality of remote killing is at least partially offset by what might be called remote intimacy.[37]

Gusterson further states:

> It is too reductive to say that the processes of re-spatialization in drone warfare simply distance drone operators from the battlefield, thus mak-

ing killing easier. It is more accurate to say that they scramble relations of distance, making them simultaneously more elongated and more compressed in ways that are subjectively confusing and paradoxical. They make killing both easier and harder, creating a new psychological topography that we are struggling to understand.[38]

Gusterson tells of drone operators who operate in trailers that come to serve as stand-in virtual cockpits, that they spend more time looking at live footage of landscapes thousands of miles away than those in which they physically live, making them more "psychologically immersed in the screen world," taking pleasure in seeing voyeuristically from a place from which they cannot be seen—a "place of the Gods . . . hurling thunderbolts from afar."[39] He also tells of drone operators who see everything from infrared-enhanced nighttime sex to people going to the bathroom and just about every kind of daily life practice of the people in distant lands. In the course of watching, they create distant narratives in their heads—running, imaginative narratives about what the people are doing that "make sense of the people they watch. In the process, they can make interpretive leaps, fill in informational gaps, and provide framing moral judgments as they integrate shards of visual information and turn pixelated figures into personalities,"[40] comparable, I would add, to the BWC ethnographer.[41]

In his work on *Drone*, Gusterson utilized force multipliers—the drones themselves that captured video data and the pilots who provided first-hand testimony of their actions, each a military data which he turned into ethnographic data through anthropological force multiplication. *Drone* created an anthropological vision in part *through* drone cameras and through drone pilots. While drone cameras were not directed at the drone operators, their camera vision illuminated the behaviors and decisions of drone operators that wielded them from distant trailers, their focused lines of sight, and the manner in which they carried out surveillance and warfare with drones.

THE BWC ETHNOGRAPHER'S RESEARCH AND WRITING EXPERIENCE

Echoing Gusterson's experience of his immersive research process, when reviewing and analyzing the BWC videos for this book, I experienced a certain sense of immersion "inside of" the content of BWC videos. This immersion is very different than the experience of watching a documentary or fictional film or even a home video. It felt like a simulation of in situ participant observation wherein I was carried on the chest of the police officer like a baby in a kangaroo sling. This approach to the videos was not automatic but rather produced by conceiving of the experience as an ethnographic one. I did my best to bracket out my geographical remoteness in order to write ethnography that attempts a more intimate, close, in-person aesthetic.

In observing the field in BWC, that is, the spaces in New Jersey where police BWC videographers went, I was not present in time or space to the officers and they did not see me. Neither did I have any agentive capacity or ability to influence the police officers' behaviors, nor could they influence the way I observed them. I was, however, emotionally affected when I watched BWC—for instance when the police officer covertly collected information for ICE to arrest and deport a man as described in the prologue's narrative. My heart pounded; I became anxious, and yet also excited at finally witnessing what I had heard about for so long from immigration advocates in sanctuary cities—something that perhaps only police, ICE, and police-targeted immigrants have seen and experienced. The remoteness seemed to be an asset to seeing the policing backstage—my personal absence from the scene allowed for it to unfold and be recorded without my physical interference forestalling it—the stereotypical objectivist position.

The emotional response should also be considered part of an in situ field experience—one in which I sat at my desk and watched remotely filmed videos of police and policing scenarios. This included pausing, rewinding, and playing certain portions of the video over and over and perhaps can be considered a form of participant research of contemporary remote surveillant work, that of people such as drone operators, department store security personnel, secret police that monitor covertly installed camera feeds, and police investigators and detectives who review camera footage of past crimes to solve a case.

The BWC ethnographer, too, puts their own body, psyche, and emotional state inside of a remote work environment in which technological infrastructures allow the ethnographer to surveil the state the way the drone operator surveils the field or the control room observer surveils policing operations. The BWC ethnographer feels isolation, witnesses state violence in a distanced yet intimately close, virtually immersive way, and creates in their mind narrative gaps that they utilize remotely to make sense of the activities and events taking place in the video. As such, remote ethnography produces the possibility of conducting participant observation of remote surveillance work in conducting it *as anthropological research* and pure observation of the places filmed with video equipment in other places throughout the world. As such, we might consider this type of anthropology as a nested, multi-scalar anthropology—studying the local scale of the immediate surroundings of the ethnographer and the multiple scales and jurisdictions roamed and captured by surveillance technologies—both at the same time in the same, singular ethnographic activity. In other words, doing remote ethnography could, in part, take the form of an auto-ethnography of the researcher's remote participant research experience working from, seeing through, thinking inside of, and emoting at, against, and toward surveillance footage of state actors.

It is also worth noting that while the police were not influenced by me individually watching the video, given my remoteness from the scene, the BWC itself influences how police act during policing events. Given that a variety of potential observers of the film—their colleagues, superiors, lawyers, judges, the public, and social scientists—may scrutinize the videos later, police "cover their asses" in the moment to meet the BWC observer's satisfaction. As one such abstract potential viewer, the BWC ethnographer therefore contributes to the policing event in an indirect manner. We give the police a reason to justify their behavior on camera, implicitly requiring them to explain themselves to us along the way in their behavior, even if we aren't there to ask ethnographic questions directly.

In extensively watching BWC footage of the police over and over, the BWC ethnographer, similar to cadets at police academies that are shown BWC videos as part of their training, gleans some procedural knowledge about how police examine particular situations and how they navigate through a field of events and apply relevant statutes. The BWC ethnographer does not however use practical reason in the field, make decisions about how to intervene in the scene, or engage with police interventions in real time as a drone operator would. As an observer virtually embedded in police chests, the BWC ethnographer is allowed a second-by-second virtual experience, a safe representation of the insecurity, uncertainty, and danger that police officers face.

Watching BWC footage, I could return to the beginning and re-watch the interactions repeatedly, focusing on different elements or on the same element in different ways. I could focus on groups of elements in the footage, proffering new insights into exactly what happened, something that participant observation simply doesn't afford. I can pause the video, modify the sound, slow the pace of the video, home in on background noises and spatial arrangements of subjects and objects, and infer the cause and effect of related elements, shifting relations, signs, linguistic registers, and the physics of power flashing about on my laptop screen while being anywhere in the world.

When transcribing the ethnographic narratives built from the videos, I created a narrative flow that is semi-fictional in that it represents how the event would have taken place *as if* I experienced the ethnographic data in a consecutive manner in organic time from the beginning of the event to the end as if I had been there. In reality, I watched portions of the video and paused the video before it ended. If something was said in a later part of the video that might have referred back to something that I had missed during earlier parts of the video, I rewound the footage to that moment and rewatched it. In that manner, I virtually duplicated my sense experience of time in certain segments and cut up the linear experience of the event into units so that I could better understand something that I might have previously missed. My sense of time was therefore virtually multiple—linear conceptually in reference to how I imagined the event playing out in New Jersey; linear with regard to the transcriptive process as a whole; but nonlinear and recurrent experientially with regard to the content of the footage. Since it was a video that was similar to how I would have seen and heard the event in person, it felt like a temporally disjointed "live" in-person experience in some way. Given its visual, auditory, and emotional likeness to an in-person fieldwork experience in its video content, it also seemed very much like experiencing organic time itself out of sequence, with experiential returns to the past and fast-forwards to the future. This ability to experience the event as temporally recurrent allowed me to write a thick description narrative that was conceptually linear and better explained because I "caught" more data as time passed through the event than if I had been there in person.

METHODOLOGY | 211

In BWC ethnography, there is no need to first take notes and then, after, from memory, reduce or expound to a cohesive narrative. The ethnographic transcription of BWC is direct, from watching to writing the finished text, and allows the writer to produce in my opinion an uncanny sense of *experience* that allows the reader to experience the field more akin to an in situ participant observer. This is different than one we might have when reading a detail-rich portrait-style text that is intentionally written to unfold a single coherent message, theme, or narrative. The ethnographic transcription of the BWC can include the anthropologist's explanations of certain coded aspects of policing and, most importantly, the in-the-moment descriptions of boredom, empty time, silence, irrelevance, and irrationality that might be stripped from thin-description ethnographies because of their general inefficiency or nonpertinence to the text's central topic.[42] Through the BWC ethnographic thick description style, something more *fieldy* is retained. Further, the composite nature of the experience of the ethnography as both no-sited and fieldy is perplexing.[43]

This also allows us a reassessment of the application of Goffman's conceptualizations of frontstage and backstage in policing research. If the unofficial but de facto rules, behaviors, and police culture of the backstage are illuminated, unearthed, or uncovered not by long-term, trust-accompanied participant observation but rather via relatively immediate public disclosure of frontstage digital BWC video documents, the distinction between frontstage and backstage nearly collapses. The behaviors of street policing, including much of the boredom, tactical maneuvering, commiserating, and reflecting how to really conduct police work—all things that police ethnographers contend is backstage and that are not contained in official police policy—are available for people who have never met the police officers in the videos.

In collecting the BWC videos as publicly disclosed records and reviewing them remotely, anthropological research for this book augmented the role of local police and their body-worn cameras from force multipliers for ICE into force multipliers for anthropology in the field, documenting interactions with the public, and recording the manner in which immigration control–related policing occurs. I engage the police here indirectly as conduits, agents, and resources of anthropological research, literally piggybacking onto their position in the field to do what no participant observer could accomplish—to accompany them long enough to actually see the presumably rare instances of immigration control assistance with ICE in a sanctuary jurisdiction. This remote approach extended my anthropological access to countless fields, targeted entry to rare policing cases, and allowed repeated digital return to the events.

From this view, anthropology is afforded a new panoramic view, to use Gusterson's term, into what immigration control and immigration control assistance in a sanctuary state is on the ground; how it works; how cultural understandings are infused in it; how policy affects it; how it is fractured among state institutions; and how it brings disparate institutions like local police agencies and ICE together as fictive kin. Further, given that such policing is imbued with logics of sanctuary—protecting, advocating for, and empowering immigrants—police and their body cameras allow me to better understand what sanctuary is when it is instantiated as a form of policing.

SURVEILLANT ANTHROPOLOGY

I call this type of anthropology surveillant anthropology, one that is surveilling the object of anthropology, in this case, sanctuary policing and immigration control, its agents, and its field, as well as being based in the objects produced by surveillance technologies of the police, BWC footage. The approach may be considered a form of sousveillance or "watching from below"—a form of "surveilling the surveillors," the term being constructed from the French words "sous" meaning "below" and "veiller" meaning "to watch."[44] This typically refers to instances when the surveilled public use their own cameras positioned opposite of, external to, and toward police, most typically now cell phone cameras.[45] Steve Mann has described sousveillant cameras as "cameras affixed to small entities such as individual people" and sousveillance as "observation or recording by an entity not in a position of power or authority over the subject of the veillance [observation/watching]."[46] When framed as a "technique," sousveillance is not dependent upon who is holding the camera, what kind of surveillance technology it is, where it is positioned, or *who* it is capturing on video, but rather the utilization of surveillance techniques of watching through surveillance technologies to watch the watchers.[47] When members of the public use their personal cameras to watch the police, sousveillance is a manner by which to disrupt the asymmetric surveillance dynamic where only the police with access to a network of cameras may watch over the public.

Surveillant anthropology as a methodological technique then can be considered akin to sousveillance, which watches police and policing, albeit *through* police cameras themselves rather than a sousveillant "filming back" at the police via nonpolice cameras. I have chosen to describe this type of anthropology as "*sur*veillant," that is, "watching over" because the anthropologist sees, listens to, documents, and analyzes police moves, speech, gestures, morals, norms, transgressions, improvisations, freedoms, elaborations, *through* properly *sur*veillant technologies of the state that are themselves "watching over" people. Second, it entails the observation of state activities by a nonparticipant in the activity, the BWC ethnographer. It is a remote-sousveillance-through-surveillance, a retooling, re-reading, and re-narration of "panoptic" data to understand and explain state power itself.[48] Though such an approach has not been thoroughly theorized—Mann has pondered whether there could be a sousveillance that he calls "underveillance" or "under-watching" that co-opts the full network of omnipresent embedded surveillance systems of contemporary society in a similar manner.[49] Given that the anthropological methodology used here focuses its vision through merely *state* surveillance technologies and not through the entire field of omnipresent surveillance cameras, for instance, all wall-mounted or lamppost-mounted cameras in public and private spaces, I have considered it "surveillant" rather than "underveillant."

Surveillant anthropology is however different than state surveillance in certain ways. It does not for instance involve *real-time* monitoring of those that the state targets, such as criminals, foreigners, political subversives, or consumers. Anthropological watching of state actors such as the police and ICE agents takes place *after* the field activity is recorded. It could very well also examine state actors through surveillance technologies in real time. In this case, it may be more akin to what Strickland and Schlesinger refer to as "lurking," a form of sociological "pure observation" that is currently being used in social scientific research for covert monitoring of online communities, including online communities that engage in online policing of criminal activity.[50]

Surveillant anthropology is further distinguished from state surveillance due to the fact that the anthropologist does not have political or legal authority over the state actors that they observe. In this sense, surveillant anthropology, with regard to state authority, is a form of studying up from below, qualitatively a form of sousveillance. But if anthropology is integrated into intelligence and military agencies and utilized toward state objectives, that form of anthropology is more generally referred to as "surveillance anthropology" and has been broadly critiqued, foremost by anthropologist David Price.[51] Should the anthropologist be hired or used as a force multiplier by one state to research and surveil another state's officials and their policing, military, or intelligence activities, that other state's authorities may not necessarily wield state power over the anthropologist-intelligence agent but rather may be the correlate to the anthropologist, albeit in another country. Surveillance anthropology, in distinction from what I have done in this book, then, is a form of studying sideways or what Mann, Nolan, and Wellman might call "coveillance"—practices of watching horizontally among "symmetrically distant organizations."[52] Surveillance anthropology therefore should not properly be considered sousveillance or the type of critical surveillant anthropology I use in this book.

As is the case with BWC ethnography, critical surveillant anthropology utilizes state surveillance technology and those state agents that wield them as scientific vectors and research auxiliaries, as anthropological force multipliers, indirectly utilizing their work as field agents and the video data they collect for other purposes—to produce knowledge about and a critique of state activities. Through an expansion of its uses, BWC as an instrument and actant expands, and it is brought into new relations with human beings, for instance, as a verifiable scientific source. It is no longer merely a mediator and actant of prosecution but also of scientific veridiction, anthropological theorization, and what Didier Fassin describes as "ethnographic exposure"—"exposing the non-evidence of self-evidence."[53] Importantly, it also makes possible the critique of policing. As such, a surveillant anthropology of the state is one that virtually inhabits and flows through state surveillance systems rather than one that stands apart from, as if purely independent of, them.

The scientific repurposing of the BWC camera as an anthropological force multiplier does not render what it newly does as that different from its originally intended purpose in the criminal justice system. In many ways, the manner in which the ethnographer uses the BWC to surveil state actors and make truth claims about them in scientific publications is similar to the manner in which police forces conduct surveillance upon members of the public through overt and covert cameras, including BWCs, CCTV cameras, and license plate readers. Police use the footage to render truth claims in police reports, court documents, and disciplinary investigations. As Bethan Loftus, Benjamin Goold, and Shane Mac Giollabhui describe in their work with undercover police who conduct covert surveillance, undercover police

> record extensive chronological accounts of the movements of the subject ("the subject is walking from the bus stop to the pharmacy along Old Road"), their physical appearance ("the subject is wearing dark blue jeans with a black jacket"), the weather ("it is currently sunny with light cloud cover"), and descriptions of any person the subject came into contact with ("the subject is speaking with a white male in his 20s with short blonde hair and wearing a black tracksuit").[54]

Such descriptions are not only produced from duplicitous interactions with the targets of surveillance but are possible pursuant to police teams installing surveillance equipment in places, including the target's home, without the target knowing about them. Loftus, Goold, and Giollabhui explain that the kinds of ethnographic descriptions that covert police produce while conducting surveillance from a distance to objectify their targets and depersonalize them are a result of the passive and distant nature of surveillance. However, they also note that "while each element in isolation appears insignificant, it is the case that, by collecting and compiling the minutiae of daily habits and rituals, a detailed and personal profile—a dossier—emerges." The aim of such police descriptions is to identify patterns emerging from the intelligence, "enabling the analyst to draw inferences so that operational decisions can be made and on which further and possibly more honed actions are taken."[55] Ultimately, as Loftus, Goold, and Giollabhui remind us, covert police surveillance, which primarily targets underprivileged sectors of society such as the homeless, drug users, and others "living on the edge," is conducted to "collate intelligence or evidence that can be used to criminalize and prosecute a person."[56] This is where police surveillance and surveillant anthropology of the state that is critical differ. Surveillant anthropology targets state actors and lacks state powers and intentions to prosecute, arrest, and jail them.[57] Further, surveillant anthropology is not conducted covertly, nor do I advocate or condone anthropologists secretly becoming involved in placing cameras where state actors are not aware of them.

A surveillant anthropology of the state marks a complementary approach to the study of how to "see like a state"[58] in that it aims to utilize surveillance technologies of the state to study the actions of state actors in a manner similar to how the state conducts surveillance on members of the public, albeit in an overt rather than covert manner. Surveillant anthropology certainly learns from surveillance studies as well—a well-developed field of scholarship in its own right that examines how surveillance is thought of, constructed, and deployed by governmental and private sector actors throughout the world. A surveillant anthropology of the state and of police in particular, on the other hand, carries out a form of sociocultural science through surveillance technologies and their products, including BWC videos.

In this book, a critical surveillant anthropology allows us to "see" how local police perform a new immigration enforcement role when using BWC at immigration enforcement events—that of videographer, camera operator, documentarian, and film producer. This role not only secures the evidence used to prosecute individuals but also produces ready-to-hand digital representations of local and state law enforcement officers, ICE agents, and immigrant arrestees—copyable and sharable digital immigration control resources that can be used toward achieving a heretofore unknown multitude of law enforcement goals.

This type of anthropology that works with materials produced by surveillance technologies and their users as force multipliers builds from the pathbreaking methods and methodologies for studying the police, policing, immigration control, and studying up more generally in anthropology, sociology, and criminology. It also builds from a variety of practices wherein researchers outside of the study of these topics have collaborated with research force multipliers—research proxies, translators, local assistants, "para-ethnographers," "key informants," and others to achieve their *scholarly* ends—to inform the anthropologist of elements of local sociocultural life that the anthropologist otherwise could not see or understand.[59]

NOTES

PROLOGUE

1 I have changed all personal names and other identifying information for the individuals involved in the incident to maintain their anonymity.
2 For a comprehensive explanation of the manner in which ICE uses NCIC to enforce immigration laws, see Sullivan 2009.
3 For an overview of the legality of ICE warrants, see Lasch et al. 2018.

INTRODUCTION

1 DOD (US Department of Defense, Joint Chiefs of Staff). 2007. "GL-11: Joint Special Operations Task Force Operations. Joint Publication 3–05.1," April 26, referenced in Forte 2016, 1.
2 For an overview history of various forms of sanctuary practice, see Rabben 2016.
3 Lippert and Rehaag 2013.
4 Rabben 2016.
5 Coutin 1994.
6 Ridgley 2011.
7 Cuison-Villazor and Gulasekaram 2018.
8 Myrna Orozco and Noel Anderson, "Sanctuary in the Age of Trump." Church World Service, January 2018, cited in Pérez 2024, 1.
9 Mann and Mourão Permoser 2022.
10 Cunningham 1998.
11 Browne 2015; Haro and Coles 2019; Stierl 2020.
12 "Sanctuary," *The Concise Oxford Dictionary of English Etymology*. Oxford: Oxford University Press, 1996, www.oxfordreference.com.
13 Perla and Coutin 2010; Menjívar 2000.
14 Vitiello 2022.
15 Pérez 2024.
16 Paik 2017; Pérez 2024.
17 Mancina 2013; De Graauw 2014.
18 Mancina 2019a; Mourão Permoser and Bauböck 2023; Fox 2023; Hermansson et al. 2022; Ahranjani 2018.
19 Marrow 2012. Also see Charity-Ann Hannan and Harald Bauder, "Towards a Sanctuary Province: Policies, Programs, and Services for Illegalized Immigrants' Equitable Employment, Social Participation, and Economic Development." Work-

ing Paper No. 2015/3, April 2015, *Ryerson Center for Immigration and Settlement*, www.ryerson.ca.
20 Coutin and Nicholls 2023; Su 2024.
21 De Graauw 2014; Cuison-Villazor 2010.
22 Mancina 2016.
23 Houston and Lawrence-Weilmann 2016; Houston and Morse 2017; Glick Schiller and Çağlar 2018.
24 McBride 2009; Bozniak 2019; Bauder 2013; Ridgely 2008.
25 Cuison-Villazor 2008.
26 Ong Hing 2011; Gardner 2019; Lenard 2022; Cade 2018; Hoye 2020.
27 Immigrant Legal Resource Center. 2024. "State Map on Immigration Enforcement 2024." Accessed July 10, 2024. www.ilrc.org.
28 Lippert 2006.
29 Bagelman 2013, 2016.
30 Bagelman 2013, 2016.
31 Walia 2014; Mancina 2016, 2019b; Paik 2017. Also see Andrea J. Ritchie and Monique W. Morris. 2017. "Centering Black Women, Girls, Gender Nonconforming People and Fem(me)s in Campaigns for Expanded Sanctuary and Freedom Cities," *National Black Women's Justice Institute*. Accessed July 10, 2024. https://forwomen.org; and Graham Hudson, Idil Atak, Michele Manocchi, and Charity-Ann Hannan. 2017. "(No) Access T.O.: A Pilot Study on Sanctuary City Policy in Toronto, Canada." Working Paper No. 2017/1, Ryerson Center for Immigration and Settlement. Accessed December 2, 2024. www.torontomu.ca.
32 Squire and Darling 2013; Darling 2019.
33 Humphris 2023.
34 Su 2024.
35 Wyn Edwards and Wisthaler 2023.
36 Immigrant Legal Resource Center. 2019. "Growing the Resistance: How Sanctuary Laws and Policies Have Flourished During the Trump Administration." Accessed December 2, 2024. www.ilrc.org.
37 Immigrant Legal Resource Center. 2019. "Growing the Resistance."
38 Collingwood and Gonzalez O'Brien 2019.
39 Martinez-Schuldt and Martinez 2021.
40 For one example, see Peréz 2024, 39.
41 See Samantha Hing, Patrick Johnson, Joseph F. Lin, Diana Woody, and Peter Mancina. 2022. "Cultivating Immigrant Trust in the Garden State: A Report on the Implementation of the New Jersey Immigrant Trust Directive." Center for Immigration Law, Policy, and Justice, Rutgers Law School. Accessed December 2, 2024. www.cilpj.org.

CHAPTER 1. IMMIGRATION CONTROL'S FORCE MULTIPLIERS
1 For a comprehensive explanation of the separation of policing powers see Gardner 2019. For an explanation of sanctuary policies as the enactment of an

"upstream discretionary" power of local law enforcement with respect to immigration enforcement, see Cade 2018.
2   The only published comprehensive account of such cooperation in sanctuary cities was provided in a "tell-all" book told from the perspective of a pseudonymous ICE officer who managed "Operation Devilhorns," a joint operation between ICE-Homeland Security Investigations (ICE-HSI) and the San Francisco police department. See Bolger and Santini 2018.
3   See BJS (US Bureau of Justice Statistics). 2018. "Census of State and Local Law Enforcement Agencies." Accessed December 2, 2024. https://bjs.ojp.gov; US Customs and Border Protection. n.d. "About CBP." Accessed July 10, 2024. www.cbp.gov; US Immigration and Customs Enforcement. n.d. "Immigration and Customs Enforcement." Accessed July 10, 2024. www.ice.gov.
4   DHS (US Department of Homeland Security). 2023. "US Immigration and Customs Enforcement Budget Overview, Fiscal Year 2023." Accessed August 14, 2023. www.dhs.gov.
5   ICE (US Immigration and Customs Enforcement). n.d. "Secure Communities." Accessed August 14, 2023. www.ice.gov.
6   Brady 2017.
7   ICE. 2023. "Updated Facts on ICE's 287(g) Program." Accessed August 14, 2023. www.ice.gov.
8   Brady 2017.
9   Ong Hing 2011. For a discussion of failed federal attempts to coerce local agencies to enforce immigration laws by withholding federal funding, see Lai and Lasch 2017 and Mancina 2016.
10 ICE 2023. "Priority Enforcement Program." Accessed August 14, 2023. www.ice.gov.
11 Peter Mancina. 2019. "Turning the Golden State into a Sanctuary State: A Report on the Implementation and Impact of the California Values Act (SB54)." Asian Americans Advancing Justice—Asian Law Caucus, Border Criminologies, and Oxford Centre for Criminology. Accessed December 2, 2024. www.asianlawcaucus.org.
12 Mancina. 2019. "Turning the Golden State into a Sanctuary State."
13 Executive Office of the US President. 2017. "Executive Order 13768: Enhancing Public Safety in the Interior of the United States," January 25. Accessed December 2, 2024. www.govinfo.org.
14 Forte 2016. For a discussion of the term "emic," see Harris 1976.
15 Forte 2016, ix.
16 Forte 2016, ix.
17 Avison 1989, 109, referenced in Forte 2016, 1.
18 DOD (US Department of Defense, Joint Chiefs of Staff). 2007 "GL-11: Joint Special Operations Task Force Operations. Joint Publication 3–05.1," April 26. Referenced in Forte 2016, 1.
19 Forte, 2016, 2.

20 Forte, 2016, 2.
21 Forte, 2016, 3.
22 Forte 2016, 4.
23 Forte 2016, 6.
24 Forte 2016, 6.
25 Forte 2016, 6.
26 Forte 2016, 4–5.
27 Forte 2016, 7.
28 Forte 2016, 8.
29 Forte 2016, 8.
30 Forte 2016, 8.
31 Kobach 2005.
32 Kobach 2005, 181.
33 Kobach 2005, 181.
34 US Attorney General John Ashcroft quoted in Kobach 2005, 181.
35 8 U.S.C. 1357(g)(1)-(3), 2000.
36 Kobach 2005, 189.
37 Kobach 2005, 190.
38 Latour 1994; Haggerty and Ericson 2000.
39 Kobach 2005, 190.
40 ICE. 2008. "Customs Cross Designation: Partnering in Support of the ICE Investigative Mission," January 31. Accessed July 10, 2024. www.ice.gov.
41 19 U.S. Code §1401 (i)—Miscellaneous, "Officer of the Customs; Customs Officer."
42 For an ethnography of police officers deputized as customs officers through a 287(g) agreement in Nashville, Tennessee, see Armenta 2017.
43 GAO (US Government Accountability Office). 2021. "GAO-21-186: Immigration Enforcement: ICE Can Further Enhance Its Planning and Oversight of State and Local Agreements," January 27. Accessed July 10, 2024. www.gao.gov.
44 GAO. 2021. "GAO-21-186," 19.
45 GAO. 2021. "GAO-21-186," 19.
46 GAO. 2021. "GAO-21-186," 24.
47 GAO. 2021. "GAO-21-186," 24.
48 ICE. 2008. "Customs Cross Designation."
49 ICE. 2011. "Customs Cross Designation Program Extends ICE HSI Authorities to Law Enforcement Officers," June 19. Accessed July 10, 2024. www.ice.gov.
50 ICE. n.d. "Homeland Security Investigations." Accessed July 10, 2024. www.ice.gov.
51 ICE. 2024. "Leader of Human Smuggling Organization Pleads Guilty to Conspiracy to Transport Noncitizens for Profit Following HSI Sells Investigation," January 26. Accessed July 10, 2024. www.ice.gov.
52 See, for instance, Amy Larson, "Santa Cruz Police Chief Blasts Homeland Security over Secret ICE Raid." KSBW Action News, February 24, 2017. www.ksbw.com.
53 OAG (Office of New Jersey Attorney General). 2019. "Attorney General Law Enforcement Directive No. 2018–6 v.2.0: Directive Strengthening Trust Between Law

Enforcement and Immigrant Communities (Immigrant Trust Directive)." November 29, 2018, revised September 27, 2019. Accessed December 2, 2024. www.nj.gov.

54 ICE. 2014. "Customs Cross Designation Program Extends HSI Authorities to 26 PRPD Officers," June 3. Accessed July 10, 2024. www.ice.gov.
55 ICE. 2014. "Customs Cross Designation Program."
56 ICE. 2014. "Customs Cross Designation Program."
57 ICE. 2014. "Customs Cross Designation Program."
58 ICE. 2008. "ICE-led Operation Arrests 149 Gang Members, Associates in Multi-Agency Action," June 8. Accessed July 10, 2024. www.ice.gov.
59 ICE. 2008. "96 Street Gang Members and Associates Nabbed by ICE Operation Throughout New Jersey," June 22. Accessed July 10, 2024. www.ice.gov.
60 ICE. 2008. "ICE Fugitive Operations Teams Nab 104 Illegal Aliens Following a Five-Day Targeted Enforcement Action in the Carolinas and Georgia," November 25. Accessed July 10, 2024. www.ice.gov.
61 ICE. 2010. "ICE Agents Arrest 28 in New Mexico, Including Child Predator," August 30. Accessed July 10, 2024. www.ice.gov.
62 ICE. 2010. "ICE Agents Arrest 28 in New Mexico."
63 ICE. 2011. "Barrow, Newton and Walton Counties Next to Benefit from ICE Strategy to Use Biometrics to Identify and Remove Aliens Convicted of a Crime," February 15. Accessed July 10, 2024. www.ice.gov.
64 ICE. 2011. "Barrow, Newton and Walton Counties." Emphasis mine.
65 ICE. 2011. "2 LA-area Men Charged with Illegally Importing $2 Million in Counterfeit Disney Pins to Sell over the Internet," May 12. Accessed July 10, 2024. www.ice.gov.
66 Ibid. ICE. 2011. "2 LA-area Men Charged."
67 ICE. 2012. "ICE, Industry Partner to Combat Brand Theft," August 23. Accessed July 10, 2024. www.ice.gov.
68 ICE. 2012. "ICE, Industry Partner."
69 ICE. 2012. "ICE, Industry Partner."
70 ICE. 2012. "ICE, Industry Partner."
71 ICE. 2011. "ICE and International Partners Hold Conference in Colombia to Combat Transnational Criminal Organizations," November 22. Accessed July 10, 2024. www.ice.gov.
72 ICE. 2024. "Illicit Pathways Attack Strategy," May 14. Accessed July 10, 2024. www.ice.gov.
73 ICE. 2011. "ICE and International Partners Hold Conference."
74 ICE. 2024. "Illicit Pathways Attack Strategy."
75 ICE. 2011. "ICE and International Partners Hold Conference."
76 ICE. 2022. "HSI Expands Permanent Presence in Haiti to Combat Transnational Crime, Help Bring Security Through Ongoing Partnership," March 1. Accessed July 10, 2024. www.ice.gov.
77 ICE. 2014. "ICE Assists Philippine Law Enforcement in Arrest of 2 Pimps and Rescue of 21 Sex Trafficking Victims," January 15. Accessed July 10, 2024. www.ice.gov.
78 ICE. 2014. "ICE Assists Philippine Law Enforcement."

79 Hornberger 2011.
80 Fassin 2012, 1, 4.
81 ICE. 2015. "El Paso, Texas, Couple Sentenced to Federal Prison for Inducing Foreign or Interstate Travel for Prostitution," January 5. Accessed July 10, 2024. www.ice.gov.
82 ICE. 2015. "El Paso, Texas, Couple."
83 ICE. 2015. "El Paso, Texas, Couple."
84 ICE. 2015. "Departments of Homeland Security, Justice and Labor Announce Phase II of Anti-Trafficking Coordination Team Initiative," June 25. Accessed July 10, 2024. www.ice.gov.
85 ICE. 2015. "Departments of Homeland Security." Emphasis mine.
86 ICE. 2012. "HSI Arrests Man Who Allegedly Threatened to Kill Texas Police, Their Families," November 28. Accessed July 10, 2024. www.ice.gov.
87 ICE. 2012. "HSI Arrests Man."
88 ICE. 2013. "NM Felon Gang Member, Heroin Trafficker Sentenced to 57 Months in Prison," March 19. Accessed July 10, 2024. www.ice.gov.
89 ICE. n.d. "Border Enforcement Security Task Force (BEST)." Accessed July 10, 2024, www.ice.gov.
90 ICE. n.d. "Border Enforcement Security Task Force (BEST)."
91 ICE. n.d. "BEST in the Midwest: HSI Kansas City Establishes BEST Task Force." Accessed July 11, 2024. www.ice.gov.
92 ICE. 2013. "NM Felon Gang Member."
93 ICE. 2013. "NM Felon Gang Member."
94 ICE. 2015. "Puerto Rico Community Leaders to Form Second Nationwide ICE-Sponsored Citizens Academy," January 22. Accessed July 10, 2024. www.ice.gov.
95 ICE. 2015. "Puerto Rico Community Leaders."
96 ICE. 2015. "Puerto Rico Community Leaders."
97 ICE. 2015. "Puerto Rico Community Leaders." Emphasis mine.
98 Verdery 2013.
99 ICE. 2015. "Puerto Rico Community Leaders."
100 ICE. 2015. "Puerto Rico Community Leaders."
101 ICE. 2015. "Puerto Rico Community Leaders."
102 ICE. 2015. "ICE-DMV Partnership Combating Identity, Document Fraud," June 22. Accessed July 10, 2024. www.ice.gov.
103 ICE. 2015. "ICE-DMV Partnership."
104 ICE. 2015. "ICE-DMV Partnership."
105 ICE. 2015. "ICE-DMV Partnership."
106 Bolger and Santini 2018.
107 ICE. 2017. "Local Partnerships Key to Transnational Gang Investigations," November 16. Accessed July 10, 2024. www.ice.gov.
108 ICE. 2017. "Local Partnerships."
109 ICE. 2017. "Local Partnerships."
110 ICE. 2017. "Local Partnerships."
111 ICE. 2017. "Local Partnerships."

112 ICE. 2017. "Local Partnerships."
113 ICE. 2017. "Local Partnerships."
114 ICE. 2017. "Local Partnerships."
115 ICE. 2017. "Local Partnerships."
116 ICE. 2017. "Local Partnerships."
117 ICE. 2017. "Local Partnerships."
118 ICE. 2017. "ICE Newark Arrests 113 Criminal Targets in 5-Day Enforcement Surge," June 9. Accessed July 10, 2024. www.ice.gov.
119 ICE. 2017. "ICE Newark Arrests."
120 ICE. 2020. "ICE Joins Local Law Enforcement in Drive-By Shooting Investigation," September 30. Accessed July 10, 2024. www.ice.gov.
121 ICE. 2020. "ICE Joins Local Law Enforcement Emphasis mine.
122 ICE. 2022. "HSI, DHS Partners Establish Joint Coordination Center in Houston to Respond to Gulf Coast Maritime Threats," June 10. Accessed July 10, 2024. www.ice.gov.
123 ICE. 2022. "HSI, DHS Partners."
124 ICE. 2022. "HSI, DHS Partners."
125 ICE. 2022. "HSI, DHS Partners."
126 ICE. 2022. "HSI, DHS Partners."
127 See "Palantir Technologies Inc.—HSCETC-15-C-00001," Contract with ICE-HSI, May 11, 2015. www.ice.gov.
128 Tsing 2019, 150.
129 This global network is what Didier Bigo has referred to as the "ban-opticon." See Bigo 2008.
130 For an exploration of the emerging field of the anthropology of becoming, see Biehl and Locke 2017.

CHAPTER 2. FORCE MULTIPLICATION IN A SANCTUARY STATE

1 OAG (Office of New Jersey Attorney General). 2007. "Attorney General Law Enforcement Directive No. 2007–3," August 22. Accessed July 10, 2024. www.nj.gov.
2 ICE. 2016. "ICE New Jersey Recognizes Local Law Enforcement for Continued Support," February 1. Accessed July 10, 2024. www.ice.gov.
3 ICE. 2016. "ICE New Jersey Recognizes Local Law Enforcement."
4 ICE. 2016. "ICE New Jersey Recognizes Local Law Enforcement."
5 OAG. 2007. "Attorney General Law Enforcement Directive No. 2007–3." Emphasis mine.
6 For a technical and theoretical overview of how sanctuary city governments in the United States operate, see Mancina 2019a. For a thorough legal explanation of the various types of policies that govern the sanctuary-related mechanisms of local government agencies, see Lasch et al. 2018.
7 See Mancina 2016 for a detailed explanation of how the city and county of San Francisco accomplishes immigration enforcement assistance through the implementation of its sanctuary policies. For an explanation of the broad history of and

sociopolitical consequences of targeting individuals accused of and convicted of crimes for deportations under the auspices of sanctuary policies, see Paik 2017.
8. OAG. 2019. "Attorney General Law Enforcement Directive No. 2018–6 v.2.0: Directive Strengthening Trust Between Law Enforcement and Immigrant Communities (Immigrant Trust Directive)," November 29, 2018, revised September 27, 2019. Accessed July 10, 2024. www.nj.gov.
9. OAG. 2019. "Attorney General Law Enforcement Directive No. 2018–6 v.2.0."
10. OAG. 2019. "Attorney General Law Enforcement Directive No. 2018–6 v.2.0."
11. Bolger and Santini 2017.
12. OAG. 2019. "Attorney General Law Enforcement Directive No. 2018–6 v.2.0."
13. Samantha Hing, Patrick Johnson, Joseph F. Lin, Diana Woody, and Peter Mancina. 2022. "Cultivating Immigrant Trust in the Garden State: A Report on the Implementation of the New Jersey Immigrant Trust Directive." Center for Immigration Law, Policy, and Justice, Rutgers Law School. Accessed July 10, 2024. www.cilpj.org.
14. Gardner 2019.
15. TRAC (Syracuse University Transactional Records Access Clearinghouse). n.d. "ICE Removals-Under Secure Communities." Accessed July 10, 2024. https://trac.syr.edu.
16. TRAC. n.d. "ICE Removals-Under Secure Communities." Also see Hing et al. 2022. "Cultivating Immigrant Trust in the Garden State."
17. Houston and Lawrence-Weilmann 2016.
18. For in-depth studies of sanctuary values, ethics, and activities as they exist in private sector spaces, including sanctuary movements, see Coutin 1994; Cunningham 1998; Haro and Coles 2019; Mancina 2019a; Paik 2017; Perla and Coutin 2010. Also see Andrea J. Ritchie and Monique W. Morris. 2017. "Centering Black Women, Girls, Gender Nonconforming People and Fem(me)s in Campaigns for Expanded Sanctuary and Freedom Cities." National Black Women's Justice Institute. Accessed July 10, 2024. https://forwomen.org. For an examination of policing in a sanctuary city—San Francisco, California—as it intersects with national security discourses see Gardner 2014.

CHAPTER 3. CAPTURING MIGRANTS WITH POLICE BODY-WORN CAMERAS

1. See ICE. n.d. "Newsroom." Accessed March 15, 2024. www.ice.gov.
2. Mann, Nolan, and Wellman 2003; also CNN. 2019. "See Immigration Activist Shut Down Attempted ICE Arrest," March 30. Accessed March 15, 2024. https://edition.cnn.com.
3. See OAG. 2022. "Attorney General Law Enforcement Directive No. 2022–1; Update to Body Worn Camera Policy," January 19. Accessed March 15, 2025. www.nj.gov.
4. St. Louis, Saulnier, and Walby 2019.
5. Michael White. 2014. "Police Officer Body-Worn Cameras: Assessing the Evidence." Office of Community Oriented Policing Services. Accessed March 15, 2024. https://bja.ojp.gov.

6 Brown 2021.
7 US Department of Justice Office of Public Affairs. 2015. "Justice Department Awards Over $23 Million in Funding for Body Worn Camera Pilot Program to Support Law Enforcement Agencies in 32 States," September 21. Accessed March 15, 2024. www.justice.gov.
8 See OAG. 2022. "Attorney General Law Enforcement Directive No. 2022–1."
9 OAG. 2021. "Final BWC Award Amounts, 2021." Tabulated spreadsheet. Accessed March 15, 2024. www.nj.gov.
10 OAG. 2021. "Final BWC Award Amounts, 2021."
11 Gusterson 2004; Albro et al. 2012.
12 Stalcup and Hahn 2016.
13 Goold 2021.
14 Jones 2021; Goold 2021.
15 Foucault 1980.
16 Agamben 2006.
17 Agamben 2006, 14.
18 Agamben 2006, 14.
19 Agamben 2006, 15.
20 Henne and Harb 2021; Haggerty and Ericson 2000; Bud 2016.
21 Haggerty and Ericson 2000.
22 Haggerty and Ericson 2000, 611.
23 Poster 1990, 97.
24 This description emanates from Donna Haraway's notion of the "cyborg." See Haraway 1991; Haggerty and Ericson 2000.
25 Browne 2015, 109.
26 Browne 2015, 162.
27 Browne 2015, 162.
28 Henne and Harb 2021.
29 Jones 2021.
30 Henne and Harb 2021.
31 Taylor and Lee 2021.
32 Browne 2015, 55.
33 P. Shah. 2020. "ICE's EDDIE Program: How ICE Uses Biometric Scanner Tech to Amp Up Raids." Mijente and Just Futures Law. Accessed on March 15, 2024. www.justfutureslaw.org.
34 P. Shah. 2020. "ICE's EDDIE Program."

CHAPTER 4. PARKING AND STANDING IN THE STREET FOR ICE

1 I have changed the name of the police department, all personal names, and other identifying information for the individuals involved in the incident to maintain their anonymity.
2 Benjamin Township Police Department "CFS Redacted" for November 14, 2019.
3 Benjamin Township Police Department Incident Report. In author's possession.

CHAPTER 5. THE MORALITY OF SANCTUARY STYLE FORCE MULTIPLICATION

1. Humphris 2023.
2. Serin Houston and Olivia Lawrence-Weilman have astutely argued that sanctuary policies in the United States problematically utilize neoliberal logics in justifying their ends. Specifically, they valorize immigrants who make political economic and cultural contributions to American societies, take private and personal responsibility for their welfare, and are, in all popular senses, good and obedient workers, and use this as an explicit ground for protection from deportation assistance activities. To the contrary, those who jeopardize the political economic order through crime, who are not good workers, and who may undermine property relations, are legislated in sanctuary policy as subject to local deportation assistance. See Houston and Lawrence-Weilman 2016.
3. Mancina 2016.
4. For instances, see the opening paragraphs of OAG (Office of New Jersey Attorney General). 2019. "Attorney General Law Enforcement Directive No. 2018–6 v.2.0: Directive Strengthening Trust Between Law Enforcement and Immigrant Communities (Immigrant Trust Directive)." November 29, 2018, revised September 27, 2019. Accessed December 2, 2024. www.nj.gov.
5. For an extensive explanation of how this occurs, see Paik 2017.
6. Mancina 2016.
7. For a historical overview of the legal and discursive construction of immigrants as criminals, see Menjívar, Cervantes, and Alvord 2018.
8. Menjivar et al. 2018, 193; Houston and Lawrence-Weilmann 2016; Houston and Morse 2017.
9. Menjívar et al. 2018.
10. Mancina 2016.
11. Gansallo and Bernstein-Baker 2023.
12. Menjívar et al. 2018.
13. "Illegal Immigration Reform and Immigration Responsibility Act," 1996, www.uscis.gov.
14. Grable 1998.
15. For an explanation of some of the inconsistencies between the New Jersey Immigrant Trust Directive and the state's local law enforcement agencies, see Samantha Hing, Patrick Johnson, Joseph F. Lin, Diana Woody, and Peter Mancina. 2022. "Cultivating Immigrant Trust in the Garden State: A Report on the Implementation of the New Jersey Immigrant Trust Directive." Center for Immigration Law, Policy, and Justice, Rutgers Law School. Accessed July 10, 2024. www.cilpj.org, 26.
16. Mancina 2019b.
17. See Mancina 2016 for an exposition of how San Francisco Mayor Gavin Newsom used this reasoning to oppose amendments to the city's sanctuary ordinance in 2008.
18. Miles and Cox 2014.

19 Miles and Cox 2014.
20 Anthropologists have long studied the manifold manners in which people around the world form family ties and ties with others in their social world. Rather than taking the nuclear family model as a universal, they have studied how family organization, which defines the roles people play for others, does not only include those who share blood ties or marriage ties, but also those anthropologists call "fictive kin." Fictive kin are those considered to be a type of family member unrelated by blood or marriage. For a discussion of the manner in which law enforcement officers identify themselves with their colleagues in the law enforcement profession in terms of a quasi-familial fictive kin, see Figueroa and Mitchell Poole forthcoming. For a discussion of the relation of the ethnographer to the police in the course of ethnographic fieldwork that Beatrice Jauregui terms "ethnographic kin," see Jauregui 2017.

CHAPTER 7. THE AUTHORITY OF SANCTUARY POLICY

1 OAG. 2019. "Attorney General Law Enforcement Directive No. 2018–6 v.2.0: Directive Strengthening Trust Between Law Enforcement and Immigrant Communities (Immigrant Trust Directive)," November 29, 2018, revised September 27, 2019. Accessed July 10, 2024. www.nj.gov.
2 For an anthropological examination of "policy worlds," the political and discursive environments, including the policy "scaffoldings" in which policies can be said to live, to be referenced and enacted, see Shore, Wright, and Però 2011.
3 Shore et al. 2011.
4 Austin 1995: Lecture I.
5 Hart 1961.
6 Postema 2008.
7 Dworkin 1986, 176–190.
8 See video embedded in Hannan Adely. 2018. "New Jersey Cops Can't Bust Residents Over Immigration Status Under New State Rules," November 29, *USA Today Northjersey.com*. Accessed July 10, 2024. https://eu.northjersey.com.
9 OAG. 2019. "Attorney General Law Enforcement Directive No. 2018–6 v.2.0."
10 Bourdieu 1987.
11 Bourdieu 1987, 820.
12 Bourdieu 1987, 839.
13 Bourdeiu 1987, 844.
14 Hobbes 1929.
15 Title 2c: 39–4, "Possession of Weapons for Unlawful Purposes," New Jersey Code of Criminal Justice, New Jersey State Legislature, 2009, https://law.justia.com.
16 Title 2C:39–9, "Manufacture, Transport, Disposition and Defacement of Weapons and Dangerous Instruments and Appliances," New Jersey Revised Statutes, New Jersey Code of Criminal Justice, New Jersey Legislature, 2020, https://law.justia.com.
17 A bookie is someone who facilitates gambling by keeping a ledger and receiving and paying off gambling bets.

CONCLUSION

1. P.L. 2023, Chapter 262, Title 34. Chapter 11. Article 5, "Domestic Workers' Wage Protections and Workplace Rights, §§1,2,13–23, C.34:11–69 to 34:11–81 §24.
2. See section 5.B, OAG. 2019. "Attorney General Law Enforcement Directive No. 2018–6 v.2.0: Directive Strengthening Trust Between Law Enforcement and Immigrant Communities (Immigrant Trust Directive)," November 29, 2018, revised September 27, 2019. Accessed July 10, 2024. www.nj.gov.
3. OAG. 2019. "Attorney General Law Enforcement Directive No. 2018–6 v.2.0."
4. Immigrant Legal Resource Center. 2019. "Growing the Resistance: How Sanctuary Laws and Policies Have Flourished During the Trump Administration." Accessed July 10, 2024. www.ilrc.org.

METHODOLOGY

1. New Jersey State Legislature. 2001. Open Public Records Act, P.L. 2001, Chapter 404, N.J.S. 47:1A-1 et seq.
2. Marcus 1995.
3. Feldman 2011.
4. Glick Schiller and Çağlar 2011, 2018.
5. Police ethnographer Matthew Bacon has suggested that during times of "exceptional circumstances" such as during COVID-19 pandemic shelter-in-place orders from 2021 to 2023, police ethnographers who cannot conduct in situ participant observation with police look to types of remote research, including the review of BWC videos. Though the current study was carried out prior to having read Bacon's article suggesting this, and not because exceptional circumstances limited the researcher but because the method illuminated *more* than in situ participant observation even in times not marked by exceptional circumstances, I agree with Bacon's suggestion and aim here to demonstrate that Bacon is correct in his assessment that BWC research is a viable alternative to participant observation. See Bacon 2023.
6. Jauregui 2016.
7. San Francisco Police Department. 2017. "Department General Order 5.15: Enforcement of Immigration Laws." Accessed July 9, 2024. www.sanfranciscopolice.org.
8. Goffman 1959.
9. Nader 2018, 16; also see Hannerz 2006.
10. Nader 2018, 12.
11. Nader 2018, 16.
12. Bourdieu 1977.
13. Nader 2018, 20.
14. Jauregui 2016.
15. For foundational police ethnographies see Banton 1964; Bittner 1970, 1974; Klockars 1980; Manning 1977, 1980; Manning and Van Maanen 1978; Skolnick 1966; Van Maanen 1973; 1978, 1981.

16 For a particularly illuminating "insider" police ethnography wherein the researcher became a sworn police officer and patrolled one of the most dangerous districts of Baltimore for a year, see Moskos 2009.
17 Jackson 2023; Pearson and Werren 2023; De Leon 2015.
18 Jackson 2023; Fassin 2013; Rios 2020; Holmes 2013; De Leon 2015.
19 Ralph 2019.
20 Bonilla and Rosa 2015.
21 Bonilla and Rosa 2015, 7.
22 Jauregui 2018.
23 Verdery 2013.
24 Verdery 2018.
25 Price 2004.
26 Price 2004, xi.
27 Knoblauch and Tuma 2024, 165.
28 Knoblauch and Tuma 2024.
29 Knoblauch and Tuma 2024.
30 De Leon 2015.
31 Goodwin 1994.
32 Gusterson 2016.
33 Gusterson 2021, 245.
34 Gusterson 2021, 245.
35 Gusterson 2021, 3.
36 Gusterson 2016, 146.
37 Gusterson 2016, 46–47.
38 Gusterson 2016, 47.
39 Gusterson 2021, 62.
40 Gusterson 2016, 66.
41 Gusterson 2016, 71.
42 Though separate from "empty time" as I describe it here, Didier Fassin brilliantly describes not only his fieldworker experience with the elite French anti-crime police squad as one of surprising boredom, but also that the police work itself is primarily composed of moments of boredom. See Fassin 2013, 2017. Also see Rowe 2021.
43 For thorough analyses of the manner in which anthropology and military projects have co-constituted one another, see Fosher 2021; McFate 2018; and Price 2011.
44 Mann, Nolan, and Wellman 2003, 332.
45 Mann et al. 2003.
46 Steve Mann. 2013. "Veillance and Reciprocal Transparency: Surveillance Versus Sousveillance, AR Glass, Lifelogging, and Wearable Computing," Conference paper, *IEEE International Symposium on Technology and Society*. DOI:10.1109/ISTAS.2013.6613094.
47 Mann et al. 2003, 337.

48 For a description of Jeremy Bentham's conceptualization of the "panopticon," see Bentham 1838.
49 Mann 2014, 42.
50 Strickland and Schlesinger 1969; Williams 2023.
51 Price 2008, 2011, 2016.
52 Mann et al. 2003, 338, 347.
53 Fassin 2023, 623.
54 Loftus, Goold, and Giollabhui 2023, 455.
55 Loftus, Goold, and Giollabhui 2023, 455.
56 Loftus et al. 2023, 457.
57 Jackson 2023.
58 Scott 1999.
59 Holmes and Marcus 2007.

REFERENCES

Agamben, Giorgio. 2006. *What Is an Apparatus? And Other Essays.* Stanford University Press.

Ahranjani, Maryam. 2018. "Universities as 'Sanctuaries.'" *The Journal of College and University Law* 44(1): 1–21.

Akarsu, Hayal. 2018. "Proportioning Violence: Ethnographic Notes on the Contingencies of Police Reform in Turkey." *Anthropology Today* 34(1): 11–14.

Akarsu, Hayal. 2020. "Citizen Forces: The Politics of Community Policing in Turkey." *American Ethnologist* 47(1): 27–42.

Albro, Robert, George Marcus, Laura A. McNamara, and Monica Schoch-Spana. 2012. "Introduction." In *Anthropologists in the Securityscape: Ethics, Practice, and Professional Identity*, edited by Robert Albro, George Marcus, Laura A. McNamara, Monica Schoch-Spana, 7–13. Routledge.

Armenta, Amada. 2017. *Protect, Serve, and Deport: The Rise of Policing as Immigration Enforcement.* University of California Press.

Austin, John. 1995 (1832). *The Province of Jurisprudence Determined*, edited by Wilfrid E. Rumble. Cambridge University Press.

Avison, John. 1989. *The World of Physics.* Cheltenham, UK: Thomas Nelson and Sons Ltd.

Bacon, Matthew. 2023. "Police Ethnography in Exceptional Circumstances." In *Routledge International Handbook of Police Ethnography*, edited by Jenny Fleming and Sarah Charmin, 373–390. Routledge.

Bagelman, Jennifer. 2013. "Sanctuary: A Politics of Ease?" *Alter-natives* 38(1): 49–62.

Bagelman, Jennifer. 2016. *Sanctuary City: A Suspended State.* Palgrave.

Banton, Michael. 1964. *The Policeman in the Community.* Tavistock.

Bauder, Harald. 2013. "Domicile Citizenship, Human Mobility and Territoriality." *Progress in Human Geography* 38(1): 91–106.

Bentham, Jeremy. 1838. *The Collected Works.* Athlone Press.

Biehl, João and Peter Locke, eds. 2017. *Unfinished: The Anthropology of Becoming.* Duke University Press.

Bigo, Didier. 2008. "Globalized (In)security: The Field and the Ban-Opticon." In *Terror, Insecurity and Liberty: Illiberal Practices in Liberal Regimes After 9/11*, edited by Didier Bigo and Anastassia Tsoukala, 20–58. Routledge.

Bittner, Egon. 1970. *The Functions of the Police in Modern Society: A Review of Background Factors, Current Practices, and Possible Role Models.* National Institute of Mental Health.

Bittner, Egon. 1974. "Florence Nightingale in Pursuit of Willie Sutton: A Theory of the Police." In *The Potential for Reform of Criminal Justice*, edited by Herbert Jacob, 233–268. Sage.

Bolger, Ray and Michael Santini. 2018. *Operation Devilhorns: The Takedown of MS-13 in San Francisco*. Rowman & Littlefield.

Bonilla, Yarimar and Jonathan Rosa. 2015. "#Ferguson: Digital Protest, Hashtag Ethnography, and the Racial Politics of Social Media in the United States." *American Ethnologist* 42(1): 4–17.

Bourdieu, Pierre. 1977. *Outline of a Theory of Practice*. Cambridge University Press.

Bourdieau, Pierre. 1987. "The Force of Law: Toward a Sociology of the Juridical Field." *Hastings Law Journal* 38(5): 814–853.

Bozniak, Linda. 2019. "Protection: Sanctuary and the Contested Ethics of Presence in the United States." In *Deepening Divides: How Territorial Borders and Social Boundaries Delineate Our World*, edited by Didier Fassin, 148–166. Pluto Press.

Brady, Katlyn. 2017. "Sanctuary Cities and the Demise of the Secure Communities Program." *Texas Hispanic Journal of Law and Policy* 23, 21–50.

Browne, Simone. 2015. *Dark Matters: On the Surveillance of Blackness*. Duke University Press.

Brown, Gregory R. 2021. "Police Body-Worn Cameras in the Canadian Context: Policing's New Visibility and Today's Expectations for Police Accountability." In *Police on Camera: Surveillance, Privacy, and Accountability*, edited by Bryce Clayton Newell, 122–148. Routledge.

Bud, Thomas K. 2016. "The Rise and Risks of Police Body-Worn Cameras in Canada." *Surveillance & Society* 14(1): 117–121.

Cade, Jason A. 2018. "Sanctuaries as Equitable Delegation in an Era of Mass Immigration Enforcement." *Northwestern University Law Review* 113(3): 433–504.

Collingwood, Loren and Benjamin Gonzalez O'Brien. 2019. *Sanctuary Cities: The Politics of Refuge*. Oxford University Press.

Coutin, Susan. 1994. "Enacting Law through Social Practice: Sanctuary as a Form of Resistance." In *Contested States, Law, Hegemony, and Resistance*, edited by Mindie Lazarus-Black and Susan F. Hirsch, 282–303. Routledge.

Coutin, Susan and Walter Nicholls. 2023. "Admigration: City-Level Governance of Immigrant Community Members." *Law and Social Inquiry*, 1–30.

Cuison-Villazor, Rose. 2008. "What Is a Sanctuary?" *Southern Methodist University Law Review* 61(1): 133–156.

Cuison-Villazor, Rose. 2010. "Sanctuary Cities and Local Citizenship." *Fordham Urban Law Journal* 37: 573–598.

Cuison-Villazor, Rose and Pratheepan Gulasekaram. 2018. "Sanctuary Networks." *Minnesota Law Review* 103: 1209–1283.

Cunningham, Hillary. 1998. "Sanctuary and Sovereignty: Church and State along the U.S.-Mexico Border." *Journal of Church and State* 40(2): 371–386.

Darling, Jonathan. 2019. "Sanctuary, Presence, and the Politics of Urbanism." In *Sanctuary Cities and Urban Struggles: Rescaling Migration, Citizenship, and Rights*, edited by Jonathan Darling and Harald Bauder, 242–264. Manchester University Press.

Das, Sonia N. and Hyemin Lee. 2024. "Racial Optics of Escalation." *Current Anthropology* 65(3): 481–502.

de Graauw, Els. 2014. "Municipal ID Cards for Undocumented Immigrants: Local Bureaucratic Membership in a Federal System." *Politics and Society* 42(3): 309–330.

De Leon, Jason. 2015. *The Land of Open Graves: Living and Dying on the Migrant Trail*. University of California Press.

Dworkin, Ronald. 1986. *Law's Empire*. Harvard University Press.

Fassin, Didier. 2012. *Humanitarian Reason: A Moral History of the Present*. University of California Press.

Fassin, Didier. 2013. *Enforcing Order: An Ethnography of Urban Policing*. Polity Press.

Fassin, Didier. 2017. "Boredom: Accounting for the Ordinary in the Work of Policing." In *Writing the World of Policing: The Difference Ethnography Makes*, edited by Didier Fassin, 269–292. Chicago: University of Chicago Press.

Fassin, Didier. 2023. "Blow Up: Ethnography as Exposure." In *Routledge International Handbook of Police Ethnography*, edited by Jenny Fleming and Sarah Charman, 610–625. Routledge.

Feldman, Gregory. 2011. "If Ethnography Is More than Participant Observation, then Relations Are More than Connections: The Case for Nonlocal Ethnography in a World of Apparatuses." *Anthropological Theory* 11(4): 375–395.

Figueroa, Alexandra Noel and Jared Mitchell Poole. Forthcoming. "#BlueBloods: Fictive Kinship, and Unethical Pro-Organizational Behavior in Police Organizations." *Academy of Management Proceedings*.

Forte, Maximilian C. 2016. *Force Multipliers: The Instrumentalities of Imperialism*. Alert Press.

Fosher, Kerry B. 2021. "Cultural Anthropological Practice in US Military Organizations." *Oxford Research Encyclopedia of Anthropology*, https://doi.org/10.1093/acrefore/9780190854584.013.232

Foucault, Michel. 1980. "The Confession of the Flesh." In *Power/Knowledge: Selected Interviews and Other Writings, 1972–1977*, edited by Colin Gordon, 194–228. Pantheon.

Fox, Cybelle. 2023. "Rethinking Sanctuary: The Origins of Non-cooperation Policies in Social Welfare Agencies." *Law and Social Inquiry* 48(1): 175–204.

Gansallo, Ayodele and Judith Bernstein-Baker. 2023. *Understanding Immigration Law and Practice*. Aspen.

Gardner, Trevor George. 2014. "The Safest Place: Immigrant Sanctuary in the Homeland Security Era." PhD diss., University of California, Berkeley.

Gardner, Trevor George. 2019. "Immigrant Sanctuary as the Old Normal: A Brief History of Police Federalism." *Columbia Law Review* 119(1): 1–84.

Glick Schiller, Nina and Ayşe Çağlar. 2011. *Locating Migration: Rescaling Cities and Migrants*. Cornell University Press.

Glick Schiller, Nina and Ayşe Çağlar. 2018. *Migrants and City-Making: Dispossession, Displacement, and Urban Regenerations*. Duke University Press.

Goetschel, Max and Jon M. Peha. 2017. "Police Perceptions of Body-Worn Cameras." *American Journal of Criminal Justice* 42(4): 698–726.

Goffman, Erving. 1959. *The Presentation of Self in Everyday Life*. Doubleday.

Goodwin, Charles. 1994. "Professional Vision." *American Anthropologist* 96(3): 606–633.

Goold, Benjamin J. 2021. "Not Just about Privacy: Police Body-Worn Cameras and the Costs of Public Area Surveillance." In *Police on Camera: Surveillance, Privacy, and Accountability*, edited by Bryce Clayton Newell, 167–181. Routledge.

Grable, David M. 1998. "Personhood Under the Due Process Clause: A Constitutional Analysis of the Illegal Immigration Reform and Immigration Responsibility Act of 1996." *Cornell Law Review* 83: 820–866.

Gusterson, Hugh. 2004. *People of the Bomb: Portraits of America's Nuclear Complex*. University of Minnesota Press.

Gusterson, Hugh. 2016. *Drone: Remote Control Warfare*. MIT Press.

Gusterson, Hugh. 2021. "Studying Up: Four Modalities, Two Challenges." *Public Anthropologist* 3: 232–252.

Haggerty, Kevin D. and Richard V. Ericson. 2000. "The Surveillant Assemblage." *British Journal of Sociology* 51(4): 605–622.

Hannerz, Ulf. 2006. "Studying Down, Up, Sideways, Through, Backwards, Forwards, Away and at Home: Reflections on the Field Worries of an Expansive Discipline." In *Locating the Field: Space, Place, and Context in Anthropology*, edited by Simon Coleman and Peter Collins, 23–42. Berg.

Haraway, Donna. 1988. "Situated Knowledges: The Science Question in Feminism and the Privilege of Partial Perspective." *Feminist Studies* 14(3): 575–599.

Haraway, Donna. 1991. *Simians, Cyborgs and Women: The Reinvention of Nature*. Routledge.

Haro, Lia and Romand Coles. 2019. "Reimagining Fugitive Democracy and Transformative Sanctuary with Black Frontline Communities in the Underground Railroad." *Political Theory* 47(5): 646–673.

Harris, Marvin. 1976. "History and Significance of the Emic/Etic Distinction." *Annual Review of Anthropology* 5: 329–350.

Hart, Herbert. 1961. *The Concept of Law*. Clarendon Press.

Henne, Kathryn and Jenna Harb. 2021. "Reading the Body-Worn Camera as Multiple: A Reconsideration of Entities as Enactments." In *Police on Camera: Surveillance, Privacy, and Accountability*, edited by Bryce Clayton Newell, 48–62. Routledge.

Hermansson, Linus, Anna Lundberg, and Sabine Gruber. 2022. "Firewalls: A Necessary Tool to Enable Social Rights for Undocumented Migrants in Social Work." *International Social Work* 65(4): 678–692.

Hobbes, Thomas. 1929 [1651]. *Leviathan*. Clarendon Press.

Holmes, Douglas R. and George E. Marcus. 2007. "Cultures of Expertise and the Management of Globalization: Toward the Re-functioning of Ethnography." In *Global Assemblages: Technology, Politics, and Ethics as Anthropological Problems*, edited by Aihwa Ong and Stephen J. Collier, 235–252. Blackwell.

Holmes, Seth. 2013. *Fresh Fruit, Broken Bodies: Migrant Farmworkers in the United States*. University of California Press.

Hornberger, Julia. 2011. *Policing and Human Rights: The Meaning of Violence and Justice in the Everyday Policing of Johannesburg*. Routledge.

Houston, Serin and Olivia Lawrence-Weilmann. 2016. "The Model Migrant and Multiculturalism: Analyzing Neoliberal Logics in US Sanctuary Legislation." In *Migration Policy and Practice: Interventions and Solutions*, edited by Harald Bauder and Christian Matheis, 101–126. Palgrave Macmillan Press.

Houston, Serin and Charlotte Morse. 2017. "The Ordinary and Extraordinary: Producing Migrant Inclusion and Exclusion in US Sanctuary Movements." *Studies in Social Justice* 11(1): 27–47.

Hoye, J. Matthew. 2020. "Sanctuary Cities and Republican Liberty." *Politics and Society* 48(1): 67–97.

Humphris, Rachel. 2023. "Sanctuary City as Mobilizing Metaphor: How Sanctuary Articulates Urban Governance." *Journal of Ethnic and Migration Studies* 49(14): 3585–3601.

Jackson, Will. 2023. "Critical Ethnography and the Study of Policing from 'the Other Side.'" In *Routledge International Handbook of Police Ethnography*, edited by Jenny Fleming and Sarah Charman, 335–352. Routledge.

Jauregui, Beatrice. 2016. *Provisional Authority: Police, Order, and Security in India*. University of Chicago Press.

Jauregui, Beatrice. 2017. "Intimacy: Personal Policing, Ethnographic Kinship, and Critical Empathy (India)." In *Writing the World of Policing: the Difference Ethnography Makes*, edited by Didier Fassin, 62–90. University of Chicago Press.

Jauregui, Beatrice. 2018. "Police Unions and the Politics of Democratic Security and Order in Postcolonial India." *Qualitative Sociology* 41: 145–172.

Jones, Richard. 2021. "Theorizing Police Body-Worn Cameras." In *Police on Camera: Surveillance, Privacy, and Accountability*, edited by Bryce Clayton Newell, 38–47. Routledge.

Klockars, Carl. 1980. "The Dirty Harry Problem." *The Annals of the American Academy of Political and Social Science* 452: 33–47.

Knoblauch, Hubert and René Tuma. 2024. "Videography and Space." In *Handbook of Qualitative and Visual Methods in Spatial Research*, edited by Anna Juliane Heinrich, Séverine Marguin, Angela Million, and Jörg Stollman, 165–176. Bielefeld: Transcript.

Kobach, Kris W. 2005. "The Quintessential Force Multiplier: The Inherent Authority of Local Police to Make Immigration Arrests." *Albany Law Review* 69(1): 179–236.

Lai, Annie and Christopher N. Lasch. 2017. "Crimmigration Resistance and the Case of Sanctuary City Defunding." *Santa Clara Law Review* 57(3): 539–610.

Lasch, Christopher N., R. Linus Chan, Ingrid V. Eagly, Dina Francesca Haynes, Annie Lai, Elizabeth McCormick, and Juliet Stumpf. 2018. "Understanding 'Sanctuary Cities.'" *Boston College Law Review* 59: 1703–1774.

Latour, Bruno. 1994. "On Technical Mediation—Philosophy, Sociology, Genealogy." *Common Knowledge* 3(2): 29–64.

Lenard, Patti Tamara. 2022. "Sanctuary as Democratic Non-Cooperation." *Politics, Philosophy, and Economics* 2(3): 291–312.

Lippert, Randy. 2006. *Sanctuary, Sovereignty, Sacrifice: Canadian Sanctuary Incidents, Power, and Law*. University of British Columbia Press.

Lippert, Randy and Sean Rehaag, eds. 2013. *Sanctuary Practices in International Perspectives: Migration, Citizenship, and Social Movements*. Routledge.

Loftus, Bethan, Benjamin Goold, and Shane Mac Giollabhui. 2023. "Reflections on the Parallel Practices of Police Ethnographers and Covert Police." In *Routledge International Handbook of Police Ethnography*, edited by Jenny Fleming and Sarah Charman, 440–460. Routledge.

Mancina, Peter. 2013. "The Birth of a Sanctuary City: A History of Governmental Sanctuary in San Francisco." In *Sanctuary Practices in International Perspectives: Migration, Citizenship, and Social Movements*, edited by Randy Lippert and Sean Rehaag, 223–236. Routledge.

Mancina, Peter. 2016. "In the Spirit of Sanctuary: Sanctuary City Policy Advocacy and the Production of Sanctuary-power in San Francisco." PhD diss., Vanderbilt University.

Mancina, Peter. 2019a. "Sanctuary Cities and Sanctuary Power." In *Open Borders: In Defense of Free Movement*, edited by Reese Jones, 250–264. University of Georgia Press.

Mancina, Peter. 2019b. "Investigating and (Not) Disciplining Violations of Sanctuary City Laws." *Southern California Interdisciplinary Law Journal* 78(3): 641–660.

Mann, Itamar and Julia Mourão Permoser. 2022. "Floating Sanctuaries: The Ethics of Search and Rescue at Sea." *Migration Studies* 10(3): 442–463.

Mann, Steve. 2014. "Veillance: Beyond Surveillance, Dataveillance, Uberveillance, and the Hypocrisy of One-sided Watching." In *Uberveillance and the Social Implications of Microchip Implants: Emerging Technologies*, edited by M. G. Michael and Katina Michael, 32–45. IGI Global.

Mann, Steve, Jason Nolan, and Barry Wellman. 2003. "Sousveillance: Inventing and Using Wearable Computing Devices for Data Collection in Surveillance Environments." *Surveillance & Society* 1(3): 331–355.

Manning, Peter K. 1977. *Police Work: The Social Organization of Policing*. MIT Press.

Manning, Peter K. 1980. *The Narcs' Game: Organizational and Informational Limits on Drug Law Enforcement*. MIT Press.

Manning, Peter K. and John Van Maanen. 1978. *Policing: A View from the Street*. Goodyear Publishing.

Marcus, George. 1995. "Ethnography in/of the World System: The Emergence of Multi-Sited Ethnography." *Annual Review of Anthropology* 24: 95–117.

Marcus, George. 2011. "Multi-Sited Ethnography: Five or Six Things I Know about It Now." In *Multi-Sited Ethnography: Problems and Possibilities in the Translocation of Research Methods*, edited by Simon Coleman and Pauline von Hellermann, 16–32. Routledge.

Marcus, George and Fernando Mascarenhas. 2005. *Ocasião: The Marquis and the Anthropologist, a Collaboration*. AltaMira Press.

Marrow, Helen. 2012. "Deserving to a Point: Unauthorized Immigrants in San Francisco's Universal Access Healthcare Model." *Social Science and Medicine* 74: 846–854.

Martinez-Schuldt, Ricardo D. and Daniel E. Martinez. 2021. "Immigrant Sanctuary Policies and Crime-Reporting Behavior: A Multilevel Analysis of Reports of Crime Victimization to Law Enforcement, 1980 to 2004." *American Sociological Review* 86(1): 154–185.

McBride. Keally. 2009. "Sanctuary San Francisco: Recent Developments in Local Sovereignty and Spatial Politics." *Theory and Event* 12(4), http://muse.jhu.edu.

McFate, Montgomery. 2018. *Military Anthropology: Soldiers, Scholars, and Subjects at the Margins of Empire*. Hurst Publishers.

Menjívar, Cecilia. 2000. *Fragmented Ties: Salvadoran Immigrant Networks in America*. University of California Press.

Menjívar, Cecilia, Andrea Gómez Cervantes, and Daniel Alvord. 2018. "Two Decades of Constructing Immigrants as Criminals." In *Routledge Handbook on Immigration and Crime*, edited by Holly Ventura Miller and Anthony Peguero, 193–204. Routledge.

Miles, Thomas and Adam Cox. 2014. "Does Immigration Enforcement Reduce Crime? Evidence from 'Secure Communities.'" *Journal of Law and Economics* 57(4): 937–973.

Moskos, Peter. 2009. *Cop in the Hood: My Year Policing Baltimore's Eastern District*. Princeton University Press.

Mourão Permoser, Julia and Rainer Bauböck. 2023. "Spheres of Sanctuary: Introduction to Special Issue." *Journal of Ethnic and Migration Studies* 49(14): 3549–3565.

Nader, Laura. 2018 (1969). "Up the Anthropologist-Perspectives Gained from Studying Up." In *Contrarian Anthropology: The Unwritten Rules of Academia*, 12–32. Berghahn Books.

Nakassis, Constantine V. 2023a. "A Linguistic Anthropology of Images." *Annual Review of Anthropology* 52: 73–91.

Nakassis, Constantine V. 2023b. "Seeing, Being Seen, and the Semiotics of Perspective." *Ethos*, 2023, 1–19.

Ong Hing, Bill. 2011. "Immigration Sanctuary Policies: Constitutional and Representative of Good Policing and Good Public Policy." Research Paper No. 2012-03. *UC Irvine Law Review* 2(1): 247–312.

Ortner, Sherry. 2010. "Access: Reflections on Studying Up in Hollywood." *Ethnography* 11(2): 211–233.

Paik, A. Naomi. 2017. "Abolitionist Futures and the US Sanctuary Movement." *Race & Class* 59(2): 3–25.

Pearson, Geoff and Charmian Werren. 2023. "Policed Ethnography: Ethical and Practical Considerations Arising from Observations of Public Order Policing in Crowd

Situations." In *Routledge International Handbook of Police Ethnography*, edited by Jenny Fleming and Sarah Charman, 216–230. Routledge.

Peréz, Gina M. 2024. *Sanctuary People: Faith-Based Organizing in Latina/o Communities*. New York University Press.

Perla, Hector and Susan Bibler Coutin. 2010. "Legacies and Origins of the U.S.-Central American Sanctuary Movement." *Refuge* 26(1):7–19.

Postema, Gerald. 2008. "Conformity, Custom, and Congruence: Rethinking the Efficacy of Law." In *The Legacy of H.L.A. Hart: Legal, Political, and Moral Philosophy*, edited by Matthew H. Kramer, Claire Grant, Ben Colburn, and Antony Hatzistavrou, 45–66. Oxford University Press.

Poster, Mark. 1990. *The Mode of Information: Poststructuralism and Social Context*. University of Chicago Press.

Price, David. 2004. *Threatening Anthropology: McCarthyism and the FBI's Surveillance of Activist Anthropologists*. Duke University Press.

Price, David. 2008. *Anthropological Intelligence: The Deployment and Neglect of American Anthropology in the Second World War*. Duke University Press.

Price, David. 2011. *Weaponizing Anthropology*. AK Press.

Price, David. 2016. *Cold War Anthropology: The CIA, the Pentagon, and the Growth of Dual Use Anthropology*. Duke University Press.

Rabben, Linda. 2016. *Sanctuary and Asylum: A Social and Political History*. University of Washington Press.

Ralph, Laurence. 2019. *The Torture Letters: Reckoning with Police Violence*. University of Chicago Press.

Ridgley, Jennifer. 2008. "Cities of Refuge: Immigration Enforcement, Police, and the Insurgent Genealogies of Citizenship in U.S. Sanctuary Cities." *Urban Geography* 29(1): 53–77.

Ridgley, Jennifer. 2011. "Refuge, Refusal, and Acts of Holy Contagion: The City as a Sanctuary for Soldiers Resisting the Vietnam War." *ACME: An International Journal for Critical Geographies* 10(2): 189–214.

Rios, Jodi. 2020. *Black Lives and Spatial Matters: Policing Blackness and Practicing Freedom in Suburban St. Louis*. Cornell University Press.

Rowe, Michael. 2021. "Understanding the Quiet Times: The Role of Quiet Periods of 'Nothing Much Happening' in Police Work." *Journal of Contemporary Ethnography* 50(6): 751–774.

Scott, James. 1999. *Seeing Like a State: How Certain Schemes to Improve the Human Condition Have Failed*. Yale University Press.

Shear, Keith Spencer. 1998. "Constituting a State in South Africa: The Dialectics of Policing, 1900–1939." PhD diss., Northwestern University.

Shore, Chris, Susan Wright, and Davide Però. 2011. *Policy Worlds: Anthropology and the Analysis of Contemporary Power*. Berghahn.

Skolnick, Jerome. H. 1966. *Justice Without Trial: Law Enforcement in Democratic Society*. Macmillan.

Squire, Vicki and Jonathan Darling. 2013. "The 'Minor' Politics of Rightful Presence: Justice and Relationality in City of Sanctuary." *International Political Sociology* 7(1): 59–74.

Stalcup, Meg and Charles Hahn. 2016. "Cops, Cameras, and the Policing of Ethics." *Theoretical Criminology* 20(4): 482–501.

St. Louis, Ermus, Alana Saulnier, and Kevin Walby. 2019. "Police Use of Body-Worn Cameras: Challenges of Visibility, Procedural Justice, and Legitimacy." *Surveillance & Society* 17(3/4): 305–321.

Stierl, Maurice. 2020. "Of Migrant Slaves and Underground Railroads: Movement, Containment, Freedom." *American Behavioral Scientist* 64(4): 456–479.

Strickland, Donald A. and Lester E. Schlesinger. 1969. "'Lurking as a Research Method.'" *Human Organization* 28(3): 248–250.

Su, Rick. 2024. "Designing Sanctuary." *Michigan Law Review* 122(5): 809–865.

Sullivan, Laura. 2009. "Enforcing Nonenforcement: Countering the Threat Posed to Sanctuary Laws by the Inclusion of Immigration Records in the National Crime Information Center Database." *California Law Review* 97: 567.

Taylor, Emmeline and Murray Lee. 2021. "The Camera Never Lies?: Police Body-Worn Cameras and Operational Discretion." In *Police on Camera: Surveillance, Privacy, and Accountability*, edited by Bryce Clayton Newell, 80–94. Routledge.

Tsing, Anna. 2019. "On Nonscalability: The Living World Is Not Amenable to Precision-Nested Scales." *Common Knowledge* 25(1–3, April): 143–162.

Van Maanen, John. 1973. "Observations on the Making of Policemen." *Human Organization* 32(4): 407–418.

Van Maanen, John. 1978. "The Asshole." In *Policing: A View from the Street*, edited by Peter K. Manning and John Van Maanen, 307–328. Random House.

Van Maanen, John. 1981. "The Informant Game: Selected Aspects of Ethnographic Research in Police Organizations." *Urban Life* 9(4): 469–494.

Verdery, Katherine. 2013. *Secrets and Truths: Ethnography in the Archive of Romania's Secret Police*. Central European University Press.

Verdery, Katherine. 2018. *My Life as a Spy: Investigations in a Secret Police File*. Duke University Press.

Vitiello, Domenic. 2022. *The Sanctuary City: Immigrant, Refugee, and Receiving Communities in Postindustrial Philadelphia*. Cornell University Press.

Walia, Harsha. 2014. "Sanctuary City from Below: Dismantling the Colonial City of Vancouver." *The Mainlander*, June 2, http://themainlander.com.

Weber, Max. 2013 (1921). *Economy and Society*, edited by Guenther Roth and Claus Wittich. University of California Press.

Williams, Andy. 2023. "Lurking with Paedophile Hunters: Understanding Virtual Ethnography and Its Benefits for Policing Research." In *Routledge International Handbook of Police Ethnography*, edited by Jenny Fleming and Sarah Charman, 406–423. Routledge.

Wyn Edwards, Catrin and Verena Wisthaler. 2023. "The Power of Symbolic Sanctuary: Insights from Wales on the Limitations and Potential of a Regional Approach to Sanctuary." *Journal of Ethnic and Migration Studies* 49(14): 3602–3628.

INDEX

Page numbers in italics indicate tables.

abolish ICE, public calls to, 66
ACAP. *See* Alien Criminal Apprehension Program
ACLU, 188
ACT Teams. *See* Anti-Trafficking Coordination Teams
"adminigration" management, 10
administrative: civil immigration law as, 59; ICE warrants as, xvi, xvii, xix, xxii, 23, 30, 89, 98, 103, 117, 123, 140. *See also* arrests, noncriminal administrative
advocacy: immigrant rights, 64, 97–102, 104, 107, 120, 121–24, 127, 165, 194–95; legal representatives with, 90, 93–94, 97, 121–22; organizations, 187; self-, 121. *See also* lawyers
AEDPA. *See* Anti-Terrorism and Effective Death Penalty Act
"aerial policing," 206. *See also* drones
Agamben, Giorgio, 69–70
"aggravated felony," 111
Air and Marine, CBP, 41
Albuquerque Police Department, New Mexico, 42
Alien Criminal Apprehension Program (ACAP), 111
Alvord, Daniel, 110
American Association of Motor Vehicle Administrators, 44
Anaheim Police Department, California, 36
ankle bracelet, xiv, xviii, xx
anthropological camera, 204

anthropologists: as force multiplier, 214; McCarthy era and surveillance on, 202–3
anthropology, 209; BWCs as force multiplier for, 214–15; studying up and sideways, 197–98, 201, 214; surveillance, 214; surveillant, 4, 18, 212–16
Anti-Drug Abuse Act (1998), 111
Anti-Terrorism and Effective Death Penalty Act (AEDPA), 111
Anti-Trafficking Coordination Teams (ACT Teams), 40–42, 50
apparatus ("dispositif"), 69–70
Arika, Samuel (pseudonym), 129–51, 153
Aristotle, 156
Arizona, 47–48, 199
"armchair anthropology," 201
arrests, 3, 24, 73, 116, 193, 205; for airsoft gun at traffic stop, 171–76; sanctuary policing, traffic stops and, 144–45, 149–50; under S-COMM, 63–64
arrests, noncriminal administrative: children at, 87–92, 94, 96, 98, 102, 103, 104, 115–17, 119–20, 122; containment and co-optation of immigrant rights advocacy, 121–24; familial force multipliers, 119–21; law enforcement morality as force multiplier, 115–19; legal representatives and, 90, 93–94, 97, 121–22; police with BWCs at ICE, 87–102, 115–19, 124–25; potential viewer of BWC footage as force multiplier, 124–25; scene security as force multiplier, 17, 87, 88, 90, 96–101, 103–5, 113, 115, 116, 119, 123, 124

241

artificial intelligence, 72
Ashcroft, John, 28
Assembly, New Jersey, 187
Atlanta, Georgia, 40
Austin, John, 156
authority: power and, 153, 155, 156, 158, 163, 165, 168; state, 194, 198, 214. *See also* sanctuary policies, authority of
Automated Biometric Identification System (IDENT), DHS, 35
auxiliaries, xx, 15, 26, 183, 198, 214
awareness campaigns, 42–44
Axon, 75

background checks, criminal, xv, xvi, xviii, 22, 78, 174–715
backstage, 196, 208, 211, 216
Bacon, Matthew, 228n5
Baltimore, Maryland, 229n16
Benjamin Township Police Department (BDP) (pseudonym), New Jersey: BWCs at ICE noncriminal administrative arrest, 87–102, 115–19, 124–25; BWCs at traffic stop, 168–76; BWCs deactivated, 170, 173, 175; collegial relationship with ICE, 89, 95, 102, 120–21; with containment and co-optation of immigrant rights advocacy, 121–24; incident reports, 103–5, 176–79; scene security as force multiplier, 17, 87, 88, 90, 96–101, 103–5, 113, 115, 116, 119, 123, 124
BEST. *See* Border Enforcement Security Task Force
binary value systems, *109*, 109–10, 117–18, 182
Biometric Identification Transnational Migration Alert Program (BITMAP), 78–79
biometrics, 35, 71–72
BITMAP. *See* Biometric Identification Transnational Migration Alert Program

Black community, police torture and, 200
"blood feud," 6
"blue code of silence," 196
bodies: dark matter and, 71–72, 101; data doubles, 16, 70–71, 84–85; desert and disappeared, 199–200, 204; whiteness and, 71, 101. *See also* fingerprinting
body-worn cameras (BWCs), 65, 195; as anthropological force multiplier, 214–15; deactivating, xxvii, 68, 102, 151, 170, 173, 175; ethnographers, 207–12, 213; ethnography, 211, 214; history of, 68; at ICE noncriminal administrative arrest, 87–102, 115–19, 124–25; with police as videographer, 16, 67, 73, 76, 181, 208, 216; potential viewers of footage, 17, 94, 124–25, 209; surveillant anthropology with, 4, 18; at traffic stops, xi–xxvii, 129, 130–51, 168–76. *See also* videos, BWC
body-worn cameras (BWCs), capturing migrants: dark matter, 71–72; data doubles, 16, 70–71, 84–85; as force multipliers, 67, 70, 73–74, 84–85; ICE-HSI raids, 66, 73–84; with police as videographers, 67, 73, 76; view of police officers versus, 72–73; whiteness, 71
Bolger, Ray, 219n2
Bonilla, Yarimar, 200–201
bookies, 174, 227n17
Border Enforcement Security Task Force (BEST), 40–42
Border Patrol, US, 41, 48
borders: crossings, desert and death, 199–200, 204; US-Mexico, 40–42, 50, 77, 199. *See also* Customs and Border Protection
Bourdieu, Pierre, 162–64, 167
BPD. *See* Benjamin Township Police Department
bracelet, ankle, xiv, xviii, xx

INDEX | 243

branding: ICE, 43, 66, 116; with ICE agents "passing" as local police, 74–75, 76, 80, 88; immigration enforcement, 42–44, 62, 63, 66, 86; protection of corporate, 36–37; sanctuary policies, 58, 62, 63
Brown, Michael, 200
Brown, Scott, 48
Browne, Simone, 70–71, 74
Bruck, Andrew, 185, 186
budgets, 22, 27, 66, 68, 108, 185
"bureaucratic membership," for immigrants, 10
Bureau of Alcohol and Tobacco Firearms and Explosives, 41–42
Bureau of International Narcotics and Law Enforcement Affairs, Department of State, 37, 38
Bush, George H. W., 23
Bush, George W., 22
BWCs. *See* body-worn cameras

California, 11, 24, 25, 40, 226n17; Anaheim Police Department, 36; Los Angeles Police Department, 204–5; San Francisco Police Department, 45, 61, 114, 194, 219n2
California Values Act (SB54), 1, 187
Camden County, New Jersey, 68
cameras, 18, 49, 207; anthropological, 204; CCTVs, 68–69, 215; hidden, 208, 215, 216; sousveillant, 212; video, 105, 200, 203, 204. *See also* body-worn cameras; cell phone cameras; photographs; videos
Canada, 44
CBP. *See* Customs and Border Protection
CCH database. *See* Computerized Criminal History database
CCTVs. *See* closed-circuit cameras
cell phone cameras: photographs, 75, 77, 79, 80, 81, 82, 83, 176; video, 67, 68, 97, 99, 100, 104, 122, 212

Central America, 7, 171
Central Intelligence Agency (CIA), 205, 206
Cervantes, Andrea Gómez, 110
Chapman, Joe, 35, 37
"*Che cose un dispositivo?*" (What is an apparatus?) (Agamben), 69
Chicago Police Department, 200
children, 2, 43, 47, 60, 84, 123, 205; DACA, 186; as force multipliers, 17, 88–89, 120, 122; at ICE noncriminal administrative arrest, 87–92, 94, 96, 98, 102, 103, 104, 115–17, 119–20, 122; sex workers, 39
church, 2, 6, 7, 165
Church World Service, 6
CIA. *See* Central Intelligence Agency
Citizen Academies, 42–44
"City of Sanctuary," United Kingdom, 13
civil immigration law, 21, 59, 159–62
civil immigration operations enforcement: as federal mandate, xv, 108; guidelines, xv–xvi, 1–2, 3, 59, 61, 160, 161
civil rights, 31, 40
closed-circuit cameras (CCTVs), 68–69, 215
CNN, 67
Coast Guard, US, 41, 48
Cochise County Sheriff's Office, Arizona, 48
collaborators, 18–19, 25–27, 29, 89, 163, 186. *See also* force multipliers
Colombian National Police, 37, 38
Colorado, 11
commander in policy: as absent "speaker," 155; defined, 163–64; as emissary of sanctuary, 158–59; godlike authority and, 163, 165, 168; Immigrant Trust Directive, 17, 155–68; the sovereign and, 156–57
command theory of law, 156
community policing auxiliaries, 15

Community Response Team, Sierra Vista Police Department, 48
Computerized Criminal History (CCH) database, New Jersey, 174–75
Congress, US, 28, 110, 202–3, 205
Connecticut, 11
Conti, Bill (pseudonym), 171, 172–73
Cop in the Hood (Moskos), 229n16
counterfeit merchandise, 36
counties: crime data, 118; with sanctuary policies, 14, 188
court: criminal, xxii, 76, 83, 178–79; immigration, xv, xviii, xix, 5, 17, 22, 23, 29, 59, 67, 76, 94, 111, 125, 127, 176; juries watching videos in, 204–5; Pre-Trial Intervention Program, 179–80. *See also* judges
Coutin, Susan, 10
"coveillance," 214
COVID-19 pandemic, 228n5
Creech Air Force Base, Nevada, 205
crime, 15, 19, 36, 41, 44, 56, 60; ACAP, 111; criminal history, xix, xxii, 2, 70, 93, 110, 112, 128, 174–75, 187; Economic Crime Unit, 83–84; felonies, 2, 110, 111, 112; joint criminal/immigration control operations, 33, 66, 67, 73, 84, 85, 182, 188; NCIC, xv–xviii, xxii, 28–29, 50, 140, 181; rates, 14, 29, 118; TCIUs, 37–39, 50; transnational, 2, 32, 33, 37–38, 50; transnational gangs and, 45–48, 61; violent, 107
criminal aliens, 34–37, 50, 55, 111
criminal background: checks, xv, xvi, xviii, 22, 78, 174–715; with previous arrests, 93
criminal courts, xxii, 76, 83, 178–79
criminal immigrant narrative, 110, 112, 113, 116–17, 125, 182–83, 185
Criminal Investigations, IRS, 42
criminalization, of immigrants, 110, 111, 112
criminal warrants, xv, xxii, 76, 117

cross-designation authority, 30–32, 34, 54, 55
Cryan, Joseph, 187
custody transfers, 10, 14, 23, 24, 30, 118, 176, 180
Customs and Border Protection (CBP), US, 21, 22, 36, 50, 111, 112, 193; Air and Marine, 41; BEST and, 41; with border crossings, 199–200; with gangs and public safety, 45, 47; JIOCC and, 48, 49; New Jersey police and, 60–61, 63
customs laws, 21, 30, 32–34, 42
"cyborg," 225n24

DACA. *See* Deferred Action for Childhood Arrivals
dark matter, 71–72, 101
data: collection, 49–50; crime, 118; doubles, 16, 70–71, 84–85; mining, 49; "panoptic," 213; "raw unbiased," 72; sharing, 14, 35, 75; spatial arrangement, 70, 71
databases, 109, 110; CCH, 174–75; fingerprinting, 161; NCIC, xv, 140
death: AEDPA, 111; border crossings, desert and, 199–200, 204; killings, 68, 205, 206–7
Deferred Action for Childhood Arrivals (DACA, Dreamers), 186
De Graauw, Els, 10
De Leon, Jason, 199–200, 204
de-linking, of LEA from ICE, 15, 17, 126, 128, 184
Department of Defense, US, 26, 28, 42
Department of Homeland Security (DHS), US, 35, 103, 112. *See also* Homeland Security Investigations
Department of Justice: Puerto Rico, 42; US, xv, 40, 45
Department of Labor (DOL), US, 40
Department of Motor Vehicles (DMV), 44, 50, 177

INDEX | 245

Department of State, US, 37, 38, 202
Department of Treasury, US, 30, 32, 45
deportations, 9–10, 12, 33, 63–64, 74, 84; can or cannot assist, *109*; deservingness of, 93, 109, 125–26; detainer policies and, 23, 24–25; harmful consequences of, 5; reasons for, 2, 111–12
desert, death and border crossings, 199–200, 204
detainees, photographs of, 75, 77, 79, 80, 81, 82, 83, 176
detainers: ICE, 30, 47, 176, 193; policies, 23, 24–25
DHS. *See* Department of Homeland Security
"digital epidermalization," 70–71
disappeared bodies, desert and border crossings, 199–200, 204
"dispositif" (apparatus), 69–70
DMV. *See* Department of Motor Vehicles
documentation, ICE collaboration, 19
DOL. *See* Department of Labor
Domestic Workers Bill of Rights, New Jersey, 186
Donello, Chris (pseudonym), 73–78, 81–84
Dreamers. *See* Deferred Action for Childhood Arrivals
Drone (Gusterson), 205–7
drones, 205–9
Drug Enforcement Administration, US, 41, 54
drugs, 37, 38, 42–44, 111, 170–71
Dworkin, Ronald, 156

East Allen Township Police (pseudonym), New Jersey: as force divider from ICE, 141; sanctuary policing with traffic stop, 129–51, 153
Economic Crime Unit, New Jersey, 83–84
EDDIE (digital fingerprinting technology), 79–83
El Paso, Texas, 35, 40–42

El Salvador, 45
emissaries: of ICE, xx, 15, 44, 183; police as policy and law, 168–78, 180; sanctuary with commander in policy as, 158–59
emotions, 5, 6, 195, 206, 208–10. *See also* fear
empty time, 211, 229n42
enforcement, 3, 24, 30, 37, 38, 41; actions, 9, 31, 34, 36, 46, 52, 61, 86, 104, 121, 185; activities, 4, 22, 28, 31–32, 70, 105, 108, 117, 159; BEST, 40–42; branding of immigration, 42–44, 62, 63, 66, 86; immigration events, 16, 86, 116, 125, 181, 188, 216; Law Enforcement Directives, 54–57, 63, 65, 86, 153, 159; law enforcement morality as force multiplier, 115–19; LESC, xvii–xxiv, xxvi–xxvii, 28, 141; sanctuary policies on federal civil immigration law, 159–62. *See also* civil immigration operations enforcement; Immigrant Trust Directive; law enforcement agencies
Enforcement Removal Operations (ERO), ICE, 32–35, 40–41, 45, 47, 50, 55, 84
English as a second language, xi, 77, 194
Ericson, Richard, 70
ERO. *See* Enforcement Removal Operations
ethnographers: BWC, 207–12, 213; police, 211, 228n5
"ethnographic exposure," 214
"ethnographic kin," 227n20
ethnographic narratives, 18, 87, 210
ethnographies, 200–201, 204, 206, 211, 214; police, 198, 203, 229n16; remote, 205, 209, 228n5
"exigent circumstances," 95–96, 103, 182
exploitation, of police, 198
extrajudicial killings, 205

familial force multipliers, 119–21
family members: border crossings and missing, 199; as force multipliers, 17, 88–89, 119–22. *See also* children

family organization, fictive kin, 227n20
"family unity," value systems, 106
Fassin, Didier, 39, 214, 229n42
FBI. *See* Federal Bureau of Investigation
fear, 2, 5–6, 25, 45, 107, 157–59, 200, 205
Federal Bureau of Investigation (FBI), US, 22, 33, 40–42, 50, 78, 128, 202–3
federalism, police, 63
federal judges, 60, 158, 160, 161
felonies, 2, 110, 111, 112
Ferguson, Missouri, 200
fictive kin, 128, 212, 227n20
"Fighting Networks with Networks through Interregional Partnerships" conference (2022), 37–38
Figueroa, Mario Cabrera (pseudonym): arrest and investigation, 175–80; traffic stop, 169–76
Final Order of Removal, 60, 160, 161
fingerprinting, 22, 50, 77–83, 112, 161, 176–78
firearms, 32, 42, 43, 44, 111, 171–76
firewall sanctuary policies, 9, 127, 129
Flanagan, Brian (pseudonym), 168–70, 172–75
"flesh-technology-information amalgam," 70
Florida, 32, 40
force (divider) division, 18, 19; LEA and, 15, 17, 126, 128, 141, 168, 183–84; sanctuary policing as, 15, 17, 126–29, 141, 152, 184, 188
force multiplication tactics, 74–76, 80, 88, 111
force multipliers: ACT Teams and BEST at US-Mexico border, 40–42; anthropologists as, 214; BWCs as, 67, 70, 73–74, 84–85; BWCs as anthropological, 214–15; Citizen Academies, awareness campaigns and branding of immigration enforcement, 42–44; criminal aliens and fugitives, 34–37; with cross-designation, 30–32, 34, 54, 55; data doubles as, 16, 70–71, 84–85; desert as, 204; drones as, 207; ERO, 32–34; family members as, 17, 88–89, 119–22; HSI, 32–34, 36–48; ICE with police as, 180; Immigrant Trust Directive as, 54, 57–60, 97; industry surveillance partners and data collection, 49–50; informants as, 39, 47, 185; JIOCC, 48–49; law with police as, 180; LEA and ICE with sanctuary policing as, 15, 65, 185; local LEA as ICE, xix–xx, 3, 21–25, 28–31, 35–42, 44–52, 54–64, 67–68, 73–91, 93–101, 103–5, 112, 115–16, 119–24, 168, 176–77, 180–82, 184, 188; mechanisms, 27–50; nonsoels of modernity contrasted with, 51; "passing" as local police, 74–75; police videographers as, 16, 67, 73, 76, 181, 208, 216; police with ICE as, 180; public safety, 29, 42, 45–48, 51, 55, 64, 116, 122–24, 181, 182; researchers as, 216; sanctuary policies as, 54, 64–65, 184–88; scene security as, 17, 87, 88, 90, 96–101, 103–5, 113, 115, 116, 119, 123, 124, 181, 183; S-COMM with, 22–25, 30, 35, 45, 50, 53; TCIUs and global network building, 37–39; Title 19, 30, 32; transnational gangs, 45–48; 287(g) agreements, 30–32; US military concept of, 3, 25–27, 50
force multipliers, morality of sanctuary style: containment and co-optation of immigrant rights advocacy, 121–24; deportations, can or cannot assist, *109*; familial, 119–21; law enforcement as, 115–19; potential viewer of BWC footage as, 124–25
"The Force of Law" (Bourdieu), 162–63
Forte, Maximilian, 25–27

INDEX | 247

Foucault, Michel, 69
Freedom of Information Act, 202
Freeman Township Police (pseudonym), New Jersey, BWCs at ICE-HSI raid, 66, 73–84
frontstage, of policing, 196, 211
Fugitive Operation Support Center, ICE, 34, 35
Fugitive Operation Teams, ICE, 35, 47
fugitives, 7, 34–37, 47

gangs, 29, 38, 45–48, 50, 61
GAO. *See* Government Accountability Office
Gardner, Trevor, 63
gender, 7, 26
Georgia, 35, 37, 40
God, 163, 165, 168, 207
Goffman, Erving, 196, 211
Goodwin, Charles, 204
Goold, Benjamin, 69, 215
governance, 4, 31, 39, 69, 189
government, 9–10, 11, 21, 26
Government Accountability Office (GAO), US, 31
Grewal, Gurbir, 154–55, 186; with Immigrant Trust Directive, xi, xvi, xvii, 1–2, 17, 54, 57–59, 63, 66, 86, 129, 153, 157–58, 165, 166; news media and, 157–58, 162; with US Securities and Exchange Commission, 185
guns, airsoft, 171–76. *See also* firearms
Gusterson, Hugh, 205–7, 212

habeas corpus rights, 23
Haggerty, Kevin, 70
Haraway, Donna, 225n24
Hart, H. L. A., 156
"hashtag ethnography," 200–201
Hebraic Cities of Refuge, 6, 183
Hernandez, Tom, 40
Herrera-Niles, Dorothy, 35
Hobbes, Thomas, 156, 163

Homeland Security Investigations (HSI), ICE: ACT Teams, 40–42, 50; BEST, 41, 42; with Citizen Academies, 42–44; force multipliers, 32–34, 36–48; with gangs and public safety, 45–48; IBFU, 44; JIOCC and, 48; with joint criminal/immigration control operations, 33, 66, 67, 73, 84, 85, 182, 188; Operation Devil Horns and, 45, 219n2; with "police" vests, 74, 75, 76, 80; raids, 66, 73–84; TCIUs, 37–39, 50
home raids, 49, 75, 83–84
hospitality, sanctuary and, 7–8, 13
Houston, Serin, 226n2
Houston, Texas, 48
HSI. *See* Homeland Security Investigations
Hudson, Roderick, 49
Hudson County, New Jersey, 55
human rights, 107, 108
human trafficking, 21, 29, 32, 39–40, 66, 75, 80, 182
Humphris, Rachel, 13

IBFU. *See* Identity and Benefit Fraud Unit
ICE. *See* Immigration and Customs Enforcement
IDENT. *See* Automated Biometric Identification System
identification, 3, 31, 44, 83, 146–47, 175, 195; BITMAP, 78–79; "digital epidermalization" and, 70–71; IDENT, 35; ITIN, 140–41, 178, 187; ORI, xvii; at traffic stops, xii, xviii, 58, 132–39, 143; TTIN, 177
Identity and Benefit Fraud Unit (IBFU), ICE-HSI, 44
Illegal Immigration Reform and Immigration Responsibility Act (IIRAIRA), 111–12
Illinois, 11
"illocutionary force," 93
Immigrant Legal Resource Center, 13, 14

immigrants, 2, 10, 111, 187; as criminals, 110, 112, 113, 116–17, 125, 182–83, 185; as informants, 15, 65, 185; rights, 12, 22–24, 64, 97, 106, 120–24, 127, 165, 189

Immigrant Trust Directive (Law Enforcement Directive 2018-6), New Jersey, 4; California Values Act and, 1, 187; commander in policy, 17, 155–68; on enforcement of federal civil immigration law, 159–62; exceptions to, 33, 60, 61–62, 91, 93, 113, 117, 161–62; "exigent circumstances," 95–96, 103; as force multiplier, 54, 57–60, 97; Grewal and, xi, xvi, xvii, 1–2, 17, 54, 57–59, 63, 66, 86, 129, 153, 157–58, 165, 166; historical context and reasons for, 159; police with, 3, 58–64, 90–91, 93, 99–101, 103–4, 114–15, 134, 140–41, 145; police with violation of, xvi–xvii, 62–63, 100–101, 103, 114, 123–24, 195; policy intent, xi, 1–2, 54, 59, 154–55, 157–58; reporting requirements for ICE collaboration, 19, 186; training, 129, 153, 186–87; value systems for, 106–7, 110, 113

immigration: civil immigration law, 21, 59, 159–62; court, xv, xviii, xix, 5, 17, 22, 23, 29, 59, 67, 76, 94, 111, 125, 127, 176; criminal/immigration raids, 33, 66; sanctuary in context of, 4–5. *See also* civil immigration operations enforcement

Immigration and Customs Enforcement (ICE), US, xi, xvi, 3, 21, 50, 56–57, 66. *See also specific topics*

Immigration and Nationality Act (INA), 28, 33

Immigration and Naturalization Service (INS), US, 111–12

immigration enforcement events, 16, 86, 116, 125, 181, 188, 216. *See also* arrests, noncriminal administrative; raids; traffic stops

Immigration Reform and Control Act (IRCA), 110–11

improvisational decisions, 16–17, 72, 113, 168

INA. *See* Immigration and Nationality Act

in absentia ("in their absence"), xv, xviii, xix

India, 198, 201

Individual Taxpayer Identification Number (ITIN), 140–41, 178, 187

informants, 15, 52, 65, 216; as force multipliers, 39, 47, 185; networks, 43–45, 47, 202

information, 70, 202; collecting, xxiv, xxv, 9, 35, 49, 51, 57, 62–63, 112, 179, 185, 186, 203, 208, 211, 214, 215; NCIC, xv–xviii, xxii, 28–29, 50, 140, 181; sharing, xvii, xxv, 3, 75, 176, 194, 216

INS. *See* Immigration and Naturalization Service

Institutional Removal Program (IRP), 111

intellectual property (IP), 36–37, 42

intent, sanctuary policies, xi, 1–2, 54, 59, 153–55, 157–58, 166

Internal Revenue Service (IRS), US, 42, 140–41, 176–79, 187

International Justice Mission, 39

"in their absence" (absentia), xv, xviii, xix

IP. *See* intellectual property

IPR Center. *See* National Intellectual Property Rights Coordination Center

IRCA. *See* Immigration Reform and Control Act

IRP. *See* Institutional Removal Program

IRS. *See* Internal Revenue Service

ITIN. *See* Individual Taxpayer Identification Number

Jail Enforcement Model, 30, 31
Jauregui, Beatrice, 198, 201, 227n20
JCART. *See* Joint Criminal Alien Removal Taskforce

Jersey City Police, 66
JIOCC. *See* Joint Intelligence and Operations Coordination Center
Johnson, Samuel (pseudonym), 102–3
Joint Criminal Alien Removal Taskforce (JCART), ERO, 35, 50
joint criminal/immigration control operations, 33, 66, 67, 73, 84, 85, 182, 188
Joint Intelligence and Operations Coordination Center (JIOCC), 48–49
Jones, Richard, 72
judges, 98, 158, 163, 187, 209; criminal court, xxii, 178–79; federal, 60, 158, 160, 161; immigration, xv, xviii, 17, 22, 23, 59, 94, 111, 125, 176
judicial warrants, xxii, 23, 98, 161, 187
juridical field, 162–63
"juridical sense/faculty," 162, 167
juries, watching videos in court, 204–5

Kansas, 27
Kansas City, Missouri, 27, 40
Kelly, Adam (pseudonym), 176–79
killings, 68, 205, 206–7
kin, fictive, 128, 212, 227n20
King, Rodney, 204–5
kinship, professional, 64, 80–81, 82, 84, 85, 89, 95, 102, 120–21, 182
Knoblauch, Hubert, 203
Kobach, Kris, 27–29, 35
Kowalsky, Grant (pseudonym), 168–76, 180

labor, 10, 11, 186; DOL, 40; worksite raids, 2, 49, 66, 73–84
language, xi, 77, 176, 194; policy, 63, 107, 109, 156, 158–62, 164; translators, xiv, 74, 75, 80–82, 146–47, 177–78, 216
Latin American surnames, 111
law: civil immigration, 21, 59, 159–62; command theory of, 156; "The Force of Law," 162–63; police as emissaries of policy and, 168–78; policy and, 156–57,

163, 164, 166, 168–78, 180. *See also specific laws*
Law and Public Safety Committees, 187
law enforcement agencies (LEA), 4; civil immigration operations enforcement as voluntary for, xv–xvi, 108; collegial relationships between ICE and, 64, 80–81, 82, 84, 85, 89, 95, 102, 120–21, 182; de-linked from ICE, 15, 17, 126, 128, 184; detainer policies and, 23, 24–25; force division and, 15, 17, 126, 128, 141, 168, 183–84; as force multipliers for ICE, xix–xx, 3, 21–25, 28–31, 35–42, 44–52, 54–64, 67–68, 73–91, 93–101, 103–5, 112, 115–16, 119–24, 168, 176–77, 180–82, 184, 188; with guidelines for civil immigration operations, xv–xvi, 1–2, 3, 59, 61, 160, 161; ICE agents "passing" as local, 74–75; with ICE warrants, xv–xix, xxii; with sanctuary policies, 14, 23–24; sanctuary policing as force multiplier for ICE and, 15, 65, 185. *See also* police; sheriff's deputies
Law Enforcement Directive 2018-6. *See* Immigrant Trust Directive
Law Enforcement Directives, New Jersey: No. 2005-1, 159; No. 2007-3, 54–57, 63, 65, 86, 153
Law Enforcement Support Center (LESC), ICE, xvii–xxiv, xxvi–xxvii, 28, 141
lawmakers, 8, 106–9, 114, 163, 188, 189
Lawrence-Weilman, Olivia, 226n2
lawyers, 18, 162, 163, 170, 178, 205, 209; with "firewall" sanctuary policies, 127; with noncriminal administrative arrests, 90, 93–94, 97, 121–22; with sousveillance, 66–67
LEA. *See* law enforcement agencies
legal representatives, 90, 93–94, 97, 121–22. *See also* lawyers
LESC. *See* Law Enforcement Support Center
Leviathan (Hobbes), 163

license plate reader cameras, 49
LIVESCAN database, 161
local partners, of ICE, xx, 3, 30, 34
Loftus, Benjamin, 215
Los Angeles, California, 36, 40
Los Angeles Police Department, 204–5
Luna, David, 38
"lurking," 213

Mac Giollabhui, Shane, 215
Madigan, Thomas (pseudonym), 87–105, 115–18, 120, 122–25
Mann, Steve, 212, 213, 214
Martínez, César (pseudonym), 176–79
Maryland, 11, 177
masks, ski, 80, 82, 83
Massachusetts, 11
mean-spiritedness, 2
media. *See* news media; social media
Melendez, Angel, 34, 44
Memphis, Tennessee, 40
Mendoza, Juan (pseudonym), xi–xvi, xviii–xx, xxii, xxiv–xxvii
Menjívar, Cecilia, 110
methodology: with BWC videos as multi-sited object of study, 193–94; research and writing experience of BWC ethnographer, 207–12; ride-alongs with police, 194; Rutgers University law student researchers, 195; studying up and sideways, 197–98, 201, 214; surveillant anthropology, 18, 212–16. *See also* participant observation; videos, BWC
Mexico, 40–42, 50, 77, 171, 177–78, 199
Michigan, 11, 37
Middle East, 38, 205
migrants, 3, 111, 199. *See also* body-worn cameras, capturing migrants
migration, 2, 33, 52, 77–79, 185
Milgram, Anne, 54–57, 59, 63–65, 86, 153
military: paramilitary, 23; US, 3, 25–27, 41, 48, 50
Minnesota, 11

Miranda rights, 175
"mobilizing metaphor," sanctuary as, 13
Molina, Jason, 46, 47
Monmouth County, New Jersey, 55
morality. *See* force multipliers, morality of sanctuary style
moralizing, at traffic stops, 138, 147
Moskos, Peter, 229n16
Moskowitz, Brian M., 37
MS-13, 45–47, 61
Mukherji, Raj, 187

Nader, Laura, 197
Nassau County Police Department, 46–47
National Crime Information Center (NCIC), xv–xviii, xxii, 28–29, 50, 140, 181
National Fugitive Operations Program, ICE, 34–35
National Gang Unit, HSI, 45
National Guard, Texas, 48
National Intellectual Property Rights Coordination Center (IPR Center), ICE, 36–37
national security, 29, 38, 41, 51, 55, 65, 111–12
NCIC. *See* National Crime Information Center
neoliberalism, 10–11, 27, 226n2
"neutralization effect," 162
Newark Department of Public Safety, 66
New Jersey, 11, 68, 174–75, 186–88, 193; Economic Crime Unit, 83–84; Law Enforcement Directive No. 2005-1, 159; Law Enforcement Directive No. 2007-3, 54–57, 63, 65, 86, 153; Pre-Trial Intervention Program, 179–80. *See also* Immigrant Trust Directive; police, New Jersey
New Jersey State Parole Board, 47, 68
New Jersey State Police, 66, 68, 74
New Jersey Values Act, 187–88
New Mexico, 11, 42

news media, 18, 67, 74, 110, 157–58, 162
Newsom, Gavin, 226n17
New York, 11, 46, 83, 162
New York City, 45, 46
New York City Police Department, 46
Nichols, Walter, 10
Nick number, xvii–xviii
9/11, 28–29, 30, 111, 112
NJLearn training portal, 129
Noland, Jason, 214
non-social landscape elements (nonsoels) of modernity, 51
nonviolence, 106–7, 108, 118
no-sited ethnography, 206

Obama, Barack, 2, 23, 24, 25, 68, 206
Office of Investigations, ICE, 34
Ohio, 36–37
Open Public Records Act, New Jersey, 193
Operation Community Shield Initiative, ICE, 34
Operation Devil Horns, 45, 219n2
Operation Devilhorns (Bolger and Santini), 219n2
Operation Matador, 45, 46
Operation Raging Bull, 45–46
Oregon, 11
Originating Agency Identifier (ORI), xvii

Palantir, 49, 50
"panoptic" data, 213
panopticon, 69
paramilitary extensions, of ICE, 23
participant observation: BWC videos versus, 210, 211, 228n5; drone warfare and, 205–6; policing and, 18, 194, 196–99, 201–2, 204, 208; remote surveillance work and, 209
"passing," as local police, 74–75, 76, 80, 88
Pecos, Texas, 41
Pennsylvania, xii, xiii, xix
PEP-COMM, 24
Philippine National Police, 39

photographs, 49, 85; of detainees, 75, 77, 79, 80, 81, 82, 83, 176; by migrants crossing borders, 199
Platkin, Matthew, 186
Plato, 156
Plousis, James T., 47
police, 14, 21, 63, 180; Albuquerque Police Department, 42; Anaheim Police Department, 36; Chicago Police Department, 200; Colombian National Police, 37, 38; *Cop in the Hood*, 229n16; as emissaries of sanctuary policies and law, 168–78; ethnographers, 211, 228n5; ethnographies, 198, 203, 229n16; as force dividers, 168, 183–84; ICE agents "passing" as local, 74–75; killings, 68; Los Angeles Police Department, 204–5; Nassau County Police Department, 46–47; New York City Police Department, 46; Philippine National Police, 39; in Puerto Rico, 34, 52; sanctuary policing as force multiplier for ICE and, 15, 65, 185; San Francisco Police Department, 45, 61, 114, 194, 219n2; secret, 43, 201, 202, 208; Sierra Vista Police Department, 48; Suffolk County Police Department, 46; torture, 200–201; undercover, 201, 215; as videographers, 16, 67, 73, 76, 181, 208, 216; view of BWCs versus, 72–73; violence, 68, 108, 189, 200–201, 204–5. *See also* body-worn cameras
police, New Jersey: auxiliaries, 198; BWCs, 68; BWCs at ICE-HSI raid, 66, 73–84; BWCs at ICE noncriminal administrative arrest, 87–102, 115–19, 124–25; BWCs at traffic stops, xi–xxvii, 129, 130–51, 168–76; as BWC videographers, 16, 73, 76, 208, 216; collegial relationship with ICE, 89, 95, 102, 120–21; with containment and co-optation of immigrant rights advocacy, 121–24;

police, New Jersey (*cont.*)
as force divider from ICE, 141, 168; as force multipliers for ICE, xix–xx, 3, 54–64, 67–68, 73–91, 93–101, 103–5, 115–16, 119–24, 168, 176–77, 180, 184; Immigrant Trust Directive and, 3, 58–64, 90–91, 93, 99–101, 103–4, 114–15, 134, 140–41, 145; Immigrant Trust Directive violations by, xvi–xvii, 62–63, 100–101, 103, 114, 123–24, 195; incident report, 103–5, 176–79; Jersey City Police, 66; New Jersey State Police, 66, 68, 74; as policy and law emissaries, 168–78, 180; with sanctuary policing, 129–52, 153; with scene security, 17, 87, 88, 90, 96–101, 103–5, 115, 116, 119, 123, 124
policed spaces, 189
policed state, 124, 183
the policed, 164, 199, 200
policing, 39, 159, 203; "aerial," 206; backstage of, 196, 208, 211; frontstage of, 196, 211; participant observation and, 18, 194, 196–99, 201–2, 204, 208; sanctuary policies and, 15. *See also* sanctuary policing
policy: intent with Immigrant Trust Directive, xi, 1–2, 54, 59, 154–55, 157–58; language, 63, 107, 109, 156, 158–62, 164; law and, 156–57, 163, 164, 166, 168–78, 180; worlds, 155, 227n2. *See also* commander in policy; sanctuary policies
Polis Solutions, 72
power, 12, 27, 167, 197, 213, 214, 216; authority and, 153, 155, 156, 158, 163, 165, 168; dynamic, 13, 93, 151
Pre-Trial Intervention Program, New Jersey, 179–80
Price, David, 202, 203, 214
Priority Enforcement Program, 24
private sectors: informant networks, 43; sanctuary, 5–6, 10, 12, 224n18; surveillance, 216

"Professional Vision" (Goodwin), 204
protests, 26, 92, 199, 200
providers, of sanctuary, 4–8, 12–13, 65, 124, 168, 183
public records requests, for BWC footage, 4, 179, 193, 195
public safety, 56, 68, 76, 93, 103, 188; as force multiplier, 29, 42, 45–48, 51, 55, 64, 116, 122–24, 181, 182; Law and Public Safety Committees, 187; threats, 33, 41, 59; value of, 107–8, 115
Puerto Rico, 34, 42–43, 52

racially-influenced policing, sanctuary policies on, 159
raids, 96, 99–100, 157; criminal/immigration, 33, 66; with fingerprinting, 77–83; home, 49, 75, 83–84; questioning during, 77, 78, 79–80, 81; worksite, 2, 49, 66, 73–84
Ralph, Laurence, 200
Reagan, Ronald, 2, 188
reentry, unlawful, 112
refugees, 6–8, 11–12, 51, 74, 107, 185
relationships, LEA and ICE, 64, 80–81, 82, 84, 85, 89, 95, 102, 120–21, 182
remote ethnography, 205, 209, 228n5
remote killings, with drones, 206–7
remote surveillance work, 209
removal: ERO, 32–35, 40–41, 45, 47, 50, 55, 84; order of, xvi, xviii, 60, 160, 161, 176; proceedings, xiv, xv, xviii, 55, 67, 176
research: auxiliaries, 214; BWC ethnographer with experience of writing and, 207–12; "videographic" tradition with social science, 203
researchers: as force multipliers, 216; Rutgers University law student, 195
resistance, 6, 11, 15
Reyes, Senan (pseudonym), xi–xxvii
Rhode Island, 11
ride-alongs, with police, 194

rights, 23, 31, 40, 186, 188, 201; human, 107, 108; *Miranda*, 175

rights, immigrant, 12, 23, 189; advocates, 64, 97–102, 104, 107, 120, 121–24, 127, 165, 194–95; community, 22, 24, 106

Rizzer, Tim (pseudonym): at traffic stop with BWCs, xi–xxvii; with violation of Immigrant Trust Directive, xvi–xvii

Romanian Secret Police, 43, 202

Rosa, Jonathan, 200–201

Rutgers University, law student researchers, 195

Ryder, Patrick, 46–47

Sanchez, Diego (pseudonym), 129–51, 153

sanctuary: commander in policy as emissary of, 158–59; connotations, 181; as governance, 4, 189; hospitality and, 7–8, 13; in immigration context, 4–5, 6, 8; movements, 7, 13, 63, 166–68, 224n18; private sectors, 5–6, 10, 12, 224n18; providers, 4–8, 12–13, 65, 124, 168, 183; seekers, 4–9, 12–13, 185; spaces, 7, 8, 11, 189; with surveillance, 6–7

sanctuary policies: benefits of, 3, 8–9; branding, 58, 62, 63; counties with, 14, 188; defined, 57; exceptions to, 33, 60, 61–62, 91, 93, 109, 113, 117, 127, 161–62; firewall, 9, 127, 129; as force multipliers, 54, 64–65, 184–88; with government services, 9–10; intent, xi, 1–2, 54, 59, 153–55, 157–58, 166; LEA with, 14, 23–24; neoliberalism and, 226n2; as path for police enforcement, 3, 4; police with violation of, xvi–xvii, 62–63, 100–101, 103, 114, 123–24, 195; policing and, 15; territorial spaces and, 11; value systems, 16–17, 63, 106–10, 113, 114, 115. *See also* Immigrant Trust Directive

sanctuary policies, authority of: commander in Immigrant Trust Directive, 17, 155–68; complaint warrant, 178–80;

police as emissaries of policy and law, 168–78; power and, 153, 158

sanctuary policing, 4, 103, 124, 181, 194; BWC videos illuminating, 196; defined, 127, 151; as force division, 15, 17, 126–29, 141, 152, 184, 188; as force multiplier for LEA and ICE, 15, 65, 185; ideological foundation for, 118; traffic stop with, 129–52, 153

San Francisco, California, 226n17

San Francisco Police Department, 45, 61, 114, 194, 219n2

San Juan Computer Forensics Laboratory, HSI, 43

Santini, Michael (pseudonym), 61, 219n2

SB54. *See* California Values Act

scene (safety) security: as force multiplier, 17, 87, 88, 90, 96–101, 103–5, 113, 115, 116, 119, 123, 124, 181, 183; police backup with, 19

Schlesinger, Lester A., 213

schools, 2, 10, 47, 69, 94, 99–100, 123

S-COMM. *See* Secure Communities

"search and rescue" organizations, 6–7

searches: probable cause, 170–71; warrants, 42, 101–2, 178–79

secrecy, 18, 196, 198, 200, 216

secret police, 43, 201, 202, 208

secret policing, 202, 203

Secret Service: Romania, 202; US, 41, 103

Secure Communities (S-COMM), 54, 112, 118, 184; arrests under, 63–64; with biometric data-sharing technology, 35; with fingerprinting, 22, 50; with force multipliers, 22–25, 30, 35, 45, 50, 53; PEP-COMM and, 24; proliferation of, 35

Securities and Exchange Commission, US, 185

"securityscape," 68

seekers, of sanctuary, 4–9, 12–13, 185

Senate, New Jersey, 187–88

September 11, 2001. *See* 9/11

services: immigrant benefits and, 185, 187; sanctuary policies and government, 9–10
sex offenders, 35, 109
sex trafficking, 39, 40, 66
sexual minorities, 26
sheriff's deputies, 1, 41, 64, 108, 165; Cochise County, 48; ICE partnered with, 23, 35–37, 65, 66, 74–77, 80, 82–83, 182
Sierra Vista Police Department, Arizona, 48
silence: blue code of, 196; about police torture, 200
"silent sanctuary," 13
Sini, Timothy D., 46
slaves, 7, 51, 74
social media, 73, 96, 110, 200, 201
social movements, 8–10, 167, 181, 201
sociocultural life, backstage of, 196, 216
sousveillance ("watching from below"), 66–67, 212–14
sousveillant cameras, 212
the sovereign, 156–57
spaces, 69, 116; policed, 189; sanctuary, 7, 8, 11, 189
spatial arrangement data, 70, 71
spatialization, drone warfare and re-, 206–7
Springer, Scott, 32
states, 6, 11, 23, 69, 209; authority, 194, 198, 214; policed, 124, 183; power, 12, 213, 214, 216; surveillance, 213–14; surveillant anthropology of, 216; US Department of State, 37, 38, 202
Strickland, Donald A., 213
Su, Rick, 13
Suffolk County Police Department, 46
Sunom, Steven (pseudonym), 87, 90–95, 97–103, 115–18, 120, 122, 124–25
Supiso, John (pseudonym), 172, 174
surnames, Latin American, 111
surrogates, of ICE, xx, 168

surveillance, 3, 110; on anthropologists, 202–3; industry partners, 49–50; sanctuary with, 6–7; sousveillance, 66–67, 212–14; state, 213–14; technologies, 4, 68, 70, 199, 209, 212–14, 216; "watching over," 4, 6, 7, 213
surveillant anthropology, 4, 18, 212–16
"surveilling the surveillors," 212

tactical armor carrier. *See* vests
TCIUs. *See* Transnational Criminal Investigative Units
technology: biometrics, 35, 71–72; fingerprinting, 22, 77–83; surveillance, 4, 68, 70, 199, 209, 212–14, 216. *See also* body-worn cameras; drones
Temporary Taxpayer Identification Number (TTIN), 177
terror, 25, 200, 205
terrorists, 28–29, 38, 44, 66, 111–12
Texas, 35, 40–42, 48
theatrical performance, 7, 121
Title 19, of US Code 1401, 30, 32, 50
torture, 200–201, 205
The Torture Letters (Laurence), 200
trafficking: ACT Teams, 40–42, 50; firearms, 111; human, 21, 29, 32, 39–40, 66, 75, 80, 182; raid, 66, 73–84; sex, 39, 40, 66
traffic stops, 17, 19, 22, 52, 126; arrest for airsoft gun at, 171–76; identification at, xii, xviii, 58, 132–39, 143; moralizing at, 138, 147; police with BWCs at, xi–xxvii, 129, 130–51, 168–76; police with violation of Immigrant Trust Directive, xvi–xvii; with sanctuary policing, 129–52, 153; terrorists and, 28–29
transfers, custody, 10, 14, 23, 24, 30, 118, 176, 180
translators, language, xiv, 74, 75, 80–82, 146–47, 177–78, 216
transnational crime, 2, 32, 33, 37–38, 50
Transnational Criminal Investigative Units (TCIUs), ICE-HSI, 37–39, 50

transnational gangs, 45–48, 61
transparency, 68, 73, 198
Transportation Security Administration Houston, 48
trauma, 5, 115
Truleo, 72
Trump, Donald, 1–2, 25, 27, 45, 188
trust, in police, 14, 68. *See also* Immigrant Trust Directive
Tsing, Anna, 51
TTIN. *See* Temporary Taxpayer Identification Number
Tuma, René, 203
Twitter, 200
287(g) agreements, 30–32, 50, 54–56, 112, 187, 220n42

Ulrich, Dennis A., 41, 42
undercover police, 201, 215
underground railroad, 7
"under-watching" ("unterveillance"), 213
United Forces of Rapid Action, Puerto Rico Police Department, 34
United Kingdom, 13
United States (US): Attorney's Office, 42; Border Patrol, 41, 48; border with Mexico, 40–42, 50, 77, 199; Congress, 28, 110, 202–3, 205; Department of Defense, 26, 28, 42; Department of Justice, xv, 40, 45; Department of State, 37, 38, 202; Department of Treasury, 30, 32, 45; DHS, 35, 103, 112; DOL, 40; Drug Enforcement Administration, 41, 54; FBI, 22, 33, 40–42, 50, 78, 128, 202–3; GAO, 31; INS, 111–12; IRS, 42, 140–41, 176–79, 187; military, 3, 25–27, 41, 48, 50; Secret Service, 41, 103; Securities and Exchange Commission, US, 185; Title 19 of Code 1401, 30, 32, 50; USCIS, 45. *See also* Customs and Border Protection; Immigration and Customs Enforcement
"universalization effect," 162

universal subject of law, 161, 162
"unterveillance" ("under-watching"), 213
US Attorney's Offices, 42
US Citizenship and Immigration Services (USCIS), 45
US Code 1401, Title 19 of, 30, 32, 50

Values Act: California, 1, 187; New Jersey, 187–88
value systems: binary, *109*, 109–10, 117–18, 182; sanctuary policies, 16–17, 63, 106–10, 113, 114, 115
Verdery, Katherine, 43, 202
Vermont, 11, 28
vests (tactical armor carrier), "police," 74, 75, 76, 80, 88
video-based ethnographies, 203–4
video cameras, 105, 200, 203, 204
videographers: amateur, 204–5; police as, 16, 67, 73, 76, 181, 208, 216
"videographic" tradition, social science research, 203
videography, 203
videos: analysis and ethnography, 203; cell phone, 67, 68, 97, 99, 100, 104, 122, 212; drone operators watching, 206–7; juries in court watching, 204–5; from members of public, 203, 204–5; protest, 92
videos, BWC: with blurred visual blocks, xxi, xxv, 195; data doubles, 70, 84–85; with incident and arrest reports, 73; as multi-sited object of study, 193–94; participant observation versus, 210, 211, 228n5; policing narratives based on analysis of, 18; potential viewer as force multiplier for ICE, 124–25; public records requests for footage, 4, 193, 195; with redactions, 195; sanctuary policing illuminated with, 196; software tools for, 72; traffic stops, xi–xxvii, 17
viewers, BWC footage and potential, 17, 94, 124–25, 209
Vigilant Solutions, 49

violators, immigration, xv, 29, 35
violence, 8, 38, 65, 115–16, 119; of desert and border crossings, 199–200, 204; non-, 106–7, 108, 118; police, 68, 108, 189, 200–201, 204–5; sanctioned, 198; state, 209

Wagner, Ryan (pseudonym), 177–79
Walton County, Georgia, 35, 37
warrants: active traffic, 140, 141, 143–44, 145, 148, 150; complaint, 178; criminal, xv, xxii, 76, 117; judicial, xxii, 23, 98, 161, 187; search, 42, 101–2, 178–79
warrants, ICE: as administrative, xvi, xvii, xix, xxii, 23, 30, 89, 98, 103, 117, 123, 140; ICE agents issuing, 22; LEA with, xv–xix, xxii; without legal force, 23, 98, 122; municipal facilities and, 14; in NCIC database, xv
Warrant Service Officer model, 30
Washington, 11, 157
"watching from below." *See* sousveillance
"watching over," 4, 6, 7, 213. *See also* surveillance
Wellman, Barry, 214
What is an apparatus?. *See* "*Che cose un dispositivo?*"
whiteness, 71, 101
Wisconsin, 11
worksite raids, 2, 49, 66, 73–84

ABOUT THE AUTHOR

PETER MANCINA is Visiting Scholar at Rutgers Law School. Mancina holds a PhD in Anthropology from Vanderbilt University, and his research has been funded by the US National Science Foundation, the Wenner-Gren Foundation, the Swedish Foundation for Humanities and Social Sciences, and the Rutgers Law School Pratt Fund.